BEYOND CONVERSATION

BEYOND CONVERSATION

Collaboration and the Production of Writing

WILLIAM DUFFY

UTAH STATE UNIVERSITY PRESS
Logan

© 2020 by University Press of Colorado

Published by Utah State University Press
An imprint of University Press of Colorado
245 Century Circle, Suite 202
Louisville, Colorado 80027

 The University Press of Colorado is a proud member of
the Association of University Presses.

The University Press of Colorado is a cooperative publishing enterprise supported, in part, by Adams State University, Colorado State University, Fort Lewis College, Metropolitan State University of Denver, Regis University, University of Colorado, University of Northern Colorado, University of Wyoming, Utah State University, and Western Colorado University.

∞ This paper meets the requirements of the ANSI/NISO Z39.48-1992 (Permanence of Paper)

ISBN: 978-1-64642-048-3 (paperback)
ISBN: 978-1-64642-049-0 (ebook)
https://doi.org/10.7330/9781646420490

Library of Congress Cataloging-in-Publication Data

Names: Duffy, William, 1981– author.
Title: Beyond conversation : collaboration and the production of writing / by William Duffy.
Description: Louisville : University Press of Colorado, [2020] | Includes bibliographical references and index. | Summary: "Outlines an interactionist theory of collaboration to explain collaboration as the rhetorical capacity manifested in discursive engagements coauthors enter into with their writing objects. Interrogates institutional politics around debates about collaboration, offers a history of collaborative writing theory, and proposes a new way of understanding the labor of coauthorship"—Provided by publisher.
Identifiers: LCCN 2020039775 (print) | LCCN 2020039776 (ebook) | ISBN 9781646420483 (paperback) | ISBN 9781646420490 (ebook)
Subjects: LCSH: Authorship—Collaboration. | Authorship—Social aspects. | Writing.
Classification: LCC PN145 .D84 2020 (print) | LCC PN145 (ebook) | DDC 808.02—dc23
LC record available at https://lccn.loc.gov/2020039775
LC ebook record available at https://lccn.loc.gov/2020039776

The University Press of Colorado gratefully acknowledges the generous support provided by the University of Memphis toward the publication of this book.

Cover photograph © Bashutskyy/Shutterstock.

CONTENTS

ACKNOWLEDGMENTS

I'll be the first to admit the irony in writing a book about collaborative writing as a single author. As I suggest in the proceeding pages, however, one way we develop as writers, especially writers who write "alone," is to also write collaboratively. The last chapter of this book, which I've coauthored with my longtime writing partner John Pell, offers a snapshot of what this development has entailed since we first started writing together as graduate students at the University of North Carolina at Greensboro. While my collaboration with John has informed much of what I've come to understand about collaboration and writing, many others have also played a part in helping me articulate the ideas in this book.

The earliest iteration of this project was supported at UNCG by Hephzibah Roskelly, Stephen Yarbrough, and Elizabeth Chiseri-Strater. My thanks to Hepsie, for encouraging students to coauthor from day one. To Steve, for shepherding bad ideas into better ones. And to The Chiz, for asking "so what?" I am indebted to this team of teacher-scholars for their mentorship.

Since that time, I've benefited from conversations with friends and colleagues who took time to help me envision what this book should become, many of whom also offered feedback on various chapter drafts, article submissions, conference presentations, and the initial book proposal. Thank you especially to Paul Lynch, Belinda Walzer, Elizabeth Vogel, David Rogers, Jacob Babb, Brian Ray, Matt Mullins, Joseph Moore, Nancy Myers, Kelly Ritter, Lisa Ede, Roxanne Mountford, Mary Beth Pennington, Meredith Love, Kelly Pender, David Beard, Risa Applegarth, Tim Peeples, Kathi Yancey, John Schilb, Bonnie Sunstein, and Kate Ronald.

My colleagues at the University of Memphis gave me the motivation and support to complete this book. I'm especially grateful to those who read and responded to various parts of this manuscript as it developed, including Scott Sundvall, Katie Fredlund, Joseph Jones, Loel Kim, Jeff

Scraba, Susan Nordstrom, Andrea Bishop, and Elizabeth Baddour. Darryl Domingo and Donal Harris showed me how to get this project off the ground. Josh Phillips said yes virtually every time I came to him with a request. This work was supported in part by a grant from the University of Memphis College of Arts and Sciences Research Grant Fund. This support does not necessarily imply the university's endorsement of research conclusions.

Thank you to Rachael Levay for supporting this project and to the staff at Utah State University Press and the University Press of Colorado for shepherding its development from manuscript to book. To the anonymous reviewers: the praise and criticism you provided was thorough, clear, and supportive; it helped me see how to make this book better, so thank you for generously sharing your experience and expertise.

Portions of chapters 1 and 3 previously appeared in "Collaboration (in) Theory: Reworking the Social Turn's Conversational Imperative," *College English*, 76 (5) (2014): 416–35, copyright 2014 by the National Council of Teachers of English, used with permission.

My family has been supportive in all the ways that matter most, many of which were easy for me to take for granted in some of the more frenzied seasons of writing this book, so they deserve the most important thanks of all. Vicki, I love you. Fiona and Sloane, yes, you can have another treat.

John, this book is dedicated to you. Now, what's next on our list?

BEYOND CONVERSATION

Introduction
ACCOUNTING FOR COAUTHORSHIP

What happens when writers compose together? This book tackles that question by introducing an interactionist theory of collaboration, one that focuses as much on the objects collaborators share as it does on the relations with one another they must negotiate. More specifically, it introduces an approach for asking questions about the work of collaborative writing by drawing attention to the complex discursive assemblages within and out of which collaborative writers compose. I call this theory *interactionist* because most scholarship positions collaboration as a dialectical engagement between individual human subjects—that is, it assumes collaboration is at root two or more people engaged in talk. But the approach developed here complicates such dialectical models to highlight the necessary role objects play in collaboration. What collaborators do is interact with and manipulate shared objects of attention, objects both material and abstract, and these objects—all the things that populate the rhetorical ecologies of a collaboration, not the least of which is an emerging text—can and do resist the "talk" collaborators invent as they write together. In other words, the genesis of collaborative composition "does not reside in a set of objective rhetorical abilities of a rhetor [or set of rhetors]"; it instead "exists at the intersection of a network of semiotic, material, and yes, intentional elements and relational practices," to echo Carl Herndl and Adela Licona's postmodern theory of rhetorical agency (2007, 137). Accordingly, successful collaborative writers must learn to recognize and adapt to the ways collaboration can fundamentally challenge the habits and expectations we associate with and bring to the practice of writing.

Indeed, I am never more aware of how I write as I am when in the midst of coauthorship. I can clearly recall an experience from several years ago, for example, when I coauthored a book chapter with two colleagues with whom I had never written. All of us had experience with coauthorship, just not with one another. After our first meeting to discuss the project, I was confident our collective experience as collaborative

DOI: 10.7330/9781646420490.c000

authors would make the process easier than it otherwise would be had we not had such experience. But as we moved from the brainstorming to inscription stages—we were constructing the draft as a shared Google Doc—I developed an anxiety about my usual method of using chunks of freewriting to serve as placeholders for ideas not yet fully conceptualized. The three of us had agreed to start composing separate parts of the draft we would then take over from one another, round-robin style, until the draft was fully fleshed out. When I write, however, I like to bounce around from one section of text to another as inspiration hits, so I often write messy placeholder paragraphs when I'm unsure how best to articulate this or that idea but nevertheless want to get something on the page. But as I read the sections of text my coauthors were writing, they looked more cohesive and polished than my own scattershot musings, devoid as mine were of a clear developmental structure. I soon grew anxious with self-doubt. Was my method going to slow down the progress of getting to a full draft? Should I send my coauthors an apology even though I had already told them this messiness is just part of my process? Moreover, had I grown too reliant on this method of drafting? Was it inhibiting me from expanding my scholarly repertoire and learning how to compose using a wider array of strategies?

The next time we met as a group to discuss the draft, one of my coauthors apologized for what she perceived as the inefficiency of her own drafting method. Indeed, all three of us confessed feeling self-conscious in one way or another about our individual habits of composing, habits that seem to get amplified and become more discernible when we know they are on display to others. As we continued to work on the draft, we also continued to discuss how each of us writes, a kind of side conversation that allowed us to step back and hold in check the anxieties all writers, especially collaborative writers, inevitably face from time to time.

By default, then, we might say collaboration invites uncertainty because writing with others often requires us to reorient ourselves to the labor of writing itself. This uncertainty is one of the reasons collaborative writing can be so difficult, and why many people shy away from it. Writing is an intimate, private activity for most of us. In this way, dialectical models of collaboration make sense insofar as they focus on practices of interpersonal exchange for managing the uncertainties that are part and parcel of writing with others, which is implied in Charlotte Robidoux and Beth Hewett's definition of collaboration, for example, which emphasizes such a dialectical focus: "Collaboration can be understood as a strategic and generative interactivity among individuals seeking to achieve a common goal" (2009, 4). But collaborative composition, like all discourse production, is materially situated in ecologies we can only ever partially distinguish by observing the various relations between and among the many objects populating these environments, including the collaborators themselves. Accordingly, I believe the discipline of writing studies, including rhetoric, technical communication, and other fields invested in the theory and practice of writing, like communication and education, can benefit from a theory of collaboration that goes beyond conversation as the conceptual locus for understanding what collaborators do when they write together.

This is not to say conversation, or the talk collaborators produce, shouldn't be accounted for as a critical component in the work of collaborative composition.[1] Far from it. Despite the many ways collaboration might be defined, most uses of this concept imply some level of focused, deliberate engagement among individuals, engagement that no doubt depends on effective teamwork, including the ability to effectively communicate with one another. Accordingly, when teachers, researchers, and other literacy professionals discuss collaboration or otherwise try to explain it as a particular kind of practice distinct from the work of solo writing, they often focus on the interpersonal dynamics collaborators must negotiate and how these dynamics relate to and inform the procedural work of coauthorship, like developing a work plan, sticking to a schedule, delegating tasks, and so forth. Consequently, after wading through advice and best practices focused on how to *set up* a collaboration—the "task design" of a collaborative project (Bremner et al. 2014)—there is usually little said in these discussions about what the actual *writing* in collaborative writing entails. To put this as a question that highlights one of the practical concerns I consider in this book, How do collaborators negotiate the labor of rhetorical invention?[2]

But this question isn't new. In fact, composition theorists began asking different versions of this question starting in the early 1980s as the field's social turn was getting underway alongside the rise of what James Berlin labeled "epistemic rhetoric," a pedagogical approach that recognizes language as "a social—not a private—phenomenon, and as such embodies a multitude of historically specific conceptions that shape experience, especially ideological conceptions about economic, political, and social arrangements," arrangements that affect "the dialectical process involved in the rhetorical act" (1987, 166). It is through such a social-epistemic lens that in her book *Invention as a Social Act*, Karen Burke LeFevre, for example, proposes that rhetorical invention "is best understood as occurring when individuals interact dialectically with socioculture in a distinctive way to generate something" (1987,

33). LeFevre goes on to outline a continuum of social perspectives that account for rhetorical invention, one of which she labels "collaborative." To explain this collaborative perspective, she draws on the sociological theory of George Herbert Mead to model collaboration as a progressive kind of dialogue: "One person acts, and in the act of making the gesture, calls out for a response in the other. Something new is created here. . . . New meanings are thus brought about into existence by means of a social interaction involving a symbolic gesture and response" (62).[3] While LeFevre challenges a "view of invention as the act of an atomistic individual producing a discrete text," the idea of collaboration in her theory ultimately gets subsumed in her social view of invention as "one in which individuals interact with society and culture" (121). In social-epistemic terms, then, collaboration is not a strategic activity as much as it is a discursive mechanism always at work in both the localized talk of specific collaborative teams and the more abstract talk that constitutes the stuff of "society and culture" writ large.

While I appreciate that social-epistemic approaches align collaboration with the rhetorical canon of invention, thus positioning it as a concept with which to understand the ways our discursive interactions function in relation to the creation of knowledge, these approaches end up falling back on generalities with little pragmatic uptake. Consider, for example, what Gregory Clark writes at the beginning of *Dialogue, Dialectic, and Conversation,* a book published just three years after *Invention as Social Act.* Clark explicitly positions *Dialogue Dialectic, and Conversation* as an extension of LeFevre's work: "In communicating we collaborate with others in constructing and continually reconstructing from our commonality the community that enables us, both individually and collectively, to survive and progress, a community comprising people engaged in an ongoing process of renegotiating the beliefs and values—and consequently, the action—they can share" (1990, 1). Clark explains such a philosophy of communication relies on two assumptions: first, our communication doesn't merely represent but actually constitutes reality; and second, we communicate with, not just to, one another. "When communication is understood on the basis of these two complementary assumptions," he goes on, "it becomes, above all, a collaborative process through which a community of people construct a shared understanding of their common experience that provides the foundation for their continued cooperation" (2).

Mindful of the risk of reducing the complexity Clark no doubt aims to capture in this theoretical articulation of how communication and knowledge are intertwined, I didn't use this philosophical explanation to better navigate the discussions I shared with my two coauthors mentioned above as we came to terms with our own writerly insecurities we believed were impeding the progress of our collaborative work. To the extent that disclosing our insecurities with one another helped establish some "common experience" that promoted "continued cooperation," Clark is correct, but what are we to do, and indeed what *can* we do with this understanding? Insofar as Clark is not making a propositional argument but a declarative one that outlines "a social perspective on the function of writing," which is the subtitle of his book, such a theory leaves agency in the wind since such collaborative processes are what, according to Clark, comprise the foundation of communication in the first place.

Herein we find one of the primary shortcomings of social constructionist epistemology as a philosophical foundation for understanding collaboration, namely that it directed scholars to focus on "the social" and its constituent abstractions like "the cultural," "the political," "the economic," and so forth as the primary sources of struggle that collaborators must negotiate if their work together is to be successful. At the same time, these articulations of a social-epistemic rhetoric made it possible to invoke the idea of collaboration itself to underscore in tautological form the import of social turn epistemology more generally, just as Clark goes on to do when he theoretically parses the concepts of dialogue, dialectic, and conversation.[4] Yet this reflects the larger social turn logic with which Kenneth Bruffee explicitly argues for the value of collaboration when he suggests how it "provides the kind of social context, the kind of community, in which normal discourse occurs: a community of knowledgeable peers" (1984, 644). By "normal discourse" Bruffee means consensus, an idea I trace the history of as it relates to the mechanics of collaboration in chapter 3, but here my point is simply that social constructionism limits how we might understand collaboration as a deliberate practice writers pursue to invent novelty, emergent ideas and articulations writers can anticipate but never predict as they enter into and pursue the discursive work of collaboration.[5]

To return to my earlier example, the three of us decided to collaborate on that particular project because we recognized each of us could bring unique disciplinary perspectives that, when combined, would allow us to engage our research subject from a truly interdisciplinary lens, one that had been expressly cultivated for that specific purpose. I knew what ideas I wanted to bring to the table, as did my coauthors, but until we sat down and started to plan what we wanted to write, the best each of us could do was speculate about how our respective ideas would and would not fit together, and what, as a result of this engagement, we would end up writing. But in large part that was the point. That is, we didn't pursue this collaboration because we figured it would be an easy way to churn out another line on our CVs. We pursued it because we knew doing so would allow us to discover and articulate ideas and observations we wouldn't have invented had we not collaborated in the first place. Indeed, I'd wager that many academic collaborators coauthor for similar reasons.

After all, consider those occasions when collaborative writers might argue the finished product of their collaboration is greater than the sum of its parts. Such a claim prompts me to think about the phenomenon of emergence. "When two separate causes simply add or mix themselves in their joint effect, so that we can see their agency in action in that effect, the result is a mere 'resultant' but if there is novelty or heterogeneity in the effect then we may speak of an 'emergent'" (DeLanda 2011, 382). Here Manuel DeLanda is summarizing George Henry Lewes, the nineteenth-century English philosopher who coined the term "emergence," but Delanda also likens emergence to the difference between physical and chemical reactions and demonstrates how with the latter the result is not a mere combination of its original parts but something new, something different. When I begin collaborative writing projects, it is this emergent discourse I most anticipate, those articulations that result not despite but because of the interactions between each of our "separate causes" as collaborators.

But social-epistemic theories can't account for emergent discourse because collaboration as such is overdetermined in those conceptual schemes. Consider how social-epistemic rhetoric offers little relief to scholars who, for instance, recognize they might be forced to account for their respective contributions to a collaboration; Naomi Miller laments that academics "are encouraged to dissect any collaboration into absurdly artificial allocations of 'responsibility.' Surely, excessive attention to 'which half is yours' can cause us to lose sight of the whole" (2003). I agree with Miller—such concerns do prompt us to lose sight of what coauthors can accomplish. Is it useful, really, to enter such critical discussions holding up a theoretical argument that shows "how texts, whether individually or jointly authored, should be considered collaborative"? (Thralls 1992, 64). But this simplification is what a social-epistemic approach to collaboration offers; it ultimately boils down in practice to the particular strategies for arguing, in theory, that all writing is social in one way or another. And as for the place of collaborative writing in the courses we teach? Following Stephen Yarbrough's criticism of social-epistemic rhetoric, "If the doctrines of social constructionism are true then it logically follows that everyone who teaches composition is already doing what can be done to help students improve their writing" (1999, 221). If collaboration *just is*, if at the end of the day collaboration is something we can't *not* do when we write or otherwise communicate, then logically speaking there is no pragmatic difference between asking students to write alone or together. At best, collaboration simply becomes a means to divide labor, delegate responsibility, and play at what is already at work shaping our discourse.

But we know better. That is, we know collaboration can yield pragmatic differences in the writing collaborators undertake together. And we also know (the *we* here specifically means those of us who were trained and work in humanities fields) we probably aren't doing enough to engage our students in the skills and dispositions needed to be effective collaborative writers. Perhaps this is why Cathy Davidson, renowned cultural historian of technology, suggests a different approach in her *Chronicle of Higher Education* column "What If Scholars in the Humanities Worked Together, in a Lab?" In this piece Davidson discusses humanities centers and the different models they assume—some provide course releases for faculty to pursue their individual scholarship, some shape various programming around a particular theme and hold events—but she also speculates about what a humanities center would look like if it was structured more like a scientific lab. As Davidson sees it, "The ideal of individual authorship and genius, so prized in the humanities, often contributes to ineffective models of intellectual innovation and creates poor departmental and university citizens," so she suggests humanities disciplines might imagine the creation of spaces that "could borrow from the collaborative aspects of the lab, where even the most senior and junior members count on one another, and where joint publication and grant applications acknowledge and formalize a structure of mutual dependency" (1999, B4).[6] Davidson draws attention to the fact that when academics engage a common project from start to finish, like a piece of collaborative writing, the potential for discovery—what I describe above as *emergence*—becomes all the more possible. But this is a commonsense claim, right? Don't most academics believe research collaborations enhance the potential for discovery?

Well, yes and no.

Popular trade books like *Where Good Ideas Come From* (Johnson 2010), *The Silo Effect* (Tett 2016), and *Group Genius* (Sawyer 2017), to name just a few in what is a very long and growing list, explain and in most cases advocate for the benefits of collaboration. They do so, however, in general terms and by drawing on examples from business, medicine, technology, and the entertainment industry—these are trade books, after all, so the examples must have popular appeal. The market for books geared toward academics about the power of collaboration is, not surprisingly, much smaller—for a very good reason. Academic collaborators must navigate disciplinary and institutional economies that define and determine how collaborative work is valued and assessed, so while it's one thing to advocate for the value of collaboration in the abstract, it's another thing to account for and promote this value in terms that have significance in the ritualized routines of academic disciplines, college and university administrative structures, and department-level policies and procedures. Abstract defenses of collaboration are thus difficult to translate in ways that carry currency across academia's myriad institutional landscapes, including what are sometimes competing authorial economies.

Most academics probably know or at least recognize the value of collaboration, in other words, but we learn to parse this value in different ways. As a result, and when it comes to collaborative writing in particular, even though coauthorship in most academic disciplines is more common now than it was in the past, undertaking a collaboration can be difficult and even a bit risky if one is unfamiliar with what counts, both literally and figuratively, in these various economies.

* * *

Navigating coauthorship in academia's authorial economies requires knowledge of three different but obviously related concerns. First, who gets to count as an author? This question is simple if not obvious, but in the physical sciences, for example, determining what counts as authorial labor can be tricky, especially when dozens or even hundreds of people participate in the design and testing of a research project.

Second, how should coauthorship be attributed? Beyond asking the question of who counts as an author, we must also decide how to ascribe singular texts to plural authors, to echo the title of Lisa Ede and Andrea Lunsford's (1990) important study of collaborative authorship. Should name order imply level or import of contribution? Should footnotes or other textual features be utilized to qualify which contributor did what? These are thorny questions, but important ones given the responsibilities claims of authorship carry.[7]

Third, and finally, how should coauthorship be credited as a form of labor? Does it make sense to assume a text coauthored by two people, for instance, took more work on the part of each of those writers than a comparable text coauthored by three people? And how should that labor be ascribed value in end-of-year reports, tenure and promotion guidelines, funding decisions, even author-impact algorhythms?[8]

No matter the discipline, academics must constantly navigate these authorial demands. In some cases, resources exist to assist with making these determinations. Professional societies and advocacy groups release policy recommendations, organizations like the American Psychological Association and the American Medical Association develop style guides, publishers adopt guidelines, and individual schools and departments establish criteria for deciding how to represent or otherwise "count" coauthorship. With that said, "No standardized policies enable collaborators throughout academe to prevent disputes about authorship," write Ann Austin and Roger Baldwin in their 1991 report on faculty collaboration for the Association of the Study of Higher Education; moreover, they continue, these decisions are sometimes made unilaterally via top-down university assessments (68). While Austin and Baldwin devote significant attention to the challenge of crediting collaborative endeavors as they review the scholarly literature and report on various data related to authorship practices in higher education, they never question the assumption that the products of collaboration must be conceptualized as the sum total of individual efforts. "In a meritocracy like higher education," they say, "it is not sufficient to recognize [equally] all contributors to a joint publication. The system demands to know who contributed more and who contributed less to the collaborative endeavor" (67).

Even though Austin and Baldwin's report was published thirty years ago, the logic it reflects concerning the nature of authorship in higher education still persists. Specifically, and despite famous assertions by the likes of Roland Barthes (1977) and Michel Foucault (1979) that the author is dead—at least the one understood as singular and autonomous—coauthorship still gets positioned as a zero-sum undertaking. As Martha Woodmansee reminds us, "By 'author' we mean an individual who is the sole creator of unique works the originality of which warrants their protection under laws of intellectual property known as 'copyright' or 'authors' rights'" (1994, 15). With that said, she notes, "The notion that the writer is a special participant in the production process—the only one worthy of attention—is of recent provenience. It is a by-product of the Romantic notion that significant writers break altogether with tradition to create something utterly new, unique, in a word, 'original'" (16).[9] T. S. Eliot, that paragon of literary modernism, illustrates the tenuousness of such conceptions of authorship when he stipulates the writer's job is to impersonally channel the tradition (i.e., defining works of a particular literary epoch) into their work as part of a "continual surrender of [them]self" so the writer's own personality remains separated from the work itself, thus positioning authorship as a kind of tapping into the collective sensibilities of a particular school of thought; yet Eliot also stipulates that true artists are masters of concentration who through acts of creation produce "a new thing resulting from the concentration" (2007, 539, 541). Even starkly anti-Romantic critics, that is, rely on conceptions of the individual author as chief controller of the creative process. As a result, the Enlightenment philosophy that positions knowledge as something humans discover, combined with Romantic conceptions of inspiration individuals conjure through focus and will, has resulted in a set of sensibilities that supports the economic rationalism that continues to influence how collaborators are conditioned to understand their work.

Even though she's not discussing coauthorship specifically, Kathleen Fitzpatrick points out how we are disposed to "draw boundaries around our texts" and to consider them distinct objects "separate from those of other authors" (2011, 72). This limited view is certainly one of the reasons coauthorship continues to be undervalued in the humanities disciplines, despite the fact that in literary studies, for example, teachers and scholars continually ask "fundamental questions about the very institution of authorship, how it came about, the aporias that underlie it, the economy that supports it, and the legal constructs invoked to justify it" (Biagioli and Galison 2003, 3). This irony hasn't gone unrecognized. In the Modern Language Association's most recent report on evaluating tenure and promotion, which is now more than a decade old, its authors acknowledge that collaboration is often treated with suspicion and assert the need "to devise a system of evaluation for collaborative work that is appropriate to research in the humanities and that resolves questions of credit in our discipline as in others" (2007, 57). The report even suggests humanities fields could learn from the "rigorous systems" devised by "academic disciplines in the sciences and social sciences" for assigning authorship credit (56–57). But the suggestion that in the humanities we should be shaping policies for collaboration modeled around authorship practices in these other disciplines implies these latter fields have figured out how such policies should work. It doesn't take much looking, however, to locate ongoing debates in these other fields that mirror those in the humanities, especially when it comes to the three criteria I mention above.

Consider the question of how to credit collaborative work. This is a challenge the natural and physical sciences have struggled to address.

For instance, consider how author-impact metrics have become ubiquitous in these disciplines, so much so that researchers are increasingly expected to quantify the impact of their scholarship as a performance measure. One of the most common of these metrics is the h-index, which is intended to assess the relative impact of a researcher based on the number and reach of their publications. Developed by the physicist Jorge Hirsch (thus the name of the metric, the Hirsch index) in 2005, the h-index works by calculating the number of citations of a scholar's work against the total number of that scholar's publications. If someone has a score of h, that means h of their publications must have been cited at least h times. For any readers who are like me and get apprehensive around what amounts to some pretty basic math, the h-index is not that difficult to understand once you see an example or two of how a score is derived from this metric. Let's say Eric has published four articles and each of these articles has been cited four times; these numbers mean his h-index score is 4. His score will remain the same even if one of Eric's publications has been cited twenty-eight times because the highest possible value of h is the total number of one's publications. Now let's say one of Eric's articles has been cited six times, one four times, and one three times, and his last publication has been cited only once; his h-index score is 3 because that is the highest shared number of citations his work has relative to the total number of his publications. What is important to note for the present discussion, however, is that the h-index doesn't take into account whether a publication has multiple authors.[10]

So, if two scholars each have an h-index score of 15, but three-fourths of the first scholar's publications are coauthored compared to one-fourth of the second scholar's, does that mean the second scholar is more productive? This hypothetical question only scratches the surface of the problems collaboration poses when it comes to author-impact metrics. "The more researchers involved in a project, the more complicated it is to quantify their individual contributions," something established metrics like the h-index can't do because they "ignore collaboration or assume equal contribution of each coauthor" (Stallings et al. 2013, 9680). So says a team of researchers who in 2013 proposed a new metric—in the same journal Hirsch's metric first appeared—that assesses "true credit shares" of coauthored publications, thus providing an avenue for "fairer evaluations of a researcher's individual scientific impact" (9680, 9685). I won't pretend to understand the mathematics at work in this proposed metric (they call it the "A-index"), but it uses three axioms to determine a set of scores that can be used to identify a so-called credit vector, which in turn is used to determine a researcher's relative level of productivity as a collaborator. What is worth noting about this proposed collaborative productivity metric is that it prevents coauthors from claiming credit shares the sum of which exceeds the total percentage of the publication. That is, two coauthors can't each claim 100 percent of the publication credit; the most they could each claim is 50 percent.

To follow this metric, in fact, requires a team of researchers to first group themselves into relative credit categories. A five-person research team, for example, might identify two credit levels, the first one worth 60 percent of the total publication credit and the second level worth 40 percent. After they split themselves into these two groups, credit share can be weighted according to each category and then distributed. One's A-index score is determined by the sum of these various credit-share weights in conjunction with another metric, like citation counts or journal-impact scores.

The point, however, is that these researchers believe quantifying collaboration is not only necessary but also possible. Biologist Cagan Sekercioglu also insists this type of calculation is necessary, but his proposed formula is much simpler: "The kth ranked coauthor can be considered to contribute $1/k$ as much as the first author" (2008, 371). If three coauthors are listed on a publication, the second author can be assumed to have contributed 50 percent of the first author's contribution, and the third author 50 percent of the second author's contribution, and so forth. In the end, what ultimately matters for proposals like these is, to use Sekercioglu's words, that "coauthors' contributions can be standardized to sum to one" (371).

There are two obvious shortcomings with proposals like these. First, despite their quantitative sheen, these formulas require collaborators to first determine a set of qualitative values. When it comes to the A-index, coauthors must invent credit-level categories and then decide which collaborators should be slotted into which categories. But these values will always be relative from one collaboration to the next, so the only way to "accurately" represent the different contributions to a coauthored publication is to specifically qualify who did what, something that, ironically, the researchers behind the A-index do in a note that indicates who designed, performed, and analyzed (three separate tasks) the research and then who actually wrote the article (Stallings et al. 2013, 9680). But there is another problem with these proposals, and that is what happens when instead of a handful of contributors to a publication, that number explodes into the tens, hundreds, or even thousands. Sekercioglu notes, for instance, that in 2006 the journal *Science* published at least one hundred papers with over five hundred coauthors, a fact that leads him to speculate, suspiciously I might add, about the legitimacy of collaboration in such scenarios (2008, 371).

But why would it be so hard to imagine that a group of 475 physicists associated with the CERN Large Electron Positron (LEP) can all be credited for the discoveries that have resulted from the collective efforts of their research? This isn't a hypothetical example. Peter Galison (2003) looks at multiple examples of collective authorship in the field of high-energy physics in his discussion of why the concept of authorship itself can be problematic when it gets treated as a zero-sum activity. After reviewing the authorship protocols of at least five large-scale "monster" collaborations, as he calls them, Galison notes that contrary to sentiments like those of Sekercioglu, who thinks too much collaboration diminishes credibility, the opposite is the case when physicists publish apart from the collective authorship of a research team.

> Disunity of authorship appeared to many if not most participants in these large collaborations as tantamount to epistemic subversion. All of these gestures of control served to create both an internal and external social-epistemic unity: they aimed at making the knowledge embodied in physics claims come from the group as such, not from its component parts. . . . The whole of these massive authorship protocols aims to form the "self" of a monster collaboration so that the "we" of the collaboration can produce defensible, authored science. (345).

The collective identity of a collaboration, in other words, holds more weight and is thus more important in these cases than individual claims of credit. Indeed, here the A-index would not only be impossible (How many different credit levels would have to be invented?), it would fundamentally undermine the epistemic authority claimed by the collective not despite, but because of, their collaboration. More to the point, and as Sarah Scripps, Soumitra Ghoshroy, Lana Burgess, and Allison Moss observe, "The vast increase in cost, scale, and complexity of scientific ventures over the course of the twentieth century" means "collaboration has become less of an option and more of a requirement" (2013, 48). In fact, single authorship in the sciences has all but disappeared, while in the social sciences it has become the exception rather than the norm (Endersby 1996; O'Brien 2012). But the fact that coauthorship has become more normalized in these disciplines doesn't necessarily mean the policies they use to account for it are unambiguous.

In the social sciences, for example, it is well established that authorial labor is designated according to the relative importance of each individual collaborator's unique contributions. But how does the APA instruct practitioners to make these determinations? Section 8.12 of the APA's guide *Ethical Principles for Psychologists and Code of Conduct* indicates that authorship attributions can only be given to individuals for work they "have actually performed or to which they have substantially contributed." Moreover, it reads, "principal authorship and other publication credits [should] accurately reflect the relative scientific or professional contributions of the individuals involved, regardless of their relative status" (American Psychological Association 2017). The double use of "relative" to qualify what is an otherwise direct statement opens up for debate the question of whether standardized practices of *attribution* can and should themselves imply standardized practices of *authorship*. That is, to what extent can a policy for representing the labor of collaborative authorship actually capture in any meaningful way what such labor consists of in any given case?

Most of us are familiar with the system of numbered authorship practiced in the social sciences and devised by the American Psychological Association: "The general rule is that the name of the principal contributor should appear first, with subsequent names in order of decreasing contribution" (2001, 350). But this system of numbered authorship doesn't address the question of what counts as authorship itself, especially when individuals might contribute to a collaboration without necessarily being responsible for generating its products, such as being directly involved in the writing of an article or report. In this case, the APA's guidance aligns with the standards outlined by the Office of Research Integrity, which is part of the US Department of Health and Human Services, in its online handbook *Avoiding Plagiarism, Self-Plagiarism, and Other Questionable Writing Practices: A Guide for Ethical Writing*. Here is the advice it offers for establishing authorship:

> Generally, examples of substantive contributions include, but are not limited to, aiding in the conceptualization of the hypothesis, designing the methodology of the investigation and significantly contributing to the writing of the manuscript. "Menial" activities, such as entering information in a database or merely collecting actual data (e.g., running subjects, collecting specimens, distributing and collecting questionnaires) are not, by themselves, sufficient grounds for authorship, but should be acknowledged in a footnote. (Roig 2015)

Even though it isn't explicit, authorship according to these guidelines implies some type of *invention*, the generation of ideas, methodologies, or text that directs or otherwise informs the overall scope of a research project. But even if we can draw a line that separates such activities from those considered "menial," it is still unclear how authorship becomes something distinct from contributorship, say, or editorial assistantship. Language should matter, obviously, so to say that "aiding" in the conceptualization of a hypothesis, for example, counts as a "substantive contribution" is to utilize a set of terms that on its face hardly clarifies the nature of authorship as a kind of labor.

Speaking of language, what significations inform distinctions academics make between the terms *research* and *scholarship?* What about the conceptual metaphor of *discovery* versus that of *creation?* To what extent does the work of writing in a particular field imply the *doing* of research as opposed to its *transcription* into a text? And where does the term *author* fit in these discussions, if at all? As Mario Biagioli (2003) points out, for example, after years of complaints about the challenges of attributing authorship, leading medical journals like the *Journal of the American Medical Association* (*JAMA*), *Lancet,* the *Annals of Internal Medicine,* and the *American Journal of Public Health* dropped the *author* designation altogether in favor of the term *contributor.* Biagioli explains the new policy adopted by *JAMA*: "Each name should be attached to a verbal description of that person's contribution, and the contributors list should be published on the article's first page" (2003, 265).[11]

But even when contributor roles are clearly qualified and delineated in a standard fashion, how should those things requiring attribution—data collection, research design, claims, written manuscript, and so forth—be understood? Are they *content, creations, constructions?* In the social sciences, the metaphors available to talk about these products often converge in ways that trouble easy distinctions between research and the inscription of research. Yet these distinctions persist. Referencing the work of Bernard Berelson's (1960) study of the first one hundred years of graduate education in the United States, Austin and Baldwin say that to understand the nature of academic coauthorship, we should distinguish between the "word disciplines" and the "data disciplines" (1991, 25). While James Endersby proposes that "modern science and the humanities can be distinguished by the likelihood of collaborative writing and research"—a comment that on its surface seems generalizable enough—he goes on to say humanities scholars "may continue to write alone as their subject matter is less likely to require the talents of others for the completion of their works" (1996, 380–81, 384). Even though this is speculation on Endersby's part, such an observation reinforces negative stereotypes about research in the humanities as being somehow less rigorous, or more basic, than research in other areas.

In humanities disciplines, where single authorship does remain the standard—one recent study concluded 90 percent of humanities scholarship is written by single authors (Scripps et al. 2013, 48)—there has been no shortage of attempts to reorient and restructure, respectively, the expectations ascribed to notions of scholarly authorship and the systems of evaluation that encourage these expectations in the first place. In her 2000 presidential address for the annual meeting of the Modern Language Association, for example, Linda Hutcheon bemoans that the organization still holds tight to "a model of the humanities researcher as, to cite Jonathan Arac [1977], 'the figure of the creator, treated as a distinctive, single isolated individual,' not unlike the Romantic genius" (2001, 524). In her own MLA presidential address two years later, Mary Louise Pratt echoes this sentiment: "Humanists' isolation or disengagement is greatly of our own doing. Humanists need to get beyond what Goldberg and Davidson [2004] call the romance of the scholar-prophet." Pratt insists on the need for "a culture of collaboration" (2004, 426). And in yet another MLA presidential address, this one more recent, Russell Berman criticizes the "garden variety illusion that scholars, and we humanists in particular, properly work in sublime isolation, when, in fact, we are always engaged in teamwork and networking," which he follows up by asserting the need for more "vibrantly collaborative scholarship" (2012, 451).

While public addresses such as these serve an epideictic function more than a deliberative one, to its credit the MLA has tried to be more forthcoming in its attempts to encourage greater recognition and reward for collaboration. Consider the opening paragraph of the "Evaluating Collaboration" section in the 2006 "Report of the MLA Task Force on Evaluating Scholarship for Tenure and Promotion":

> Solitary scholarship, the paradigm of one-author–one-work, is deeply embedded in the practices of humanities scholarship, including the processes of evaluation for tenure and promotion. Collaboration, however, offers significant opportunities for enterprising, untenured scholars to tackle problems or interdisciplinary topics too formidable in scale or scope for an individual. Sometimes collaboration simply offers the most satisfying way to approach an issue or problem in an article or a monograph. In fact, recent technological advances have made collaboration with distant colleagues easier, faster, and more efficient. And the special challenges involved in creating digital scholarship have led to new forms of collaboration in that arena as well. (MLA Task Force 2007, 56)

Notice the emphasis on practice in this statement, specifically its invocation of "recent technological advances" as a warrant for embracing a more welcome outlook on collaborative work. To what extent do appeals like this one, which point to changes in the infrastructure available to writers, presume that just because the potential for collaborative authorship has become more ubiquitous, more scholars will actually pursue these opportunities, especially when such work remains undervalued in their home institutions? That is, there remains an obvious disconnect when in an organization like the MLA there can be repeated calls from diverse voices for more and better recognition of collaborative work, but in terms of policy, the most that is offered are suggestions wrapped up in an if-you-build-it-they-will-come ethic.

But the MLA is light years ahead of other humanities organizations. Not only does the American Historical Association (AHA) have nothing on order in terms of policy statements or task-force initiatives that compare to the MLA's, at the AHA's annual meeting in 2017, the speakers on a panel titled "Is Collaboration Worth It?" collectively agreed that, yes, collaboration is worthwhile and should be pursued if possible, but they also agreed such work will be at best undervalued and at worst completely discounted when it comes to tenure and promotion. According to an *Inside Higher Ed* article about the panel (apparently the panel was enough of an anomaly at the convention to garner media coverage), audience members suggested "that the AHA might strategically or explicitly—perhaps through some document or set of guidelines—encourage institutions to reward collaborative research" (Flaherty 2017). Writing about the session in the AHA organ *Perspectives on History*, Seth Denbo (2017), an AHA staff member, acknowledges that the field has a distorted view of authorship, especially when one considers how much interaction takes place among historians, archivists, curators, editors, peer reviewers, and the like. But as Flaherty (2017) reports, one of the speakers on the AHA panel, Joseph Locke, nevertheless insisted "historians might be surprised by the appetite for collaboration, despite prevailing attitudes, as evidenced by scholars' willingness to contribute to his project," an open-source, collaboratively written history textbook. As other responses to the "Is Collaboration Worth It?" panel attest, Locke seems to be right about the growing desire among historians to pursue collaborative work; what's missing are accessible outlets for exploring different models of coauthorship that can be studied and replicated (Oatsvall and Scribner 2017; Poska and Amussen 2018).

If these responses are representative, the primary challenge to collaborative writing in the humanities has less to do with the material structures of support that make coauthorship possible, or even with the persistence of a narrowly conceived author construct, than it does with its collective inability to make visible the work of collaborative authorship in practice. It's not that there are disciplinary or institutional resistances to collaboration so overwhelming that coauthorship should be completely avoided, that is, nor is there a dearth of sound arguments for abandoning the myth of the solitary author. When it comes to the latter, humanists have them in spades; with the former, efforts to discourage collaboration increasingly come across as anachronistic, if not draconian. The problem is that humanists by in large have a difficult time imagining the viability of coauthorship as a creative rather than strategic resource.

It's easy, after all, to imagine the strategic benefits of collaboration when cowriters come together because they hope to capitalize on how their different backgrounds or sets of expertise might be mutually beneficial—this is what initially brought the three of us together in the example from my own experience I discussed earlier. It's much harder, however, to anticipate the novelty cowriting has the potential to manifest when you believe a writing project can be just as effectively, not to mention more efficiently, completed as a single author when you have been implicitly trained to think this way.

So what do we offer by way of authorship practices in writing studies, a multifaceted field that increasingly exerts its disciplinary authority as one that bridges the humanities with the social sciences? The closest thing to a policy guideline devised by compositionists can be found in a position statement released by the Conference on College Composition and Communication that describes the field's range of research practices. Tucked onto the end of a section titled "How Rhetoric, Writing, and Composition Scholars Conduct Research" is the following statement: "Scholars in rhetoric, writing, and composition often conduct and publish work collaboratively, and often eschew traditional notions of 'first author,' both because the field typically regards collaborative work as equal partnerships and because the order of names may not indicate contribution levels" (2018).[12] This statement is neither prescriptive, like the APA's system of numbered authorship, nor particularly suggestive, like the MLA's recommendations in its report on evaluation for tenure and promotion; if anything, it reads like a passing observation, one more suited for the fine print of a prescription-drug advertisement than an official guideline collaborators might reference to support their work. But as I've been discussing in this brief review of authorship economies, even the most articulated guidelines for accounting for and crediting collaboration often raise more questions than they answer. Moreover, standardized terms like *principal*, *lead*, and *first author* are at best semantic designations that do little more than reinforce systems of evaluation that atomize scholarly labor.

While attribution policies certainly have their place in debates about how to credit coauthored work, the more pressing need is for greater recognition of the complexity coauthorship entails. We should not conflate a generic system of attribution, in other words, with the labor required of coauthorship. Rather than ask for clearer guidance on how to attribute this or that piece of coauthored scholarship, then, I believe those of us invested in promoting the benefits of collaborative writing should pursue the more complicated inquiry of trying to better understand what coauthorship entails and why this labor often exceeds standardized practices of attribution in the first place.

Such is the work I begin to undertake in this book by sketching the contours of an interactionist theory of collaboration that draws attention to the complexity of the discursive ecologies collaborators are invented by just as much as they invent, which in turn points to the possibility for more creative and potentially more disruptive inquiry into the economies of authorship that permeate the institutions in which we work. Thus the foray into these economies I just offered so we have a baseline for articulating the stakes collaborative writers are up against if we want to disrupt these prevailing logics that continue to overwhelmingly position collaboration as a zero-sum undertaking.

* * *

In the chapters that follow I make an argument for rethinking our prevailing theories of collaborative authorship by drawing attention to the discursive mechanics that allow coauthors to produce writing in the first place. Given that digital platforms have increasingly evolved to facilitate new and streamlined methods for collaborators to share and produce work, and given that rhetoricians and compositionists are starting to contemplate the uses of new materialist and posthuman theories for understanding writing, now is an opportune time for such inquiry. But my hope for this interactionist theory of collaboration goes beyond my personal investments as both an advocate and practitioner of collaborative writing to echo Fitzpatrick's desire for all academics who are motivated to rethink the ways we approach conceptions of authorship in our theories and practices as teachers and writers, "not only because new digital technologies are rapidly facilitating new ways of working and imagining ourselves at work, but also because such reconsidered writing practices might help many of us find more pleasure, and less anxiety, in the act of writing" (2011, 51)—and, of course, the act of cowriting.

In chapter 1, I consider the current status of collaboration as a critical concept in writing studies by examining in detail a popular commonplace that circulates in the field, the claim that all writing is collaborative. As widespread as this claim is, I suggest it has little pragmatic value for collaborative writers who assert the quality of their work has been

multiplied because of their collaboration. Put another way, the claim
that all writing is collaborative flattens the ontological status between
texts single authors claim and those claimed by multiple authors. But
what is the origin of this claim? And how does it actually get used by
scholars and practitioners? The line of history I trace to answer these
questions begins with one of the field's most preeminent theorists of
collaboration, Kenneth Bruffee, and moves through a discussion of
how scholars have tried to come to terms with collaboration alongside
another concept that assumed new significance as a result of the social
turn, the idea of community. I then turn to recent disciplinary interest
in new materialist philosophies to consider an alternative set of ideas
about the nature of collaboration—ideas more mundane but also more
empirical—as the starting place for speculating about the work of collaborative composition.

In chapter 2, I step back to reconsider the function of talk in collaborative composition. Insofar as social turn approaches have foregrounded
the role of dialogue, or conversation, as constitutive of collaboration
itself, conceptually we are left with something resembling a chicken-and-
egg problem. In what ways can we say collaborators deliberately wield
their talk—Do they just take it up, that is, and tackle the work at hand?
If collaboration slows down writing processes, which I discuss in chapter
1, and if collaborative writers, like all writers, can't always anticipate what
their writing will produce, is it not disingenuous to present collaboration as a process or activity that can be controlled? To engage these
questions, I propose the advantage of framing collaborative composition
as a noninstrumental technology that affects the capacities writers bring
to and foster in collaboration when they engage composing processes
together. Taking up my own definition of collaboration as a mutual
intervention and progressive interaction with objects of discourse, I
position coauthorship as labor that hinges on the ability to anticipate
remedies to the various limit-situations (a term I borrow from Paulo
Freire [1970]) that all cowriters face, not the least of which is how to
account for the development of a draft that does not "belong" to any
single writer, or agent, within the collaboration. As I suggest at the
beginning of this introduction, social turn theories of collaboration fail
to account for the work of rhetorical invention, so this chapter begins
such an accounting by calling into question just what it is collaborators
control with their talk when they compose.

In chapter 3, I extend the discussion started in the previous chapter
to consider the question of agency and how to understand the discursive *techne* that allows coauthors to compose in ways that transgress

the boundaries of their rhetorical capacities as individual composers. Concern about the dynamics between individual and group agency in collaborative endeavors has been at the forefront of the field's scholarship on collaboration, which I review in this chapter by focusing explicitly on the politics of consensus in these debates. Taking up the work of Byron Hawk (2007), Marilyn Cooper (2011), Laura Micciche (2017), and others who have proposed or contributed to theories of rhetorical agency that take seriously posthumanist and new materialist approaches, I theorize cowriting agency as an emergent capacity coauthors develop in relation to the developing object of a shared text. But I also locate this cowriting agency in the sociological theory of George Herbert Mead, who articulated a philosophy of communication that was problematical in scope, meaning that communicative interaction between interlocutors is always motivated by the desire to maintain a common world, one that "is continually breaking down" (1964, 341). In this way, I position cowriting agency as a set of discursive relations collaborators produce that allows them, however contingently, to maintain a "common world" with/in their writing.

Chapter 4 tackles the fraught question of practice and what, if anything, an interactionist theory of collaboration means not just for how we teach collaborative writing but for how we pursue it ourselves. In this chapter, I turn to Bruno Latour and actor-network theory, specifically Latour's notion of what it means to write a "risky account," as a potential site of practice for enacting the rhetorical mechanics of collaborative composition in ways not just more visible but also more useful and interesting, if not provocative. Here I consider what collaborators might do if they want to inscribe their own risky accounts, but this discussion ultimately leads me to suggest that while I do not believe we can accurately render collaborative writing *in practice*, that is, represent the complex rhetorical assemblages of coauthorship in terms that reduce those assemblages to step-by-step processes, I do think we can depict, and see depicted, some of the traces (to borrow a term from Latour) of the ideas and impressions left in the wake of coauthorship as they are processed and articulated by the very people who experience them.

In chapter 5, I return to the topic of authorial economies and suggest that questions about how to qualify coauthorship are ultimately questions about how to coauthor. In an attempt to trouble the major schemes with which academics are asked to account for the labor of collaboration, I turn to a discussion of postqualitative inquiry, which is an increasingly popular approach to research in the social sciences, especially in educational research and psychology. Postqualitative theorists draw on an array of philosophical influences, perhaps none more heavily than the poststructuralist and psychoanalytical work of Gilles Deleuze and Félix Guattari. The primary project of postqualitative inquiry is to question the representationalist assumptions—including the strict boundaries and normative structures—of what its practitioners term traditional "humanist qualitative methodology." One of these assumptions is that a set of data speaks for itself and hence it is the qualitative researcher's job to make sure such data get rendered as objectively as possible. In response, postqualitative thinkers have embraced writing as a mode of inquiry, the methodological interest in which has led to a robust postqualitative conversation about collaborative writing and the politics of authorship in qualitative research. Building from this work, I suggest the possibility of what I call, adapting concepts from Deleuze and Guattari, a *minor literature of collaboration* as an active response to the "major languages" of authorship that circulate in most academic disciplines.

Finally, John Pell and I enact our own version of a minor literature of collaboration in chapter 6 to evidence some of the debts and influences that have impacted how we've developed as collaborative writers and how the ideas presented in this book (which I've written "alone") and across some of our other collaborative work together have influenced how we understand the work of writing in general, not just coauthorship.

Before proceeding, however, I'd like to point out two things about the organization and scope of this book. As you can see from the table of contents, the six chapters that compose the body of the book are organized into two parts, which I've respectively labeled "Speculations" and "Enactments." Even though the chapters in part 1 are more theory oriented and the chapters in part 2 are more practice oriented, I eschew such theory-practice dichotomies because like Thomas Kent (1997) I've come to recognize theory itself as a kind of practice, one that finds its virtue in allowing us to continually critique and reconstruct our beliefs and assumptions about phenomena that matter to us as we experience them (158). In part 2, the practices I discuss, and the ones John and I enact, are speculative and thus meant to suggest potential consequences for the ideas developed in part 1, but I hope my articulation of these possibilities remains elusive enough that readers are encouraged to develop their own ideas and observations about the potential uptake for the theory proposed in these pages.

And this gets to my second point. While this project doesn't pursue the kinds of empirical or qualitative research other scholars of collaboration have undertaken, my aim with this book is not to cast aside the research on collaborative writing that practitioners in rhetoric and composition have produced over the last three decades. It is instead to engage a specific line of inquiry that outlines a different set of theoretical starting points for understanding what happens when writers compose together, ones I hope might reinvigorate how we advocate for the importance of collaborative writing in the work we do as teachers, scholars, and administrators. With that said, the field of writing studies has no shortage of experienced collaborators who are passionate about their work and more than capable of accounting for it. Thus I hope this book can serve as an invitation to renew these conversations as we continue to develop as teachers and writers who promote the benefits of writing together.

PART 1

Speculations

1

IS WRITING INHERENTLY COLLABORATIVE?

UNDERSTANDING A COMMONPLACE

Compositionists interested in the subject of collaboration and its place in writing studies have at their disposal a well-established body of scholarship. If citation frequency is any indication of significance, standing at the forefront is Kenneth Bruffee's 1984 "Collaborative Learning and the 'Conversation of Mankind'," an article whose status as one of the field's foundational pieces of scholarship is affirmed by its inclusion in *The Norton Book of Composition Studies* and all three editions of *Cross-Talk in Comp Theory*.[1] Even though the article is ostensibly about classroom teaching, Bruffee "offers no recipes" for actually staging collaborative learning activities in practice; instead he offers a philosophical examination premised "on the assumption that understanding both the history and the complex ideas that underlie collaborative learning can improve its practice and demonstrate its educational value" (1984, 636).[2] At the time of this article's publication, teachers and theorists of writing were coming to terms with social constructionist epistemology and the idea that discourse is epistemic. As Bruce Herzberg explained it at the 1986 Conference on College Composition and Communication, discourse "is a form of social behavior" and "a means of maintaining and extending a group's knowledge and of initiating newcomers"; therefore, a group's discourse is "epistemic or constitutive of the group's knowledge" (qtd. in Bizzell 1992, 223). Even though educational psychologists had been studying collaborative learning for several decades—two of the more influential studies were M.L.J. Abercrombie's (1960) *Anatomy of Judgment* and Edwin Mason's (1970) *Collaborative Learning*—Bruffee saw an opening for using the idea of collaboration to unpack the significance of this social constructionist philosophy of language for teachers of writing and literature.[3] Drawing principally on Thomas Kuhn (1962) and Richard Rorty (1979), with nods to other social constructionists like Stanley Fish (1980) and Clifford Geertz (1983), Bruffee helped to clarify this line of

DOI: 10.7330/9781646420490.c001

theory by reframing the philosopher Michael Oakeshott's (1959) "conversation of mankind" figure to explain collaboration as the discursive mechanism that facilitates knowledge production.

The key to Bruffee's theory is located in the double meaning of "conversation" in this scheme, which not only signals what collaborators do when they work together—they talk—but also stands in metaphorically for the knowledge discourse communities produce, knowledge that is, to echo Herzberg, constituted by the group's discourse.[4] Bruffee thus theorizes collaborative learning to help illustrate the function of discourse communities, which is to say collaboration as an idea unto itself is not the focus of his concern in this article (or really any of his work on collaborative learning). But Bruffee's impact on how teachers of writing have subsequently come to understand the concept of collaboration has nonetheless been substantial, and not just because of the frequency with which his work has been cited.[5]

Consider the claim that all writing is collaborative, which is a commonplace for many compositionists. As Lisa Ede and Andrea Lunsford have noted in *PMLA*, for example, "The socially constructed nature of writing—its inherently collaborative foundation—functions as an enthymatic grounding for much contemporary research in the discipline" (2001, 355). James Reither and Douglas Vipond suggest that to imagine "writing as a collaborative process gives us more precise ways to consider what writers do when they write, not just with their texts, but also their language, their personae, their readers" (1989, 856). Similarly, Victor Vitanza argues that because our writing is always stimulated and informed by others, "Our acts of composition are always collaborative" (1994, xi), which is similar to the logic James Leonard and Christine Wharton utilize when they argue "any [piece of] writing is essentially collaborative" because "all textuality is intertextual" (1994, 36). It thus follows that, according to its entry in *Keywords in Composition Studies*, "collaboration signifies not only the phenomenon of two or more authors working on a single project but also extends to the view that all writing is collaborative" (Goggin 1996, 35). In sum, writes Jeanette Harris, to claim all writing is collaborative is "an assumption that cannot be dismissed lightly" (1994, 77). Even though none of these scholars point exclusively to Bruffee to defend their claims about the collaborative nature of writing, to make this claim in the first place relies on a conversational imperative that conflates collaboration with talk; and this conversational imperative, one emblematic of the social turn in rhetoric and composition studies more generally, can indeed be traced back to the double meaning of "conversation" in Bruffee's germinal work.

Indeed, consider Bruffee's otherwise innocuous claim that collaboration is at its core a social activity rooted in talk. Under the aegis of social constructionist epistemology, however, this claim assumes an overdetermined quality when it gets linked to another piece of social turn logic: that conversation, or discourse, is a function of community. As Bruffee sees it, it is through the give-and-take of conversation that a "community" of peers deliberates, so to understand the social construction of knowledge in this way is to understand the basic mechanics of collaboration insofar as this latter term can be used to describe what happens when knowledgeable peers work together to produce knowledge. Here is what Bruffee says to this effect:

> To the extent that thought is internalized conversation, then any effort to understand how we think requires us to understand the nature of conversation; and any effort to understand conversation requires us to understand the nature of community life that generates and maintains conversation. Furthermore any effort to understand and cultivate in ourselves the kind of thought we value most requires us to understand and cultivate the kinds of community life that establish and maintain conversation that is the origin of that kind of thought. To think well as individuals we must learn to think well collectively—that is we must learn to converse well. (1984, 640)

It is largely through this progression of warrants about the nature of conversation leading to his claim about the connection between thinking well and conversing well that Bruffee anticipates a conversational imperative, one later theorists of collaboration have negotiated by cataloguing *types* or *degrees* of collaboration to explain collaboration itself.[6] Moreover, this conversational imperative has made it seemingly impossible to define collaboration in positive terms without also relying to some degree on definition by example.

But this problem of definition has not gone unnoticed. As Ede and Lunsford write in *Singular Texts/Plural Authors*, "The meaning of *collaborative writing* is far from self-evident" (1990, 14), adding "the shifting and conflicting nature of *collaborative writing* seems to call not for simplification or standardization but for a Burkean complexifying—a series of perspectives by incongruity" (16). In the introduction to *New Visions of Collaborative Writing*, Janis Forman references the same Burkean concept to argue for "illuminating the complex discussions" about the meaning of collaboration (1992, xi), while John Trimbur and Lundy Braun, who contribute an essay to Forman's collection, suggest the idea of collaboration "has now entered into the discourse of studies of writing as part of the conventional wisdom," but rather than define what the term might mean, they simply explain "it has come to refer to a set of practices in the teaching of writing—collective work, mutual aid, nonauthoritarian styles of classroom life—that no one would think to dissent from" (1992, 21). In *(First Person)²*, Kami Day and Michele Eodice question the utility of specific definitions because "there are as many definitions of co-authoring as there are co-authoring teams—so we necessarily must define collaborative writing polytypically" (2001, 23). I agree, and for this reason I have no intention of proposing a standard for judging what activities should or should not be called *collaborative*. But this doesn't render useless the observation that under the rubric of social constructionism, it is difficult to explain collaboration as anything other than an engagement with talk.

Indeed, what Ede and Lunsford identify as the simplification and standardization of collaboration is more or less what I understand to be one of the long-term consequences of the social turn's conversational imperative. To return to Bruffee, conversation functions as the primary mechanism through which knowledge takes shape, for it is through conversation that peers deliberate. But as the challenges inherent in defining collaboration illustrate, the figurative value of conversation too often assumes a literal significance; collaboration can then only be explained by depicting what it looks like in different contexts. Thus we see at work an unfortunate consequence of Bruffee's initial theorizing of collaboration: any scenario in which conversation transpires becomes a space in which to see collaboration at work.

Accordingly, insofar as one can discern traces of literal or metaphorical conversation (i.e., social influence) in a piece of writing, such writing can be said to have a collaborative quality. And insofar as *all* writing has social influences of one kind or another, the claim that all writing is collaborative is thus a warrantable assertion.

But as evidenced by the above examples, when scholars similarly suggest the social dimensions of writing can be understood in terms of collaboration, just how the idea of collaboration itself can be accounted for in these respective contexts is difficult to say. What is clear, however, is that collaboration is often used to name a wide array of specific activities related to the production of writing that could well be described without invoking this notion at all: peer review, small-group work, writing center tutorials, joint research, brainstorming sessions, even metaphoric dialogues with other thinkers and writers far removed from the present moment. So on the one hand collaboration is an overdetermined process that directs the social construction of knowledge in discourse communities, but it also names an array of tactical configurations of individuals in proximity sharing a common task. When these two approaches to understanding collaboration as a critical concept in writing studies are examined side by side, the epistemic uptake this concept yields is more or less inconsequential because what it means, what collaboration *is* in any given context, is dependent on the contextual factors that inform however one chooses to invoke the concept in the first place. In other words, we should not assume collaboration means anything in particular when it is used to name a particular activity.

I'm nevertheless curious about the meaning of collaboration for those of us in writing and literacy studies interested in wielding this concept more deliberately, especially when it comes to promoting collaborative writing, something many of us do ourselves and in some cases—although probably not enough—require of our students. To state my concern directly, I believe we need to rehabilitate the idea of collaboration in general and collaborative writing in particular. As Ede and Lunsford have recently noted, the state of collaborative writing as a practice in rhetoric and composition, as well as the humanities more generally, "is no better than when we began writing together several decades ago" (2011, 190). In part this lack of progress is because, as they explained a decade earlier, "despite vigorous debates over theories and methods surrounding issues of subjectivity and authorship, ideologies of the individual and the author have remained largely unchallenged in scholarly practice" (2001, 358). To wit, commenting on the rise in popularity of digital publishing platforms and the ways they make collaboration easier to pursue, it is not lost on Fitzpatrick that "however communally minded our publishing practices might become, within our current practices writing is still something that we must undertake—and be evaluated on—alone" (2011, 50). In other words, even though composition and other literacy scholars have been asserting all writing is collaborative for over three decades, we have not figured out how to transform this bromide into a set of practices that have wide-scale influence on how collaborative work gets understood and valued in our institutions. In this way, what Louis Menand says of "interdisciplinarity" as a buzzword in postsecondary education holds true for collaboration: it isn't actually "subversive or transgressive or transformational or even new"; it is really just "a ratification of existing arrangements" (2010, 96).[7]

What, then, does this discussion have to do with the claim that all writing is collaborative? As I've already summarized, this claim points to what is the logical consequence of relying on social constructionist epistemology to theorize collaboration, namely the endowing of a conversational imperative that makes it difficult to explain collaboration as anything other than talk. And if that is what collaboration is, literal or figurative talk between peers, what is collaboration not? Keith Rhodes and Monica McFawn Robinson argue this is the kind of reasoning that plagues social turn epistemology in general, namely its existence as a "functionally tautological" philosophy (2013–14, 9). It operates on a closed feedback loop, one that makes it easy to assert certain ideas about the social—*all writing is collaborative*, for example—that have no clear meaning in practice. I thus echo Kathleen Blake Yancey and Michael Spooner, who submit, "If our theory must call all writing collaborative, then 'collaboration' becomes moot and useless as a theoretical construct" (1998, 56). But I'm not interested in simply reiterating critiques of social constructionism or underscoring what scholars like Yancey and Spooner have already said about our notions of collaboration.[8] Nor am I interested in the semantic elements of these debates; that is, I have no interest in calling people out who use *collaboration* vaguely. I want to instead interrogate the claim that all writing is collaborative as a starting point for imagining a more useful conceptual framework for understanding the mechanics of collaboration in terms that go beyond its conflation with conversation.

In particular, I'm interested in understanding collaboration, specifically collaborative writing, by way of the attributes we ascribe to it as both a product and a process. I'm curious about not just the agency cowriters bring to their work but also about the push and pull they experience from all the objects that impact the processes of constructing a shared text. How do cowriters identify and account for the various matters of concern that constitute the stuff of collaboration in any given instance? As Bruno Latour points out, accounting for such matters of concern requires a "multifarious inquiry launched with the tools of anthropology, philosophy, metaphysics, history, sociology to detect *how many participants* are gathered in a *thing* to make it exist and to maintain its existence?" (2004, 246). Instead of social turn epistemology, I believe new materialist philosophies like Latour's actor-network theory (ANT) offer a more revealing lens through which to consider questions about the mechanics of coauthorship because they hold in check what Latour in another context calls the "phantoms" of sociological study: nature, society, and power (2011, 802). For Latour, these concepts are reifications that often obstruct more than they reveal when posited as reasons for or sources of specific social phenomena. In chapter 3, I provide a more detailed description of how this new materialist theory can help us understand the agency cowriters construct to write together, but for now I'll simply say that getting at the idea of collaboration in terms of the things it assembles and is assembled by offers the beginning of a new critical vocabulary with which to discuss both the dispositions needed to pursue collaborative authorship and the qualities that make collaboration distinctive from one instance to the next.

But there are further reasons to question the claim that all writing is collaborative. First, such a claim tends to overlook actual collaborative writers, that is, writers who intentionally decide to coauthor. Compositionists' arguments for the inherently collaborative nature of writing make it harder to explain the qualities that distinguish collaborative composition from individual composition, which is a problem because many coauthors believe their writing has value *because* it was produced collaboratively. Coauthors' suggestion that their writing is better because it is coauthored is rarely an indictment of their individual abilities as writers; instead, this observation usually signals the coauthors' realization that collaboration allows for what Donna Qualley and Elizabeth Chiseri-Strater call, channeling Hans-Georg Gadamer, a "fusion of horizons" that leads to "an enlargement of one's perspective, what we might call a more complicated understanding" (1994, 111). The claim that all writing is collaborative by default, then, gives short shrift to the labor needed to successfully coauthor.

This leads to another reason we should question claims about the inherently collaborative nature of writing, which is that they don't actually tell us anything useful about collaboration itself. In addition to doing a disservice to collaborative writers who consider their coauthored work unique, calling all writing collaborative is ultimately a claim about writing, not collaboration. If one is curious about the work of collaborative composition—what it is, how it works, how best to pursue it—the idea that all writing is collaborative and the tradition of social turn theory that underwrites it don't actually point the way to useful knowledge about how collaborators compose apart from the individual processes they bring to a shared project. In fact, if all writing is collaborative, the best way to learn to coauthor is to learn to write as an individual author—that is, simply learn to write. Or better yet, simply keep doing what you have always been taught to do as a writer. I'm being facetious, of course, but to the extent that collaboration is understood as what happens when "two 'I's contribute pieces both with and independent of the other" (Mazzei and Jackson 2012, 450), this suggestion isn't actually bad advice. If what is ultimately at stake is my autonomy as a writer, and if all writing is collaborative in one way or another, what collaboration will always boil down to is the arrangement of coordinated, individual efforts. Accordingly, a good collaborative writer is first and foremost a good individual writer.

But such a nominal approach to collaboration hasn't gotten us very far. Again, I turn to Ede and Lunsford:

> What is to be gained by blurring the distinction between coauthorship (a specific, material practice where one or more persons collaboratively draft a document) and the inherently collaborative (or social) nature of writing and learning in general? We have claimed on many occasions and in numerous venues that writing is collaborative "all the way down." But to what extent have claims like this made it easy for both scholars and teachers to metaphorically pat themselves on the back for holding enlightened views even as they continue pedagogical and disciplinary business as usual? (2011, 193)

As most of my readers know, Ede and Lunsford are two of the most recognized scholars of collaborative writing, yet these coauthors reveal a palpable sense of frustration that "business as usual" continues alongside our "enlightened views" about the social dimensions of writing. These "enlightened views" have especially failed to register in our classrooms where single authorship is practiced almost exclusively. Moreover, when we do ask students to write collaboratively, how often do these assignments get assessed according to the individual contributions of each student? As Ede and Lunsford observe in *Singular Texts/Plural Authors*, "Students may work together on revising or problem solving, but when they write, they typically write alone in settings structured and governed by a teacher/authority in whom power has been vested" (1990, 118).

So, where do we go from here?

If we believe collaboration presents writers with a unique set of benefits single authorship does not, and if we want to not just defend but actively campaign for the value of collaborative writing in our own work and the work we require of students, we must do better than vague, token assertions about the social nature of writing. But we also must go beyond instrumentalist discussions that explain collaboration according to predefined activities. To echo Qualley and Chiseri-Strater, what we first need is a "more complicated" understanding of collaboration itself (1994, 111), one that suggests a method for talking about the rhetorical work of collaborative composition in terms general enough to hold across contexts but still remain flexible to the unique practices individual teams of collaborators construct out of their local circumstances. As evidenced above, I am not the first to question some of the commonplaces teachers of rhetoric and writing associate with collaboration. In fact, reviewing how rhetoric and composition scholars have pushed back against some of these commonplaces helps me to establish the value of what is not so much an intervention *in* but more of a departure *from* these previous lines of inquiry my own work in this book aims to accomplish.

THE HOPE FOR DEMOCRATIC COLLABORATION

One reason it can be difficult to make sense of the claim that all writing is collaborative is that as generalized concepts, writing and collaboration are much too unwieldy for such aphoristic compression side by side. Even so, the social turn logic behind this claim suggests defining either of these terms too closely limits the potential for the collaborative dimensions of writing to be actualized in practice. This is the concern Day and Eodice raise in (*First Person*)[2] when they suggest coauthors should feel empowered to define collaboration in whatever terms they choose because otherwise we risk circumscribing or quantifying the complexities of collaborative writing (2001, 24). In chapter 4, I elaborate on how this idea of giving collaborative writing teams the room to define their practices is paramount to the theory of collaboration outlined in this book, but there is an obvious futility at work when this freedom to name what we do as collaborative writers is paired alongside claims about the inherently collaborative nature of all writing. After all, social turn collaboration theory presents us with categorical claims difficult to actualize in practice because what these claims mean is categorically indeterminable. As Patricia Roberts-Miller explains of this logic more generally, "The pragmatic consequences are not very good" (2001, 103). So, what other concepts have been used to understand collaboration?

At this juncture, it might first be useful to identify the different forms collaborative writing can embody. By *forms* I mean the perceived relations between how a coauthored text is composed and then attributed. Despite their own caution that these categories are generalizations and shouldn't be reified, Ede and Lunsford's (1990) distinction between "hierarchical" and "dialogic" modes of collaboration (the former designating cowriting practices guided by a generic framework in which each contributor plays a specific role, and the latter designating cowriting practices to which each coauthor contributes equally throughout the process) has continued to be invoked by teachers and scholars since it was first articulated almost three decades ago. Paul Lowry, Aaron Curtis, and Michele Lowry suggest that five of "the most prevalent CW [collaborative writing] strategies can be described as group single-author writing, sequential single writing, parallel writing, reactive writing, and mixed mode writing" (2004, 74). Sequential single writing and parallel writing are two more nuanced designations for what Ede and Lunsford identify as the hierarchical mode;

the primary difference between the two is temporal, that is, whether a draft is passed around from one author to the next or all the authors contribute to the draft simultaneously. Group single-author writing is what happens when, say, a member of a committee writes a report on behalf of that committee; and reactive writing denotes collaborative writing undertaken in real time, what some might call *joint writing*. Mixed-mode writing, of course, designates some combination of these methods. Lowry, Curtis, and Lowry also identify six different authorial designations, or roles, collaborative writing teams might utilize to specify the nature of who did what during the process: writer, consultant, editor, reviewer, team leader, and facilitator (88). It's worth noting these schemes reported by Lowry, Curtis, and Lowry come from the sectors of professional and technical writing, which is to say they don't necessarily capture the collaborative processes of writing teams in other disciplines, nor do they account for the kinds of distributed and fragmented practices of collaboration described by Frances McDonald and Whitney Trettien (2017) that now occur in social media and other digital environments.

One thing all of the above forms have in common, at least in how they get discussed as methods, is in how they presuppose the need for well-defined roles among the members of a collaborative writing team. Without such structure, after all, conflict among individual collaborators is sure to result. I want to linger on this problem of interpersonal conflict because it is often pointed to as the primary challenge to a productive collaboration. As Bruffee notes, "The rocks and shoals of social relations" are always tricky and often impede the progress of collaborative projects (1984, 644–45). Too often, however, these social relations are imagined only in dialectical terms—as the interpersonal dynamics between individual collaborators—and collaboration in practice thus gets figured as whatever scheme has been established to manage a shared task while maintaining parity between or among collaborators.

As a result, there has been no shortage of theoretical debate focused on managing the proverbial meeting of minds needed to maintain the democratic ideals presupposed in social turn collaboration theory.[9] Perhaps the best way to illustrate this point is to examine how compositionists have accounted for another social turn keyword, *community*, and how debates about this concept have spilled over into debates about collaboration. Indeed, and to return to my question about what other concepts rhetoric and writing scholars have used to theorize collaborative writing, there is an interesting overlap in how concern for so-called community developed alongside and informed how social turn collaboration theory took root in the 1980s and 1990s.

When Joseph Harris published "The Idea of Community in the Study of Writing," he channeled Raymond Williams to suggest "the extraordinary rhetorical power one can gain through speaking of community," describing the term as not only seductive and powerful but also empty and sentimental (1989, 13). By this point social constructionist epistemology had reached its apogee in academic disciplines across the university, and Harris wondered whether the idea of community adequately represented what students encounter when they are introduced to scholarly writing, specifically the idea of academic discourse. While acknowledging the important work of theorists like David Bartholomae (1985) and Patricia Bizzell (1992) for helping compositionists understand the purpose of discourse communities in the teaching of writing, Harris pointed to several problems imagining such communities in practice.

> First, recent theories have tended to invoke the idea of community in ways at once sweeping and vague: positing discursive utopias that direct and determine the writings of their members, yet failing to state the operating rules or boundaries of these communities. . . . Recent social views of writing have also often presented university discourse as almost wholly foreign to many of our students, raising questions not only about their chances of ever learning to use such an alien tongue, but of why they should want to do so in the first place. And, finally, such views have tended to polarize our talk about writing: One seems asked to defend either the power of the discourse community or the imagination of the individual writer. (12)

It is one thing to grant the basic premises of a social constructionist theory of writing, Harris implies, while it is something else to understand the material consequences of such a theory in practice. As he questions, What good does it do to posit the ubiquity of discourse communities without also explaining the "rules or boundaries" that make them negotiable? How useful are these theories, moreover, if they impair what we can actually talk about when we talk about writing? These questions led Harris to wonder about the metonymic significance of *community* for abstract claims about the social nature of discourse, which in turn provoked him to argue how the use of this term to explain how discourse works begs more questions than it answers.

For other compositionists, such as Gregory Clark, the idea of community is central to any conceptualization of discourse that implies the possibility of democratic cooperation. If discourse is constitutive of the epistemic practices that define the identity of a group, Clark argues, we need the idea of community to acknowledge the shared values that inform those commitments that maintain a group's epistemic coherence. Turning to moral philosophy and care ethics, Clark points to Edith

Wyschogrod's (1990) and Nel Noddings's (1984) respective notions of "work" and "striving" to argue that negotiating disagreements is a necessary activity in the life of a community. Indeed, without disagreement we would be unable to enact the democratic ideals that underwrite the idea of community in the first place. As Clark explains, the work of building community "assumes collectivity is a process rather than a state of being, that it is itself an ongoing discourse in which people continually redefine their commonality in terms that emerge from discussion of their differences" (1994, 63). Community in this sense is not an empty and sentimental signifier, as Harris believes, but instead a kind of practice or discipline, one with ethical implications insofar as we must constantly push back against those homogenizing tendencies that impair a community's ability to accommodate and welcome diversity.

Below the surface of their apparent disagreement about the value of community as a critical concept for the teaching of writing, Harris and Clark basically argue for the same thing: the need to recognize conflict as an indispensable component in the construction and maintenance of discourse communities. Where these positions are really at variance is in their respective assessments of what should be the primary nomenclature for describing this kind of work. Harris thinks the idea of community is too commonplace and begs questions of agreement; he also thinks it does not offer enough upfront utility. Clark thinks the idea is necessary for conveying the relational commitments that make cooperation possible; he also appreciates its connection to democratic ethics. At the risk of oversimplifying the matter, I maintain these arguments are at root over issues of style. Deciding whether or not to use the idea of community in our talk about writing boils down to something that is equal parts taste and expediency.[10] But I have summarized these respective positions because of the emphasis these scholars put on the metaphoric significance of a specific keyword for teasing out the pedagogical implications of social constructionist epistemology.

In fact, Harris proposes a different metaphor he believes is better suited for this work. The image he chooses is a city because cities are easily recognizable as conglomerates of competing and overlapping communities (1989, 20). Indeed, the vitality of a city is dependent on the multiplicity of perspectives, values, histories, and talents that inform the identities of those who live and work within its borders. The idea of a city also provides conceptual space to account for writing as an indeterminate process without sacrificing the social constructionist imperative that, according to Bruffee's oft-quoted explanation, "understands reality, knowledge, thoughts, facts, texts, selves, and so on as community-generated and community-maintained linguistic entities—or, more broadly speaking, symbolic entities—that define or 'constitute' the communities that generate them" (1986, 774). In Harris's formulation, the city metaphor is therefore a better "symbolic entity," to echo Bruffee, for teachers and theorists of writing because it lends itself less problematically to the realization that conflict and disagreement are both precursors to and necessary for whatever can be said to approach the types of democratic engagement the idea of community implies when it is invoked to describe the discourse of a group as constitutive of the group itself.

Five years after Harris's proposal, Susan Miller also put forward the city metaphor as a concept that might be useful for teachers of writing interested in the pedagogical potential of social constructionist epistemology. But Miller isn't concerned with the idea of community; what she suggests the metaphor is better suited to represent is the work of collaboration. Specifically, Miller wants to make sense of the antagonistic negotiations that idealized conceptions of collaboration too often elide, or as she puts it, the "interactions that result when oppositions remain after all these well-intentioned and well-theorized processes" of collaboration have been explained (1994, 285). These "well-intentioned and well-theorized processes" are those put forward, according to her, by pedagogues such as Bruffee, Lunsford and Ede, Karen Spear, John Trimbur, David Bleich, and Anne Ruggles Gere, all of whom by that point were recognized advocates of collaboration and the social turn more generally. As for Miller herself, she is unapologetic in her commitment to "these [social turn] logics of collaboration" (284), so it was never a question for her as to whether she would apply this theory to her teaching. Accordingly, she recalls several experiences trying to enact with her students the kinds of collaboration she had come to associate with these well-theorized processes; one such experience even resulted in a jointly authored essay with five of her students that was published in *College Composition and Communication.*[11]

Overall, however, her students resented having to collaborate, which made sense, Miller realized, because nowhere else in the university were they encouraged to adopt such a collaborative mindset. As she writes, "What the students were *experiencing* as they moved through their first year of the university was, after all, the isolated, competitive, capitalist situation opposed by all who promote collaborative teaching, learning, and writing" (1994, 288). In the end, Miller concludes, "my informed understanding of social constructions of knowledge . . . hadn't been worth a damn" (289). The takeaway for Miller is that while social turn collaboration theory is sound *in theory*, it nevertheless fails to answer how the experience of collaboration *in practice* is supposed to alter "bourgeois visions of individuality" (296). In fact, she is afraid it might actually have the opposite effect: "My experiences, special efforts, and knowledge and teaching of collaborative theories together produced a successful article and by all accounts a valuable, highly interactive course. But they did not appear to change attitudes toward knowledge and knowledge-making, nor produce 'communities,' at least not as we now understand them in the literature of collaboration" (292). In other words, it wasn't that her students couldn't cooperate and work toward shared goals—they could—it was that they resisted adopting mutual identifications while doing so.

Here is where Miller finds utility in thinking about collaboration through the metaphor of a city, specifically a "discourse city," because such an "urban incarnation" better frames what kinds of agreement are and are not necessary for successful collaboration (1994, 299). Miller thus adds another layer of criticism to what Harris and Clark more or less recognize, that without having the opportunity to account for differences of opinion, aims, and techniques in the work we ask students to engage together, as well as the time and space in which to allow these differences to influence such shared work, social turn collaboration theory is inherently flawed. The model she proposes, her discourse city figure, thus calls on instructors to recognize that the purpose of collaboration should be to maintain movements of mutual exchange and recognition, not to force generic attempts at community.

What's important for the present discussion, however, is that even though she questions the utility of social turn collaboration theory, she doesn't actually abandon it. After all, she says, "most ideas and all published texts result from the presence of more than one person"; moreover,

> I am aware that learning done in discussion and engagement with others is retained better than the results of isolated study. As a theorist, I accept that ideas and texts reiterate and displace other ideas and other texts in social interactions that comprise intertextual exchange, not individualistic or inspired referents. I know that "meaning" resides in language rather than in extrinsic referents, and that agreements about meaning and about the significance of texts are produced by negotiation about words and cultural purposes, not agreements about a truthful, or valid, arrangement of an unmediated "reality." (1994, 284)

Although not word-for-word, Miller's confession of her philosophical commitments echoes Bruffee's (1986) definition of social constructionism. And while Miller doesn't explicitly proclaim all writing is collaborative, the balancing act she performs trying to account for the resistances that make collaborative writing difficult while still holding fast to the social turn epistemology that convinced her of the importance of collaboration in the abstract nevertheless evidences the primary challenge that has led scores of other writing theorists to draw this conclusion.[12]

But this is what happens when we start with overgeneralized premises about collaboration. It is easy to make the leap from theory that posits the social nature of writing to the conclusion that writing is collaborative *all the way down*. I've singled out Harris's, Clark's, and Miller's work because they evidence how concerns about the nature of discourse communities have informed how the field of writing studies understands collaboration, which is to say theorists have overwhelmingly concerned themselves with questions about conflict and consensus as constitutive features of collaboration itself (a topic I take up more closely in chapter 3). Miller was nonetheless on to something with her recognition that social turn theory doesn't offer much in the way of a conceptual orientation for experimenting with methods of coauthorship in ways that reveal the differences collaboration makes for those who deliberately choose to coauthor.

But it's one thing to challenge the utility of these social turn concepts and something else entirely to set them aside. To do the latter, I suggest, we must direct our attention to the missing masses of collaboration our social turn theory has largely left behind. That term, "missing masses," comes from Bruno Latour, who uses it to designate the many different types of objects that disrupt cursory conceptions of human agency. Depending on the context, these missing masses might be xerox machines, laws, instruction guides, weather patterns, social-networking apps, bank-account balances—anything and everything that could be said to impact how we do things in the world.[13] For Latour, what really matters is the *matter* at play in those situations we wish to understand, that is, all the things that give a situation its material significance. While Miller was far from anticipating the type of inquiry Latour proposes, we must give her credit because she was nevertheless interested in tracing actual engagements of collaboration that challenged her assumptions about this slippery concept and the assumptions writing theorists were bringing to it. Like all writers, collaborative writers rely on innumerable objects and artifacts to articulate texts, not the least of which are the discursive objects that assemble in the talk collaborators produce as they write. This brings me to my own definition of collaboration, which I share in this book's introduction: *a mutual intervention and progressive interaction with objects of discourse.* Even when collaborators write separately and then combine their respective texts after the fact, they still must mediate shared objects of discourse: questions, ideas, propositions, theories, vocabularies, interpretations, and innumerable combinations thereof.

When we recognize that collaborators must always share objects of discourse, then, it gets harder to chalk up the resistances collaborators negotiate as the natural consequences of interpersonal conflict. Collaborators indeed must constantly negotiate conflict, but this conflict is never dialectical in the social turn sense; rather, this conflict is always triadic. That is, collaborators don't just negotiate a shared relationship with one another, they must negotiate a set of shared *relations* with the objects of discourse that populate the rhetorical ecologies of their collaboration. These relations thus figure the very things through and about which collaborators compose. As those who have experience with coauthorship no doubt understand, navigating these relations is in turn what makes collaboration difficult; or, to borrow from Latour, these relations are what can render it a "trial."[14]

WRITING SLOW: WHAT COLLABORATION DOES

> *In fact, writing's distinguishing feature might be that it unfolds*
> *in increments, revealing and becoming itself over time.*
> —Laura Micciche, *Acknowledging Writing Partners*

At this point I want to shift gears. Most of what I've done so far is to outline a set of reasons for looking beyond the social turn logic that continues to influence how the field of writing studies talks about collaboration. But at this juncture I want to suggest a thought experiment of sorts. Perhaps the claim that all writing is collaborative isn't necessarily wrong, its logic just needs to be reversed. To start with the premise that collaboration animates writing doesn't do much by way of inspiring us to change how we actually compose. But if we believe collaboration has the potential to offer writers advantages not available to them when they compose alone, what if we simply reverse the logic at work in this claim? That is, instead of using major premises about collaboration to make deductions about particular instances of composition, what if we start with particular instances of collaboration to inductively speculate about composition itself? In other words, what does the experience of collaboration stand to teach us about the work of writing more generally?

Part of the inspiration for this line of inquiry comes from Latour's distinction between "actants" and "actors," key concepts in actor-network theory. In his Tanner Lectures at Yale entitled "How Better to Register the Agency of Things," he explains that actants can be thought of as a list of performances that, once observed, reveal traces of their transformation in objects that can then be called upon to explain future action. Most of these transformations are "trivial," he notes, and he offers the hypothetical example of a cotton pad:

> For instance, episode one, a pad of cotton absorbs water; then, episode two, it is named "hydrophilic." The difference between the two episodes . . . is that absorbing water is an action performed on some lab bench with some material contraption by some people who don't yet know what the "properties" of the material under scrutiny are, while "hydrophilic cotton" is a well known substance that has as one of its attributes the property of absorbing water. (2014, 82–83)

Latour is famous for employing mundane examples to illustrate his theory, and this one is no different. But his central point is nonetheless clear: to make reliable claims about what a thing can do—to talk about a thing's "competence" in Latour's idiom (83)—requires careful observation of that thing's properties. If the scientific tenor of this example is off-putting, Latour notes "the situation is exactly similar although reversed for those who write in the humanities or in the social sciences. The specific opacity of their accounts comes from the hard work they have to do so as to counteract the familiarity their readers believe gives them access to the characters acting in the narrative" (8). The function of most scholarship in the humanities and social sciences is to reconstruct "actors" (texts, theories, behaviors, events, histories, interpretations) by returning to the actants that inform what these things are and how and why we recognize them as such. In the humanities, that is, we tend to take more interest in the things that inform how specific concepts and beliefs function in the world and the consequences that result.

To discuss a familiar concept like collaboration in the way I'm suggesting, for instance, the tricky part is convincing writers to reverse what is an otherwise deductive course of inquiry and move away from generalized claims that bypass the particular toward a position that allows for close observation of the various properties of collaboration in specific times and places. This latter kind of inquiry is what Latour is getting at when he says, "Let us 'increase the dictionary' by slowing down a bit and being unabashedly speculative" (2014, 82). Playing on a line from Alfred North Whitehead, he is saying that by slowing down our generalizations, we stand to enlarge the critical vocabulary available for studying the phenomena in question.

But how would this work for studying collaboration, especially since collaboration itself is already such an overgeneralized concept?

To return to my definition of collaboration as a mutual intervention and progressive interaction with objects of discourse, one of the first moves is to develop an appreciation for the three-part arrangement this definition implies: (1) to involve oneself *with another* (2) in a *developing* engagement (3) with a particular set of *objects* that mediate what can be mutually articulated together. I hesitate to use the word *language* and opt instead to employ *objects of discourse* because the philosophies that inform this definition, including interactionist rhetorical theory and new materialism, do not assume the relationship between thought and speech (or agency and action) is governed by closed systems that determine what we can know, speak of, or do in advance of a given situation. Accordingly, collaboration shouldn't be conceptualized as the two-way, or dialogic, interactions shared between coauthors because such interaction is always at least partially mediated by the shared objects of their attention. And the meaning of such objects, including the complex discursive object of an emerging coauthored text, will always be dependent on how well collaborators can triangulate their interactions.

Triangulation is the term the analytic philosopher Donald Davidson uses to name the process of discursive exchange through which we communicate with others. According to Davidson, to understand how we communicate requires first and foremost an awareness of how interlocutors share meaning in passing, not a systematic theory of meaning that exists prior to actual moments of discourse (2006). In "A Nice Derangement of Epitaphs," Davidson argues that to understand discursive interaction, we must make a distinction between what a speaker *intends* their words to mean and how those words are actually *interpreted* in the moment. He points to malapropisms to show this distinction at work. I might say to a friend, for example, "You're still welcome to drop by on Friday, but for all intensive purposes the party is canceled," without realizing the conventional phrase is *for all intents and purposes*. I *intend* my utterance to convey the meaning "for all practical purposes," but the literal meaning of my utterance (if we consider the conventional meaning of *intensive*) is something altogether different. If my friend picks up on the malapropism, it might elicit a guffaw, but my misspoken phrase is likely to go unheeded because we both understand what I intended to say. What is needed to understand discursive exchanges like this one, says Davidson, "is a firm sense of the difference between what *words* mean or refer to and what *speakers* mean or refer to" (98). We deduce the meaning of a word or phrase according to a convention, or theory, based on prior experience (how specific words and phrases tend to be interpreted). But our theories of what words mean are not always sufficient for interpreting another's discourse. More often than not, however, we can adjust our "prior theories" to quickly arrive at "passing theories" if we realize another person is using discourse in a way that does not align with our expectations. As Davidson explains, "For the hearer, the prior theory expresses how he is prepared in advance to interpret the utterance, while the passing theory is how he *does* interpret an utterance. For the speaker, the prior theory is what he *believes* the interpreter's prior theory to be, while the passing theory is the theory he *intends* the interpreter to use" (101). To put this more directly, we often can understand what someone means just by paying attention to the contextual information supplied in the course of speaking.

Seasoned composition instructors, for instance, are usually adept at interpreting the writing of even our most inexperienced students. Part of our job, after all, is to help novice writers identify and negotiate the prior theories of audiences who expect written discourse to perform in certain ways. But we also know, of course, that following conventions does not always result in effective writing, just as we know that following conventions too closely might occasionally produce bad writing. Scholars in rhetoric and discourse studies have explained Davidson's philosophy of language and its implications for teaching composition, so I will not rehearse what has already been done.[15] Important for my purpose here is to underscore that Davidson takes the process of interpretation out of the minds of individuals and locates it in their discursive interactions with one another *and the world.* Here is where the concept of triangulation is relevant. As Eli Dresner notes, "Davidson maintains that we assign meaning to another's utterances not by translating them into our own language, but rather by associating them with things in the world surrounding us" (2009, 124). Triangulation therefore names the process through which interlocutors adjust their talk (or conversation) to share objects of discourse—to triangulate with whatever things in the world, even abstract things like ideas, they intend to discourse about.

To understand the concept of triangulation as a critical component in the discursive work of collaboration, we must recognize that what collaborators foster with one another is an enhanced capacity to triangulate meanings. The more effectively collaborators anticipate the passing theories necessary to share meaning, the more efficiently they can use their talk to reflexively interact within the discursive ecologies that inform the purposes of their work. This idea extends what Day and Eodice observe in their qualitative study of academic coauthors, that collaboration "consists of a great deal of talk, which involves negotiation and invention that leads to decision-making" (2001, 127). It also reinforces Karen Spear's observation about the discourse collaborators produce: "The act of talking is a process of discovering, articulating, and clarifying meaning based on the flow of verbal and non-verbal cues the interaction generates" (1988, 6). What Spear doesn't say is that this "flow of verbal and non-verbal cues" doesn't just transpire between and among individual collaborators; it involves all the objects, or actors, that influence the talk generated in collaboration. Moreover, the talk collaborators foster is hardly seamless. Indeed, to effectively share discourse, collaborators must continually confront resistances that hamper their ability to triangulate meanings. Thus, consider how this line of speculation about the work of collaborative writing leads us to a different point from which to understand composition more generally.

To return to the question I posed in the opening of this section, What if we were to begin with specific instances of collaboration as a way into a more general speculative inquiry about the work of writing? If we did, we would start with the actual discourse collaborators foster, which must include not just their habits of conversation but also a consideration of the material-discursive ecologies that provide the complex of objects with which they interact *as collaborators* to write together. And if Davidson's notion of triangulation is a helpful starting point for understanding the rhetorical labor needed for collaborators to share objects of discourse, I think we can anticipate two general, if not obvious, conclusions about collaborative writing that probably hold from one instance to the next. First, collaboration inevitably *slows down the writing process*; second, as a result of this slowdown, the writing process itself becomes *more observable*, or as Latour would say, *more traceable*.

I don't necessarily mean to suggest collaboration slows down the writing process in a diachronic sense, although many teams of coauthors would no doubt say their work together takes longer. Rather, I mean the temporality of writing is intensified—how we experience the work of composition in passing. "Writing time is thick with bodies, feelings, materials, others," writes Micciche; moreover, "what finished writing obscures is not only the daunting amount of *real time* that goes into making scholarly work, but also the traces of a writer's changing interests that form *over time*" (2017, 65, 68; emphasis added). Keep in mind that collaborators not only must continually triangulate with objects of discourse to foster their shared conversation, but they also must mediate their work around myriads of other resistances, both material and abstract, those missing masses that may not get taken up directly in the discourse collaborators inscribe but nonetheless influence the development of that discourse *in time*.

At the time of this writing, for example, I'm in the early stages of two separate writing projects with my frequent collaborator, John Pell. For one of these projects, we are writing about a subject fairly new to us, whereas the other is on a subject we've been studying and writing about, both together and independently, since graduate school. I mention this because this second piece will inevitably prove harder to complete even though we have made roughly the same amount of progress on both. I can make such a prediction because the rhetorical ecology of that second project is more complex, or, rather, more developed than that of the first project, by which I mean there are far more objects we will inevitably conjure and confront by virtue of our collective experience with this subject, objects that will slow down, in the Latourian sense, the progress of our writing. But I can also predict that as we continue working on these projects, our conversations about each will bleed into each other as we assess where we are with each piece: *What needs to happen next? What can be put to the side? What needs to be reconsidered?* and so forth. What I'm saying is that even if we were to set aside one of these projects to just focus our efforts on the other one, it would be difficult to *not* have to acknowledge and account for the objects that have emerged and will emerge from the project we've set aside (not to mention all the various other responsibilities we manage), these missing masses, so to speak, that will bear upon how we experience the labor of writing together *in* and *over* this specific period of time.

Of course, as all collaborative writers know, collaboration sometimes takes too much time to justify pursuing a collaborative writing project in the first place. But I venture the time factor itself is not always the primary reason some writers shy away from collaborative work. It is also because of all the other various resistances that come to light when the slowdowns of collaboration manifest: insecurities, idiosyncrasies, unanswered questions, hurt feelings, misunderstandings—the things, in other words, that make the labor of writing with another all the more immediate than the labor we typically associate with the writing we undertake alone. In short, to claim collaboration slows down the writing process is simply to say it intensifies our recognition of its myriad fits and starts and the many obstacles revealed therein.

But to leave aside for a moment all the nondiscursive resistances that impact how writers compose—things like scheduled writing times, internet connections, how hungry or tired or distracted we might be, a sticky M on the keyboard, or the noise of a new parking garage under construction across the street from one's office—what is always most taxing about collaborative writing is the basic work of triangulating with the discourse collaborators struggle to invent. Articulating questions, identifying problems, interpreting data, clarifying suggestions, refining meanings—all of this requires *producing a lot of talk,* a lot of *conversation.* But insofar as collaboration can be understood as a mutual intervention and progressive interaction, the discourse collaborators foster eventually becomes an actor in the collaboration, something that begins to push back against the attempts of its coauthors to develop it. But the processes of triangulation can be further honed as this discourse gets inscribed, as it becomes an artifact. It will no doubt lack clarity at points, reveal inconsistencies in organization, and, in the way all developing writing often acts on our psyches, suggest to its collaborators that it isn't very good. But like Latour's example of a hydrophilic cotton swab, as the contours of this developing artifact emerge in ways observable to its coauthors, it will gradually reveal the writing it might or even should become.

So, finally, is this an adequate response to the claim that all writing is collaborative? Stepping outside the currents of social turn epistemology, I think what we can tentatively conclude is that while this claim is not necessarily false, it certainly is not useful because its logic is moving in the wrong direction. Instead of calling all writing collaborative, let's instead consider how collaboration is always an attempt at composition—an attempt at writing. On the surface this latter claim is trite and maybe even uninteresting; it also lacks epigrammatic appeal. But it does point the way toward another commonsensical idea that should nonetheless be asserted: just as we know that no two *individual* writing processes are the same from one instance to the next, neither are the *collaborative* processes coauthors negotiate.

If we recognize collaborative writers are like all writers insofar as they must renew and sometimes reinvent the processes through which they compose each time a new exigence presents itself, it becomes clear that overgeneralized claims about the social nature of writing rooted in the idea of collaboration elide the very thing we can say with relative confidence about collaboration itself: it almost always slows down the work of writing and in that slowdown reveals more of the resistances all writers confront. In this way, collaboration *enlarges* the work of writing as it invites us to be more attuned to the processes we engage every time we compose, whether alone or with others.

So, what happens if we follow Latour's invitation to "increase the dictionary" by learning to take advantage of the slowdown collaboration affords?

In the early pages of *Reassembling the Social,* his popular treatise on actor-network theory, Latour explains that in situations where "innovations proliferate" and "where group boundaries are uncertain," we must "follow the actors themselves" (2005, 11, 12). Critical of how sociologists often cast their subjects of study as entities only understandable according to the terms of their own "master vocabulary," Latour admonishes sociologists to "keep as their most cherished treasure all the traces that manifest the hesitations actors themselves feel about the 'drives' that make them act" (36, 47). To mix proverbial wisdoms, don't put the cart before the horse, and remember actions speak louder than words. In short, slow down and let subjects speak for themselves. Don't be in a hurry, moreover, to ascribe a particular phantom force as the reason for this or that behavior in an attempt to nail down the meaning of whatever is the thing under study.

Insofar as we are concerned with how better to understand and in turn promote what collaborative writers do when they compose, Latour becomes especially useful in his insistence that we slow down our observations to consider the ways actors work together to form unique assemblages that can ever only be defined momentarily and in retrospect according to the relations the actors themselves perceive. In order to observe what collaboration is we must allow coauthors to observe what it is, which is to say we shouldn't make sweeping generalizations about the nature of collaboration that we expect to hold true—and more important, useful—from one instance to the next. But this doesn't mean we cannot identify the kinds of questions that might productively direct our general knowledge about what collaborative composition entails.

TO BEGIN AGAIN

I've spent this chapter interrogating the commonplace that all writing is collaborative because of its metonymic connection to the social turn philosophy that underwrites it. I've explained why I don't believe this commonplace—and by extension social turn epistemology more generally—offers us much of anything in terms of practical value, by which I mean I don't believe it points the way to a useful philosophy of collaboration that can be drawn upon to enhance our own understandings and experiences of collaborative composition *in situ*. Furthermore, neither does it point to a persuasive set of premises from which to argue for the value of collaborative composition, especially in the humanities where our economies of authorship overwhelmingly dictate that we prioritize single authorship in not only our own writing but also in the writing we ask of our students.

In this way, I have been trying to show why those of us interested in the work of collaborative composition might consider whether there might be something better on offer than the social turn collaboration theory that has guided research in this area for over three decades.[16] I believe there is, and I've started to articulate an interactionist theory for approaching collaboration drawing upon externalist language philosophy and new materialist ontology. While subsequent chapters flesh out this theory, I view my work in this first chapter as an experiment in what I. A. Richards calls "practical criticism" (1930), which Ann Berthoff explains as the work of "tracing the sources of misunderstanding so that remedies [can] be arrived at more rationally" (1991, 23).

More than half a century before Latour's critique of contemporary sociology, Richards posed a similar argument about literary criticism. Frustrated with what he perceived as a reliance on diffuse, nonsystematic methods of interpretation, Richards proposed a framework for literary criticism as an empirical enterprise. "All of the great watchwords of criticism," says Richards, "are ambiguous pointers that different people follow to different destinations." He continues, "Even the most sagacious critical principles may, as we shall see, become merely a cover for critical ineptitude; and the most trivial or baseless generalization may really mask good and discerning judgment. Everything turns upon how the principles are applied" (1930, 12). This last sentence anticipates an idea Richards later developed in *The Philosophy of Rhetoric*, that to understand what a theory means, just study how it is used, or as he puts it, "how we use a theorem best shows us what that theorem is" (1936, 27). Indeed, the claim that all writing is collaborative is for compositionists a case in point of what Richards probably meant when he said a critical maxim uncritically deployed is no more helpful than "a will-o'-the-wisp" (1930, 12).

Practical criticism is pragmatic; it approaches theory as an instrumental engagement with ideas. That is, how people use ideas is often the best indicator of what those ideas mean—what differences they make. The claim that all writing is collaborative has been ripe for such practical criticism for a long time, so as we consider other ways to talk about the work of collaborative composition, let's take as a guiding ethic this reminder: what a theory is ultimately depends on how others take it up. Such an ethic will surely be useful as we turn in the next two chapters to the vision collaborators foster for their work and the agency they must negotiate to complete it.

2

THE TECHNOLOGY OF TALK

Very early in my research on collaborative writing, before I even knew what exactly I was researching, I came across an essay titled "Collaboration in Practice" by Chris Anson, Laura Brady, and Marion Larson. Published in 1993 in *Writing on the Edge*, a journal with "a pronounced touch of belletrism" that exists "on composition studies' border with creative writing" (Hesse 2019, 387), Anson, Brady, and Larson's essay was unlike the other scholarship on collaborative writing I had read up to that point. Manifesting as a mix of process essay, scholarly literature review, and pedagogical reflection, the piece chronicles the history of its authors' collaboration while assessing in personal terms the scholarly and pedagogical terrain for collaborative writing as a viable practice in postsecondary education. What makes the essay different, or at least what made it different to me at that particular stage of my professional development, is the scope of its provisionality as a piece of scholarship: no direct claims, no positing of theory, no close engagement with data. Instead, these cowriters treat their readers to a story about how they became collaborators and what they have so far learned about collaborative writing, and writing collaboratively, through the process.

That last point about no close engagement with data isn't quite correct because Anson, Brady, and Larson do engage some data, and rather closely. It's just that these data comprise entries from, as they describe it, an "informal, collaborative journal" they began keeping several years prior to composing their essay (1993, 83). When it comes to the essay's structure, these coauthors share selected entries from their journal, explicate these moments retrospectively, and then read these explications alongside the then-current literature on collaboration in composition studies. Indeed, and despite my initial questions about the structure and scope of their writing, Anson, Brady, and Larson creatively represent what is an otherwise persuasive scholarly portrait of "collaboration in practice," to echo their title.

But reading this essay when I did, almost twenty years after it was originally published, I was drawn to one detail these cowriters included

DOI: 10.7330/9781646420490.c002

when discussing how they pursued their collaboration. After noting how they "wanted to proceed slowly" so as "to explore [their] collaborative terrain carefully, to be aware of the risk of competition and other obstacles," they say this about their journal: "This single, 'dialogic' notebook—composed on a computer disk and exchanged among the three of us (a hybrid compromise between e-mail and regular correspondence)—allowed us to identify other textual goals by conversing about different aspects of collaboration" (1993, 83). These writers, as you can read, maintained their growing text, a collaborative journal that was being used to explore the subject of their collaboration, on *a computer disk* they passed back and forth.

Chalk it up to my status as a millennial, but I fixated on this detail. How was the disk labeled? Did they keep any backup disks? I imagined scenes in which these collaborators meet at a conference, say, and one of them passes a little blue or black or grey computer disk to their fellow collaborator, who then stows it in the side pocket of a satchel or slips it into an envelope that is then deposited into a suitcase, where it stays for several days until this person arrives back at their campus office where they have the available hardware, a desktop computer, to read the journal's latest entry. But how soon until they compose a new entry? And what happens after that? In my mind I could imagine this writer hitting the Save button, ejecting the disk, and then sending an email (or do they make a phone call?) to their two collaborators to plan the next hand-off.

I share this memory here because I can now articulate that what so intrigued me by Anson, Brady, and Larson's essay is how it reflects these collaborators' engagement with emerging technology to engineer a kind of sociotextual experience that until then was probably hard for many people to imagine as a viable method for coauthorship—this sharing of a single, digital document that belongs to none of the writers individually even though they can individually add, delete, and write over the text in ways that give the text itself a kind of agency. Keep in mind that "track changes" wasn't a feature available in word processors at this time. So each time one of these collaborators opened their journal after the previous collaborator passed it along to them, they encountered a text that had changed, that had grown or morphed in ways that influenced not only how these writers experienced this coproduction of writing but also how they envisioned its possibilities. Indeed, Anson, Brady, and Larson hacked together a method of cowriting that resembles what is now a fairly standard practice: sharing documents and writing collaboratively on cloud-based platforms. True, these three collaborators couldn't write in their journal synchronously, nor could they access it with the ease we can access such documents today. But their makeshift method allowed Anson, Brady, and Larson to experiment with collaboration in a way that forestalled potential narratives of attribution that might easily account for each of these collaborators' individual contributions to their writing. Just consider the disclaimer these coauthors offer to those who may be curious about the voices that come through in the text: "Once in a while you'll hear a first-person pronoun which reflects one of our more individual entries, but clear from your minds any connection between these entries and us as individuals. Since we all entered the dialogic notebook and wrote into (sometimes over) each other's entries, we can no longer tell where one person's words end and another's begin" (1993, 83–84). As they go on to explain the experience of this method, what it was like to share their journal via this drawn-out process of circulating a computer disk, these coauthors note that their collaborative writing expanded how they understand composition more generally. "Collaboration doesn't replace other processes," they observe, "it extends the scope and possibilities of writing (and other) practices" (85), a claim that gets at the idea of how collaborators can foster capacities not available to writers otherwise.

Collaboration itself can therefore be imagined as a technology that "extends the scope" of what writers can do when they are able to manipulate this technology for productive ends. When it comes to their experimentation with collaboration as a method of textual production, then, we can provisionally observe how Anson, Brady, and Larson engaged with various material technologies to cultivate a discursive technology, one that, once underway, "erased discourse boundaries, erased ownership, and foregrounded the practical negotiations involved in creating a collective text" (1993, 87). But I'm not the first person to suggest such a connection between the technology of collaboration and the technologies that help facilitate it. Ellen Schendel, Michael Neal, and Cecilia Hartley, for instance, have examined "CMC [computer-mediated communication] and collaboration as separate but intertwined and interdependent technologies" (2004, 195). They note in particular that processes of collaboration influence technology just as technology influences these processes, or as they say more specifically, "The ways in which people contribute to and the technologies they use to participate in the system largely influence the work that can be accomplished collaboratively" (202, 203). While they don't use these terms, Schendel, Neal, and Hartley are essentially drawing attention to the ways the technology of collaboration is constrained by the material conditions of the technologies writers utilize to collaborate. But I neither want to assume nor imply a neat distinction between collaboration as a kind of technology in the abstract and the more material technologies we use to collaborate. Technologies of collaboration assemble in ecosystems that alternately encourage and constrain interaction, so understanding the mechanics of collaboration in any given case depends in part on understanding the dynamics between and among the various things, both material and abstract, collaborators take up.

But in most theoretical discussions of collaboration, focus is directed not on these things but on what results from the interactions we negotiate with these things, *the thing* that has been produced and the nature of its quality. I have pointed to the commonplace refrain that collaborative writing often results in texts greater than the sum of their parts. When Anson, Brady, and Larson tell their readers not to assume too much about their occasional use of singular pronouns, for example, they are telling us not to focus on their writing as something that has been constructed by individual contributors; they are telling us to focus on the text as a singular object, one that exists separately from each of these writers individually. One challenge to such a request, however, is that we do not have robust language for talking about writing in such ways. What terms are available for invoking the singularity of a collaboratively composed text? Given that most economies of authorship require collaborators to be able to account for their individual efforts, the language we have available for talking about collaboration is often vague, if not fleeting. Anson, Brady, and Larson acknowledge this struggle as they try out different metaphors for their writing together, even though they "quickly decided that no single description or definition could capture the range and complexity of collaborative dynamics" (1993, 89).

With that said, there are some terms popular among advocates of collaboration. One in particular, *synergy*, often gets invoked to name the shared capacity coauthors foster through processes of collaboration. The word itself has etymological roots in theology that date back to the fifteenth century, but today its most popular use is as shorthand for mutually reinforcing cooperation or coaction, which is how Carol Mullen and Frances Kochan use the term when they say academic writers "who collaborate with others to accomplish mutual aims can experience a fertile synergy that enhances the work of all" (2001, 128). Moreover, compositionists have used this term to name the capacity that allows collaborative writers to claim the exponential quality of their writing. Reither and Vipond, for example, say collaborators create a "synergy" that allows them "to accomplish things together that neither could have accomplished alone" (1989, 858), which is almost word for word what Ede and Lunsford say in their first coauthored article about collaborative writing when they point to "a kind of synergism" they detect when cowriting, "the felt sense that by combining our efforts we could in some instances achieve more together than alone" (1983, 155). Perhaps this synergistic quality is what LeFevre attempts to name when she invokes the term "resonance" to describe collaboration, a quality that "comes about when an individual act—a 'vibration'—is intensified and prolonged by sympathetic vibrations" (1987, 65).

While I like LeFevre's use of "resonance" to explain what happens when writers compose together, I must admit *synergy* is a word I don't care for in these contexts. It reminds me of those tacky inspirational posters you sometimes find in corporate-office environments, the ones depicting a scene from nature, or perhaps a group of athletes, that have a single word labeling the scene, one like *persistence* or *integrity* or even, let's be honest, *collaboration*. But what in rhetorical terms does *synergy* point to when writers invoke it to note collaboration allows them to produce texts better than what they would have written alone? I ask this question sincerely even though I imagine that if given time to unpack the term, most collaborators who use it might explain *synergy* in a way that mirrors the idea of emergence as described by DeLanda (2011). That is, when collaborators use this term, they are probably suggesting their respective agencies as writers have merged in ways that allow them to create a product or outcome whose properties cannot be reduced or otherwise explained by tracing a set of initiating causes. The biggest problem with *synergy*, then, is that too often it is deployed in ways that minimize how difficult it is to conjure (let alone represent) this complex emergence. But I believe it is possible to probe the rhetorical capacity collaborators foster to better understand what collaborators gesture to when they invoke the idea of synergy.

At this juncture I'd like to return to my own definition of collaboration as a mutual intervention and progressive interaction with objects of discourse. Such a definition is not constrained by a narrow sense of technique or method, nor does it imply the dialectical focus most definitions of collaboration assume. It also attempts to capture, or at least imply, this potential for emergence that advocates of collaborative writing point to as one of its benefits. With that said, the practical value of this definition might not be obvious at first glance, but it offers something most social-epistemic definitions of collaboration lack: a third character at work in the equation, those objects collaborators interact with and discourse about. Collaborators do not just converse; they deliberately engage and interact with objects of discourse. What distinguishes this definition of collaboration is the role of whatever it is collaborators attempt to share with their discourse, whether an idea, proposition, question, data set, observation, or some combination thereof. In reality, of course, collaborators are always navigating complex assemblages of discourse that cannot be isolated into such tidy categories. One obvious value of this definition, then, is that it is flexible to potential adaptations because it leaves room for a range of approaches to the talk collaborators foster. Such adaptations are possible because this definition works out of *interactionist rhetorical theory*, a banner term I use for philosophies of language that explain communication in paralogic terms by positing the relationship between thought and speech as intersubjective and therefore dependent on the actual interactions between interlocutors to understand how language means in any given instance.

One immediate consequence of defining collaboration in these interactionist terms is that it becomes a difficult activity to identify as such. To simply point to a discrete activity and call it *collaborative* isn't sufficient without attempting to understand how collaborators are interacting with similar objects at a given instance. Of course, this claim might lead to questions about what types of interactions do and do not count as collaborative. Are some iterations of talk more collaborative than others? And how should we differentiate collaboration from the related concepts of cooperation, teamwork, or mutual aid? Setting semantics aside, I don't think such questions are that interesting or even that useful because if these are the primary concerns we take up, we risk treating collaboration instrumentally as something that can be identified before writers begin the work of actually composing together. As Ede and Lunsford caution, after all, we should view "collaboration and collaborative writing as richly complex, situated, and materially embedded practices" (2011, 202). Accordingly, I believe there is pragmatic value in shifting how we talk about the benefits of collaboration away from whatever textual products it might yield to the kinds of enhanced perception collaborators foster to negotiate the work of composition. Yes, here I mean that elusive notion some collaborators use the idea of synergy to capture, this emergent capacity that results in the felt perception of shared agency, that capacity Anson, Brady, and Larson, for example, struggle to name in their consideration of how they have benefited from their experiences with coauthorship.

Such inquiry is important because collaborative composition may not always produce discrete texts. To unpack the rhetorical complexities that underwrite practices of collaboration, it is important to first recognize collaborative composition as something that can but may not always result in textual products. We should therefore avoid using collaboratively composed texts as the primary evidence for evaluating the successes and failures of the collaborations that produced them. To put this as a question, Must we always imagine collaborative composition as being temporally constrained by the beginnings and endings of isolated writing projects? What might it mean to imagine collaborative composition as something entered into and enacted over time, the discursive relationship collaborators foster from one project to the next?

We should therefore consider more closely the rhetorical mechanics that allow collaborators to share objects of discourse from the start, which brings me back to the idea of approaching the talk collaborators foster to write together as a kind of technology. Indeed, to understand the emergent function of collaborative composition, we need to understand how collaborators use their interactions to intervene in and enhance how they produce discourse about shared objects of concern. When collaborative writing is viewed in these terms as a deliberate engagement that aims to enhance the production of discourse, we can further refine this notion of collaboration as a technology to view collaboration as a site where craft knowledge, or *techne*, is developed.

Thinking in terms of techne offers a more rhetorically nuanced starting point for theorizing the capacity cowriters foster to negotiate the processes of collaboration itself. After all, the talk collaborators foster requires more than the dialogic back-and-forth we often imagine conversation to entail. Anson, Brady, and Larson, for example, demonstrate how they used their collaborative journal and the ideas discussed therein as a set of objects around which to progress their understanding of collaboration itself. But all collaborative writers do this insofar as they identify and share a set of discursive objects that assemble in ways that inform the purpose and scope of what they write or attempt to write. This doesn't mean coauthors must necessarily think about or approach their collaborations in such abstract discursive-material terms, of course. But any inquiry into the role of talk in coauthorship must necessarily begin with the recognition that collaboration implies some degree of mutual interaction with objects of discourse. In this way, collaborative composition is necessarily an activity interlocutors pursue as they interact *with* and not *through* discourse.

This point is important because if discourse is something collaborators interact with, something they manipulate, it can more easily be conceptualized as a technology, or a techne. As Robert Johnson argues, "Language and other technologies are tools that can serve practical or mundane functions like making, shaping, or fixing" (1998a, 18). To illustrate the utility of such thinking, Johnson connects this idea of language as technology to a conception of rhetoric as a productive, teachable art: "Rhetoric is a systematic series or collection of techniques that makes the production and dissemination of language strategic for the orator or writer, and, due to its systematic and thus transferable nature, is teachable to others" (22). He goes on to quote Janet Atwill and Janice Lauer's interpretation of Aristotle on what the *telos*, or end, is of a productive art. As they explain,

> The end of the art is *not* a product, but the use made of an artistic construct. The end of the art of housebuilding, for example, is neither the builder's use of the art nor the house itself, but rather the use made of the house by those for whom it was constructed. Similarly, the end of rhetoric is an active response in the auditor, not the speech itself. By identifying rhetoric as an art as opposed to theoretical or practical knowledge, Aristotle attempted to ensure that rhetoric could neither authorize itself as knowledge for its own sake nor be the instrument of a specific social and political objective. Instead, rhetoric was situated in a space where values were in contest and claims to knowledge were assessed according to competing situational demands (29).

Based on this definition of rhetoric as a productive art that finds its end in the *uses* of the things created with it, Johnson theorizes technical discourse as a techne, a generic definition of which is "knowledge of a determinate field (or subject matter), knowledge of how to shape specific material into a useful product" (Roochnik 1996, 22). To wield a techne therefore means one has the know-how necessary to conceive of and execute the production of something useful. Writers of any kind who are conscientious of the productive value of their work probably recognize how the artfulness of composition is bound up in a deliberate utilization of prior knowledge with the various skills necessary to produce and render language for particular ends.

Dialectical models of collaboration rooted in a social-epistemic theory of rhetoric often position the talk between collaborators as a tool for negotiating shared tasks and thus align with the above conception of techne as an art aimed at producing a desired result. In fact, I take it as a given that most teachers of writing who require collaboration in their courses want students to recognize its technical value, how it is a skill that can be put to use alongside the other skills we encourage students to foster in the writing courses we teach. As one team of collaborators explains in the journal *College Teaching*, coauthorship is a useful "tool" because it "creates a forum for participatory problem-solving, reflection, and action" (Reed, McCarthy, and Briley 2002, 22). This conception of the value of coauthorship hits the necessary notes for conceiving of collaboration as a technology, at least insofar as it is understood as a "way of engineering materials in order to accomplish an end" (Baron 2001, 71). Accordingly, a defining characteristic of collaboration-as-techne in this context is its instrumentality. We might thus say that collaborative writing as understood in these technical terms is useful to the extent that it is useable. When it comes to using collaborative writing in our teaching, an emphasis must therefore be placed on the technical knowledge individuals bring to processes of collaboration, like how to talk to one another "productively" so as to render a preconceived end, which is how Richard Young defines his "new classicist" approach to teaching rhetoric as a techne in his essay "Arts, Crafts, Gifts, and Knacks": "It means the knowledge necessary for producing preconceived results by directed action" (1980, 56).

But this instrumentalist approach to rhetoric as techne has been contested in ways that can be extended to how we might envision the technical work of collaborative composition. Johnson, for example, has focused on the problem of identifying ends and follows in the footsteps of Atwill and Lauer to recognize that users of technology "operate in a world where things are constantly changing," where even the most entrenched practices eventually require reform; thus "technologies must be described or explained through a lens of contingency, probability, and/or mutability that accounts for shifting contexts and situations" (1998a, 24). Moreover, Joseph Petraglia recognizes that an instrumentalist rendering of rhetoric might limit how we imagine its indeterminacy, so he questions rhetoric and composition's "pedagogical link to techne, or the belief that rhetoric is the practicable and perfectible art that enables one to be eloquent" (2000, 90). Elsewhere Petraglia points to the rise of process pedagogy as the crucial moment when a reliance on rhetoric-as-techne came to dominate composition pedagogy, because, as he puts it, "a faith in both the describability and the manipulability of the process by which writers produce texts allowed teachers to do their job in a more academically legitimized manner" (1999, 51). Such criticisms take aim at writing pedagogies that primarily focus on heuristic skills, which Petraglia notes is how many first-year writing programs incorporated rhetoric into their curricula, not as a tool for invention but for navigating established academic conventions.

But how does this line of critique related to rhetoric's instrumentality inform how we might envision collaborative discourse as a technology, especially in light of my proposal to define collaboration as a kind of mutual intervention and progressive interaction? As part of

Johnson's critique, he differentiates between "systems-centered" and "user-centered" models of technology: the former refers to technological design that emphasizes "the artifact or system as primary"—the thing that has been designed—and the latter emphasizes how "users are active participants in the design, development, implementation, and maintenance of the technology" (1998a, 25, 32). But in collaborative composition, to what extent is the system, so to speak, also its users? Is it possible to differentiate between *means* and *ends* in collaborative writing if the discursive interaction of collaborators is the "tool" they manipulate to compose together? This is not an easy question to answer, but it is an important one if we shift the focus from the textual products of collaboration to its discursive mechanics as the locus for whatever might constitute the technological know-how of collaborative composition.[1]

Instrumentalist guides to collaboration, those "how-to" manuals that are not hard to find, certainly assume its technical nature in this regard, especially insofar as such guides, to echo Petraglia, betray a faith in the describability and manipulability of its processes. But I don't believe collaboration can be described and manipulated so easily, at least when it comes to fostering the emergent potential of collaborative composition. As advocates of writing-to-learn pedagogies attest, at best we can only anticipate what a finished text will be each time we sit down before the proverbial blank page. For this reason, I'm interested in the potential for imagining the techne collaborators develop within an ecological model that emphasizes the location of individuals within complex rhetorical environments, and one conceptual path for pursuing such inquiry can be found in Hawk's approach to techne grounded in what he calls "complex vitalism."

What is essentially a combination of philosophical vitalism with complexity theory, complex vitalism encourages writing theorists to look beyond "simple notions of cause and effect" to understand the techniques writers utilize to produce texts (Hawk 2007, 168). Technology does not exist in a vacuum, after all, so theories of techne fall short if they fail to consider the environmental constraints that reveal how human beings and technology exist in complex relationships with each other and the surrounding world. Influenced by Martin Heidegger's phenomenological method of investigating how technological objects help constitute the environments in which those who uphold a more instrumental understanding of techne argue human beings exist over and above, Hawk makes clear that technologies "are never distinct objects: they are only experienced in relation to other entities arranged in complex constellations to form particular environments" (171).[2]

Hawk also reminds us that for Heidegger, a tool is experienced by situating it in relation to other equipment that forms assemblages that set "the conditions of possibility for particular acts, processes, or products" (2011, 82–83). In sum, what a writer or set of writers can do with their writing, so to speak, in any given rhetorical context is conditioned by the experience of those interactions that reveal the various resistances posed by and in that rhetorical context. The takeaway is that we should develop a conception of techne that promotes an ecological awareness of how bodies act in and are acted on by particular rhetorical environments.

This ecological understanding of techne is relevant for unpacking my understanding of collaboration because it does not locate the technician (in this case, collaborative writers) situated over and above their product, whatever discourse they have produced and intend to inscribe as text. Rather, what collaborators produce is an enhanced capacity to interact with the various objects, including objects of discourse, that exist in the environments in which they compose, environments that constrain how their writing might unfold at any given moment. In other words, the discourse collaborators produce (and, by extension, the written product of this discourse) is influenced by the ecologies in which collaborators are located, so these ecologies influence the craft knowledge of the collaboration just as much as the collaborators do (although, of course, not in the same way or to the same degree). This craft knowledge, or techne, I'm describing as the capacity collaborators foster to write together results from the deliberation or talk between collaborators as they interact with the various objects that comprise the discursive environments they are attempting to share.

But the capacity to negotiate these environments is not located separately in the mind of each individual; it emerges as a consequence of the ways collaborators experiment with—and experience—their discursive interaction. In sum, the shared perception collaborators foster to anticipate and direct the interaction that will produce whatever discourse they intend to inscribe is what we might say constitutes the techne of collaboration.

I recognize these claims are fairly abstract and might therefore be hard to process even though what I'm ultimately trying to describe is how collaborative writers come to experience the materiality of their shared discourse. Here I could point back to Anson, Brady, and Larson's progressive engagement with their own collaborative writing that unfolded in the digital pages of their collective notebook and how these cowriters eventually recognized this series of individually inscribed entries pushed them to see their journal (and the discourse they generated about it) as an object that posed its own resistances. As they chronicle how their discussions about collaboration evolved as the text itself evolved, for example, they note how "the tension between individual and collective voice was one of the most essential issues we negotiated together" (1993, 84). We might say, then, that these cowriters' technical capacity as collaborators was partially dependent on their ability to engage with that felt tension emanating from the collective voice speaking back to them from the pages of their journal.

But we can also see how coauthors come to experience their capacity as collaborators by turning to what Laurie JC Cella and Jessica Restaino say about their own collaboration in a recent essay that is similar to Anson, Brady, and Larson's piece insofar as Cella and Restaino also offer an autoethnographic snapshot of their writing together as a method for considering the benefits of collaborative composition. The medium through which Cella and Restaino constructed their shared voice was not a digital notebook shared via a computer disk; it was email, the back-and-forth of which gave them the imaginative space to recognize the potentiality of their collaboration. They write, "Our own relationship strengthened with each communication, even when our own interaction didn't yield immediate reward" (2014, 70). Borrowing Morris Young's notion of "little [literacy] narratives," Cella and Restaino craft a little narrative about how their "collaboration as writers and editors has taught [them] to embrace an uncertain kind of progress, one that starts and stops, races and slows" (72)—progress that in the little moments of their interactions as collaborative writers might not even feel like progress at all, especially through the otherwise mundane exchange of email.

Cella and Restaino explicitly suggest the point I make above about the limitations of imagining collaborative writing as an activity with clear temporal boundaries. But they also highlight how collaboration can be understood as a discursive capacity that ebbs and flows—"an exercise in possibility (if not always productivity)" (2014, 67)—which is why I need to further qualify my proposal that we theorize collaboration as a techne.

Even though collaboration can be framed as an activity that requires deliberate engagement with others to produce a specified result, we should envision collaboration as a *noninstrumental* technology when it comes to matters of coauthorship. By this I mean we should recognize collaboration as an artificial resource or tool, but not one that can be wielded generically or that functions according to whatever procedural strategies collaborators bring to their work prior to those engagements, especially when the discourse between collaborators reveals possibilities for their writing that until that moment were unrecognized. This framing of collaboration as a noninstrumental technology offers a rhetorically grounded starting position for interrogating the potential for rhetorical invention that advocates of collaboration often praise. Here I mean the potential for emergence, what Hawk identifies in terms that echo DeLanda as those moments "when the interaction of parts or system components generates unexpected properties not present in any of the local parts" (2007, 184). And here is yet another way into conceptualizing the techne of collaboration: as the rhetorical work of exploiting the "unexpected properties" of what can be articulated in specific discursive environments or rhetorical situations. Here I am describing the quality that in my own definition of collaboration I gesture to with the term *intervention*, one of the things collaborators pursue with their discourse.

To speak of a rhetorical or discursive intervention leads me to Atwill's understanding of techne as "a domain of human intervention and invention," one that "is often associated with the transgression of an existing boundary—a desire for 'more' that challenges or redefines boundaries" (1998, 7). If collaborators foster a techne that allows them to jointly compose, the "boundaries" that must be transgressed will necessarily include whatever habits or hindrances constrain the progression of their discourse in the ways they are attempting to inscribe it. This can, of course, include transgressing the limits of their individual apperceptions of objects of discourse. As a kind of intervention, this collaborative techne therefore serves two primary functions. First, it allows collaborators to converge around a set of common objects and share contingent positionings in relation to these objects, a kind of third space always in flux because it belongs to no one collaborator in isolation from the other's discourse. In the previous chapter, I elaborate on a version of this process using the philosopher Donald Davidson's notion of triangulation, but my point here is that for collaborative writers to jointly engage in rhetorical invention, they must be capable of converging their respective interpretations of common objects in ways that allow for shared meaning. The second function this collaborative techne serves is one I've already been explicating, and that is the expectation that some level of novel discourse will emerge as collaborators compose—that this collaborative third space, in other words, will yield perspective that allows for further discursive interaction and production about an idea, problem, question, or whatever is the thing being inscribed into text, perspective that cannot be completely traced back to a set of individual causes, that is, the singular contributions of specific collaborators (unless, of course, such attributive markers are deliberate).

To put this in terms that highlight the pragmatic work of collaboration, one's rhetorical agency is influenced by the limitations one perceives in any given time or place, constraints that can be transgressed as one develops the capacity to recognize how these limitations are not markers of inability but instead just lapses in technical vision. As collaborators develop a shared capacity to see discursive remedies to these constraints, they foster the techne necessary to intervene in and transform those boundaries.

If we are looking for a rhetorical term that speaks to this capacity, perhaps *dynamis* is most apt. Atwill uses this term (which is usually translated from the Greek as a "capacity" or "power") in her definition of techne as a transformative power or engagement that transforms limits and transgresses restraints (1998, 2, 7). In this complex, dynamis is a capacity one must develop over time with practice and patience even though it is not a skill in the instrumental sense. Technicians bring to their craft unique visions for what their reasoned capacity will produce, but these visions change and develop as the craft is enacted, evolutions partially dependent on the power, dynamis, inherent in those visions.

In this way, dynamis can also be understood as potentiality. Poulakos's well-known definition of rhetoric as "the art which seeks to capture in opportune moments that which is appropriate and attempts to suggest that which is possible" (1983, 36) certainly overlaps with what I am suggesting about the dynamic component of this techne that emerges as a capacity "appropriate" to the vision that results from the unique engagements engendered by collaboration—and the vision that points to what is "possible" because of these engagements.[3] Yet insofar as dynamis can be conceptualized here as the power to anticipate something that does not yet exist, we must remember such anticipation does not guarantee the emergence of what is anticipated because potentiality is not the same as genesis. Collaborations can always fail. But even if cowriters don't follow through with their writing—if for whatever reason they decide to discontinue a project—the potentiality suggested by this capacity to envision what is possible through a collaboration is nevertheless real. How much richer is this notion of a dynamis for describing the capacity cowriters negotiate than explanations that rely on a bland notion like synergy?

In short, collaboration opens opportunities to widen the scope of discourse available at any given moment if cowriters are prepared to exploit it—if they are able to recognize this inventive potential when it manifests. If in this way collaboration does make possible work that is better than what each individual would have produced alone, it makes sense to characterize collaboration as a techne. Gregory Semenza models this understanding, for example, when he notes collaboration can be an "antidote for stagnancy and myopia" because it "teaches us new ways—often better ways—of doing things we've grown too used to doing our way" (2015). But it might seem that here I'm moving away from an ecological to a more humanist approach to techne, one that presupposes an agency or set of agencies collaborators bring to their work that allows them to manipulate their writing processes in ways that produce these emergent effects. As I have tried to explain, however, we can view collaboration as a noninstrumental technology that positions the "material" of collaborative composition, shared discourse, as something always contingently constrained by the rhetorical ecologies collaborators navigate as they compose.

The techne of collaboration can in this way be just as easily understood as a discursive relationship always in development as it can be a reasoned capacity, which is to say, following Atwill, this techne is to a certain extent a strategic sense of purpose for engaging uncertainty. Perhaps the thing that mediates these contingent qualities is what is often characterized as techne's opposite, *tuche*, which means "chance" or "luck." In a passage reminiscent of Atwill and Lauer's description of techne, Paul Lynch says that if techne is understood as the "deliberate application of human intelligence," tuche "is what happens when you are making other plans. A carpenter may build a house well enough to withstand a storm but not the earthquake that collapses it. Likewise, a rhetorician may build an argument to persuade a hostile audience, only to discover—for reasons she could not anticipate—a much friendlier audience for whom the original arguments seem condescending or aggressive" (2013, 60).

If chance, or tuche, is always at work in the application of techne—Lynch says the two are interdependent (2013, 63)—one concept that mediates this tension between intelligence and chance is Paulo Freire's "untested feasibility," which is his term for the possibility of action in the face of limit-situations. For Freire, a limit-situation is the material effect of historical instances of oppression (1970). We can think of it as the extent to which one has agency in structural conditions that are or were designed to limit such agency in the first place. But like so many other of Freire's concepts, a limit-situation can be adapted to understand literacy development more broadly, in this case how writers come to recognize what is and is not possible in a specific rhetorical situation. Accordingly, the extent to which collaborators can engage limit-situations speaks to Atwill's definition of techne in that it implies the transgression of boundaries, but with the added qualities of imagination and hope.[4] These latter terms sometimes assume wishy-washy connotations. What does hope have to do with techne? Hope has more to do with chance and luck, with tuche, right?

As I've said, however, collaboration requires writers to be open to possibilities they may not have considered prior to their engagement with one another. And how collaborators respond to such possibilities—whether they can tap into the untested feasibility of their collaboration—will affect how well they engage the starts and stops of their work. Hope is therefore not the handmaiden of luck in this context but a disposition that helps us recognize when the limits of our discourse can be transgressed and transformed through collaborative composition. If collaborative writers are cynical about the labor of cowriting, if they view limit-situations as contests of strength or individual will, they limit the untested feasibility that might be exploited with the creation of novel discourse. Just consider the negative attitudes toward collaboration many of our students have cultivated over the course of their schooling, attitudes that must be unlearned if they want to recognize and in turn take advantage of what collaboration makes possible.

There is always a temptation with Freire to overromanticize, or in some cases simply write off, his critical vocabulary, infused as it is with the liberation theology that defined his own philosophical commitments. But this critical vocabulary is what gives his work its sense of urgency. Of course, the context of this urgency is what critics of most North American applications of Freire's pedagogy point to when they recoil at the way some so-called critical pedagogues apply his work in contexts notably removed from the oppressive material realities out of which he wrote.[5] To encourage readers of Freire to connect his critical pedagogy to the tradition of philosophical pragmatism, Kate Ronald and Hephzibah Roskelly consider how each promotes the testing of experience as a method for transforming the limits of belief. "Being able to break through limit situations," they write, "means being able to see them as problems rather than as givens and thus being able to act to change them as well as reflect on the consequences of that action" (2001, 615). Untested feasibility can thus be related to the idea of emergence as I've been discussing it; it names what collaborative composers anticipate as a consequence of their discursive interaction. Collaboration as a technology of talk is in this way not so much a reasoned capacity to *make* as it is a reasoned capacity to *anticipate*.

Of course, to emphasize the consequential value of the interventions collaborative composers learn to anticipate naturally invokes a pragmatist sensibility. In fact, I am reminded of how John Dewey defined pragmatism in 1925: "an extension of historical empiricism, but with this fundamental difference, that it does not insist upon antecedent phenomena but upon consequent phenomena; not upon the precedents but upon the possibilities of action" (1984, 196). It also speaks to Hawk's ecological rendering of techne when he suggests that instead of "technology causing effects or humans determining purposes, technology and humans combine with many other elements in the environment to create the conditions of possibility that suggest potential futures" (2007, 172). If collaborative writers consider how their shared discourse makes possible different opportunities for intervention, this realization might provoke new ways to describe the various techniques they negotiate to compose together, which in turn might offer teachers and theorists of writing alternative avenues for imagining the scope of composition in general and the work of collaboration in particular. As Hawk suggests, "Composition theorists should be striving to develop methods for situating bodies within ecological contexts in ways that reveal the potential for invention, especially the invention of new techniques, that in turn reveal new models for action within those specific rhetorical ecologies" (206). As I have so far argued, what marks the value of collaborative composition is the opportunities it provides writers to examine how they are situated within ecologies that constrain articulation and how through such examination such constraints can be transgressed and transformed. As many collaborative writers would no doubt suggest, it is because of this opportunity to engage the limit-situations of writing that collaborative composition carries a greater potential than solo writing for revealing "the invention of new techniques" for rhetorical action Hawk encourages composition theorists to propose.

Whether composing a shared document that lives on a computer disk or building an archive of email correspondence or using some other particular method a team of collaborators has invented to write together, what constitutes collaboration—what defines it in any given case—should not just be chalked up to strategic planning. If this is how we end up defining collaborative writing, we should not chafe at questions concerning attribution or ownership, especially those questions that aim to reduce collaborative writing to the sum of its individual parts. If collaboration can be instrumentally orchestrated, it can be instrumentally disassembled.

But this reductiveness is not in line with what many of us who have been trained to study and teach writing understand about the nature of collaboration. While it can be done in some instances, the textual artifacts that emerge in collaborative writing cannot and should not always be reducible in terms of "who wrote what" because, as I demonstrate in this chapter, the complexity of collaborative composition is better captured when we approach it as a techne rather than a generic set of practices. Insofar as I've been discussing the capacity collaborative writers cultivate to produce texts that can exceed the technical vision, so to speak, of what each individual collaborator brings to their work, I now want to tackle the idea of agency and how collaborative writers negotiate the tricky work of managing the power they exert through coauthorship. It is one thing, in other words, to consider what collaborators envision, how they anticipate what their work together will produce; it is another thing to consider how collaborators account for the influence they exercise once a collaboration is underway.

3

COWRITING AGENCY

INVENTING A COLLABORATIVE FUTURE

*This book was first written over 5 days (Jan 18–22, 2010)
during a Book Sprint in Berlin. 7 people (5 writers, 1
programmer and 1 facilitator) gathered to collaborate and
produce a book in 5 days with no prior preparation and with the
only guiding light being the title "Collaborative Futures."*
—*Collaborative Futures*

So begins the second chapter of *Collaborative Futures*, a book about collaboration in the wake of Web 2.0 when websites like YouTube, Wikipedia, and Facebook arrived on the scene with their interactive interfaces that encouraged and made possible virtual forms of social engagement that didn't exist before the early 2000s. A group of semi-anonymous open-source software activists, the authors of *Collaborative Futures*, use their second chapter to narrate the book's origins. After this initial opening, each member of the collaboration is named; they then note the book "was revised, partially rewritten, and added to" several months after its initial publication by a group of further collaborators, who are also then named (2010, 6). The entire chapter spans little more than 350 words. It includes an epigraph attributed to the popular novelist Tom Clancy ("Collaboration on a book is the ultimate unnatural act") and two photographs ostensibly depicting the group's collaboration in progress. The first photo shows three people arranging dozens of Post-It notes on a wall; the second shows five people sitting around a pair of portable tables that have been pushed together and on top of which rests the detritus of an active writing scene: laptop computers, stacks of papers, cups and water bottles, plates of food, cell phones, more Post-It notes. The chapter also includes an inset block of text labeled "Glossary: Inconsistencies" that in part reads as follows:

> In this book there are inconsistencies, occurring in the shifts between the distinct voices that constitute the text in its entirety. By constantly re-writing, over-writing, and un-writing the book, the residual material

DOI: 10.7330/9781646420490.c003

(that which remains unseen in the printed version) is also the material that expresses the mode of collaboration at work here. Each collaborative (futures) book is fundamentally a reference to a very particular micro-community. In this sense it can be seen as attributing to a social study. There is no generality in collaboration. (7)

Most of the book's forty-three chapters resemble this one, which is to say *Collaborative Futures* is an interesting amalgamation of brief stretches of narration, inset glossary entries that wax philosophical, the occasional photograph or illustration, and long or short quotations upon which the authors may or may not directly comment.

To the extent that a book can be described as disheveled, *Collaborative Futures* fits the bill, yet its messiness is what also makes the book compelling. It hasn't been professionally typeset, for instance, and there is no discernible rhyme or reason to the arrangement, length, or detail of each chapter.[1] On the other hand, and despite what the authors say about its aforementioned "inconsistencies," the book's delivery is often bolstered by an active, first-person-plural voice that narrates a persuasive call for rethinking the idea of collaboration and the methods we use to pursue it. Specifically, the authors argue that even though Web 2.0 gave us a slate of tools for interacting with one another in new and more complex ways, such technology has also artificially limited what counts as meaningful social engagement on these platforms. What on the surface may appear to be free and open digital landscapes for expanding the possibilities of "social life" and "peer production" (2010, 16) are really platforms that often compel users to interact with one another in very specific ways.

What the *Collaborative Futures* writers are talking about here is what technologist Jaron Lanier says in *You Are Not a Gadget* about the phenomenon of "lock-in." Lock-in occurs when users of digital platforms conform their behaviors to the structure and design of the platforms themselves. "The process of lock-in is like a wave gradually washing over the rulebook of life, culling the ambiguities of flexible thoughts as more and more thought structures are solidified into effectively permanent reality," writes Lanier (2010, 9). Take the phenomenon of trolling, for instance, or the rise of the Like functionality on social media platforms that not only facilitates quick, nonqualitative responses to posts but also stands in as a kind of impact-assessment tool that measures how popular our posts are with friends and followers. The growing scores of anonymous bullies who take pleasure in harassment, or the various ways our social media activity gets rendered into performance metrics, are possible in large part because the interfaces of these applications facilitate such behavior in the first place. In this way, Lanier says, design comes before ethics in the digital world (62), an idea that composition-ist Rebecca Tarsa (2015) has recently considered in relation to literacy education.[2]

But for the *Collaborative Futures* authors, the desire to rethink the idea of collaboration has a strong ethical imperative that goes beyond arguments about interface design. In fact, they want to problematize how we understand the social value of collaboration in the first place.[3] To illustrate these stakes, they juxtapose their own collaboration with that of the hacker group Anonymous, famous for its cyberattacks on organizations it deems oppressive, such as the Church of Scientology, the KKK, even the North Korean government. But as *Collaborative Futures* points out, the methods Anonymous uses to carry out its "hactivism" rely on a spectacle, a collective agency greater than the power of any one of its individual hackers. And, more often than not, Anonymous wields the specter of its collective agency like a weapon, one that can be deployed to wreak havoc anywhere, anytime. What kind of power is this? While Anonymous might at times be reaching for supposedly just ends, its method is built on the cultivation of cynicism, fear, and distrust.[4] If this is the future of collaboration digital culture has inaugurated, posits the *Collaborative Futures* collective, "it is a ter-rifying one in which anonymity and structurelessness permits total absolution of social responsibility"; it is a "P2P, collaborative, digitized 'Lord of the Flies'" (2010, 5).

The real problem with Anonymous as an example of collaboration goes beyond the group's dubious actions as a vigilante hacker collective because what the group celebrates is not collaboration but anarchism. In promoting as a value its refusal to materialize its procedures or share its resources, Anonymous champions a world where shared agency can be created and readily proliferated without the traces of any actual col-laboration. Conversely, the writing in *Collaborative Futures* often turns in on itself to trace the agency that gets created in the spaces between the subjectivities of its authors. "At the outset we must admit this book might be useless," one chapter begins. "To imagine that we could write a book about collaboration is to imagine there is such a thing as *not* collaborat-ing. And to imagine a long history of *not* collaborating with each other. And the ability as 'individuals' (Western liberal subjects) to operate sep-arately from the 'others' and the world, environment, context around them. And all of that is false. How can we even begin?" (2010, 21).

Here *Collaborative Futures* enacts the subject of its inquiry by anticipat-ing novel forms of peer production that counter attempts to posit the mechanics of collaboration as procedures that hold value only when they remain hidden. At the same time, the book reconsiders the most common concerns that influence how collaboration plays out at any given time, like how to identify shared goals, articulate organizational structures, set guidelines for participation, and establish rules for attribution. To echo the programming speak in which much of the book is written, *Collaborative Futures* is an attempt at articulating the ideal conditions in which collaborations execute, which implies production not just in a material sense (producing the things a collaboration sets out to make or achieve) but also a functional sense (improving the processes of a collaboration's operations). That is, collaboration must work, and do work, before it yields work. So what does this mean for collaboration in contexts of coauthorship and writing instruction?

I suggest in chapter 1 that what collaborative writing ultimately does is slow down the writing process while expanding the scope of discourse available to coauthors because one of the fundamental differences between cowriting and solo writing is that cowriters don't have to imagine an immediate audience for their work—another writer or writers always figure directly into the labor of writing in ways that have a material effect on the process itself. Then in chapter 2, I outline an argument for defining collaboration as a noninstrumental technology that coauthors wield, but only contingently. Collaborative writers cannot control their collaboration, in other words, at least not in the sense that generic procedures can be established that will produce the same effects from one instance of collaboration to the next. When these ideas are taken together, we might say collaborative writing is less something "processed," so to speak, from the outside than something processed from the inside out. Put differently, what the processes of coauthorship really entail can only be identified once they are already underway. This should not be a provocative claim, especially given the many ways social constructionists have drawn on the language of collaboration to posit the social nature of writing.

With that said, the most interesting question *Collaborative Futures* points us to in this regard is one that social turn collaboration theory has largely avoided: In what ways does collaboration *produce its own subjects?* This is essentially what Lanier wonders when contemplating the consequences of lock-in as he speculates about how interactions on social media are manipulated by the design of the various interfaces we use for such engagement, but Fitzpatrick points us to a similar concern: "The networks of electronic communication carry embedded values within the codes that structure their operation, and many of the Internet's codes, and thus its values, are substantially different from those within which scholars—at least those in the humanities—profess to operate" (2011, 53). Given the growing concern for the ways digital technologies both encourage and constrain social interaction, it seems necessary to consider *how*, not *if*, various modes of collaboration influence the subjectivities of participants. Accordingly, I think it is useful to consider how the construct of collaboration in any given context thus assumes the quality of an *assemblage*, the term Deleuze and Guattari use to denote "a collection of animate and inanimate bodies, actions and passions, and enunciations and statements constantly in motion" (Hawk 2011, 78). Hawk uses this term to describe the ecologies within which writers compose, the "relations of things with each other, relations of ideas with each other, and the relations of things and ideas with each other" (2007, 45). This comingling of things and ideas is implicit in the definition Kathleen Blake Yancey and Stephen McElroy offer in the introduction to their recent edited collection *Assembling Composition*: "Assemblage refers to and sanctions the makingness that textuality affords and its use, reuse, and repurposing of materials, especially chunks of texts, in order to make something new" (2017, 4). An assemblage is a collection of things—bodies, passions, words, ideas, objects—that aid and constrain the actions that transpire within it. In a chapter included in Yancey and McElroy's collection, Alex Reid notes how "assemblage theory articulates language and symbolic behavior as a relational capacity that emerges within a network of human and nonhuman objects," which suggests, as he goes on to say, "a human being's ability to write only becomes real within a network of actors that facilitate writing" (2017, 27, 32). When it comes to collaboration, the agencies collaborators bring to a writing project should therefore be understood as both contributing to and developing from the assemblages within which they endeavor to compose. We might thus say collaborators cowrite the agency of their collaboration as it develops.

This brings me to the idea of *cowriting agency*, which I intend to be read as both a subject and a predicate. Cowriting agency signals a kind of object as well as a kind of action; it is something cowriters share as well as something they do. This term is stylistically playful, and I find the ambiguity in it advantageous because to productively talk about the idea of agency in collaborative writing requires moving beyond conceptual binaries like subject/object and process/product that reify notions of authorship as "singular, originary, autonomous, and uniquely creative," as Lunsford once put it (1999, 529). Indeed, I do not believe we can talk about the agency coauthors wield at any given time without also talking about its origins as a kind of power or dynamis coauthors cultivate in the rhetorical ecologies—or assemblages—of their collaboration, a quality that links cowriting agency to techne, which I discuss in the previous chapter when considering how to understand the talk collaborators produce as a noninstrumental technology. When I invoke the idea of cowriting agency, I am therefore deliberately trying to complicate "questions of epistemic hierarchies," to echo Richa Nagar, ones that might "betray the logic and investments emanating from our own locations" (2014, 3).

But the double meaning at work in this term also suggests a temporal concern that speaks to the identification of a thing that has already emerged, as well as the anticipation of a quality that does not yet exist. Cowriting agency is thus a Janus-headed moniker for the ability that allows coauthors to negotiate their collaboration. To understand cowriting agency in these terms thus requires an accounting of agency that looks beyond the individual subjectivities collaborators bring to their work. To do this, I turn to compositionists who have been drawing on new materialist and posthuman schools of thought as resources for theorizing rhetorical agency as an emergent, distributed phenomenon.

But new materialist and posthuman philosophers were hardly the first to suggest such a revisioning of agency. When it comes to collaboration in particular, feminist scholars made early inroads in critiquing modernist conceptions of authorship while promoting models of distributed agency.[5] In "Rhetoric, Feminism, and the Politics of Textual Ownership," for example, Lunsford points to this feminist tradition to "promote alternative forms of agency and ways of owning that would shift the focus from owning to owning up; from rights and entitlements to responsibilities (the ability to respond) and answerability; from a sense of the self as radically individual to the self as always in relation" (1999, 535). Such an "owning up" is no doubt visible in the interview Mary Belenky gave to *JAC* in which she explains how her, Blythe McVicker Clinchy, Nancy Rule Goldberger, and Jill Mattuck Tarule's landmark *Women's Ways of Knowing* "could not have been written by any single one of us" because the book "has a scope that reflects a wide range of experiences in a wide range of institutions, and a single person couldn't have created that" (Ashton-Jones and Thomas 1990, 280).[6] Accordingly, Micciche notes that feminist theorists have significantly reapproached corporeality and embodiment to underscore the ways identity and agency emerge from material environments and the diversity of objects and forces located therein (2017, 44).[7]

Nagar in particular takes this line of inquiry even further as she considers the political implications of such emergent agency as feminist researchers wrestle with questions of identity, power, and representation in transnational contexts. *Muddying the Waters: Coauthoring Feminisms across Scholarship and Activism,* her 2014 book that includes essays written with and alongside fellow scholars as well as project participants, details research practices that attend to "the specificities of geographical, socioeconomic, and institutional locations of those who enter into intellectual and political partnerships," as well as the "processes, events, and struggles underway" in those specific locations and partnerships (2014, 5). In research collaborations that grow out of and promote feminist epistemologies, "the possibilities of alliances are inseparable from a deep commitment to critique"; for those who claim allegiance to feminist epistemologies, that is, collaboration is impossible without also being "radically vulnerable" to "critiques of identity and meanings and possibilities of authorship" (5, 6). One line of inquiry Nagar offers that I find especially compelling for its import on how we understand the agency coauthors negotiate has to do with the focus on reflexivity much feminist scholarship has promoted. Writing with Susan Geiger about the way feminist ethnographers are often compelled to disclose their own identities as markers for situating their biases as a rite of passage that authorizes themselves as researchers, they "challenge and resist this demand to uncover ourselves in specific ways for academic consumption" so as to problematize "the essentialist nature of social categories, which are, in reality, created, enacted, and transformed" (Nagar 2014, 84). Similarly, in what ways are coauthors more generally asked to "uncover themselves" for "academic consumption" via a kind of essentializing of writerly labor?

The theory of cowriting agency I develop here builds on these lines of inquiry to outline a framework collaborative writers can use to account for their shared labor, especially on those occasions when a collaboration yields a text its authors want to resist accounting for within neoliberal frames of intellectual property, that is, "who wrote what." The aim of this chapter is to thus offer a new set of answers to questions like the following: What's happening when coauthors see possibilities for a text that neither writer anticipated individually? When cowriters say what they have written is greater than the sum of its parts, what can this mean? Conversely, what might be happening when coauthors *don't* make progress on a text, even if there is consensus on what they wish to write? As I discuss in the previous chapter, the social turn theory that has informed so much of rhetoric and composition's understanding of collaboration hasn't offered anything close to an adequate answer to these questions outside the occasional bromide about synergy or how two minds are greater than one. Indeed, what might it look like to instead theorize such agency as a state of emergent potential?

But even when a coauthored text doesn't elude economies of individual attribution—when coauthors are both willing and able to account for who wrote what—such questions are still relevant for developing a more sophisticated understanding of the agencies collaborative writers must negotiate, even if the recognition and manifestation of cowriting agency in these cases is only minimal. Before proceeding, however, I think it is useful to take a slight detour to review where and how compositionists have raised concerns about agency and subjectivity in the field's scholarship on collaboration, and what new ideas, if any, these concerns have encouraged the field to consider.

THE POLITICS OF CONSENSUS

While the *Collaborative Futures* authors encourage fellow writers and activists to welcome the transformations in subjectivity that come when one submits to a collaborative project (2010, 44), they neither downplay the interpersonal struggles such transformation might entail nor suggest such struggles don't have negative consequences. When casually invoked to name a "methodology of production," they write that the idea of collaboration sometimes "occludes more than it describes" (60). There is always more happening behind the curtain, so to speak, that will never be reflected in the products a collaboration yields.[8] When rhetoric and composition scholars in the 1980s started to position collaborative learning as the pedagogical consequence of social constructionist epistemology, many teachers recognized the need for interrogating what exactly collaboration "occludes" when it gets deployed in our teaching practices. Most pervasive here were questions about the role of consensus in collaborative learning, especially when accounting for differences in identity and privilege that might affect the way conflicts among collaborators get resolved. As I discuss in chapter 1, it should thus be no surprise that the earliest defenses of collaborative pedagogies were rooted in the belief that they better enacted the social principles of democratic learning: the value of debate, the importance of equal representation, and the benefits of compromise.

Indeed, these were the liberal values Bruffee identified in his early attempts at outlining a social turn theory of collaboration. As Bruffee puts it, "If we regard knowledge as a social artifact, as socially justified belief, then we seem bound to reinterpret education as a social process" (1985, 233). The idea of *socially justified belief* is easily the most important concept to influence Bruffee's understanding of collaborative learning, as well as what he sees as its ultimate goal. Socially justified belief is a hallmark of Richard Rorty's philosophy of epistemological behaviorism, which Bruffee was introduced to in Rorty's 1979 landmark book *Philosophy and the Mirror of Nature*.[9] Rorty's nonfoundational epistemology emphasizes that socially justified belief represents the most tenable starting position for epistemological inquiry since it rejects the Cartesian split between mind and nature. The problem with this latter model, as Bruffee summarizes, is it "assumes that knowledge is a mental construct and it draws its authority, on one hand, from the quality of that mental construct and, on the other hand, from the quality of reliability of mental constructs' reference to a reality external to the mind" (1985, 231). Rorty's basic argument, which Bruffee supports, is that knowledge is a social artifact rooted in talk. In fact, by 1982, Bruffee had already formulated a working model of Rorty's social justification that clearly anticipates his use of conversation as the conceptual mechanism for understanding collaboration.[10]

What Bruffee eventually takes from Rorty is a philosophical argument for theorizing collaborative learning as the only adequate model for actualizing socially justified belief in classroom learning. "If I say, then, that knowledge is socially justified belief," Bruffee suggests, "we seem to be saying that knowledge results from *acknowledgement*, the mutual agreement among knowledgeable peers that a belief expressed by a member of that community has been socially justified or is socially justifiable" (1982, 106). The social justification of belief therefore functions for Bruffee as the epistemological starting point for grounding a pedagogical theory that positions consensus as the practical goal of conversation among collaborators.

Another critical term in social constructionist epistemology, *consensus*, comes from Thomas Kuhn and his theory of paradigm shifts articulated in *The Structure of Scientific Revolutions* (1962), which influenced Rorty's theory of socially justified belief. Moreover, it is from Kuhn that Rorty adapts the concepts of "normal" and "abnormal discourse" to describe the means through which knowledge becomes socially justified, concepts that are in turn central to Bruffee's explication of collaborative learning. Normal discourse denotes whatever habits of talk a particular group considers legitimate. For Bruffee, like Rorty, to understand normal discourse, one must recognize how "knowledgeable peers" are the agents of this discourse. "A community of knowledgeable peers," writes Bruffee, "is a group who accept, and whose work is guided by, the same paradigms and the same code of values and assumptions"

(1984, 642). Normal discourse in collaborative learning therefore signals the uninterrupted flow of conversation among knowledgeable peers. When new ideas or what are otherwise novel or even unfamiliar utterances—abnormal discourse—are introduced into a conversation, they might stop the progression of the group's normal discourse, so the group of knowledgeable peers must account for these utterances to determine their legitimacy. The virtue of abnormal discourse, as Bruffee notes, is that it "sniffs out stale, unproductive knowledge and challenges its authority, that is, the authority of the community which that knowledge constitutes" (648). Collaborative learning therefore requires participants to negotiate whatever abnormalities—points of disagreement, for instance—that might stymie the group's proverbial conversation so as to develop consensus about the task at hand.

Bruffee avoids detailed discussion of the potential problems of positing consensus as the goal of collaboration, which is to say the debate he is ultimately concerned with is over what he views as the philosophical givens of social constructionism as a justification for collaborative learning. Hence the long arc of Bruffee's work amounts to a general theory of collaboration that largely ignores the weeds of classroom practice, which is not to say Bruffee didn't concern himself with pedagogy—after all, he did publish a popular textbook—but this does account for why many of the responses to Bruffee's work questioned the consequences of adopting wholesale the social constructionist principles that largely define his arguments about the nature of collaboration.

For many of the compositionists responding to and writing in the wake of Bruffee's work, the particulars of classroom practice most concern them. In this way, Bruffee's theory is quickly subjected to composition's so-called pedagogical imperative, or what Paul Lynch calls the "Monday Morning Question": "This theory (or idea, or philosophy) you're proposing is great and everything, but what am I supposed to do with it when the students show up on Monday morning?" (2013, xi). In this case, fellow scholars and practitioners wanted to tease out the philosophical jargon Bruffee appropriates from Rorty, like "normal" and "abnormal discourse," to speculate about what is at stake when teachers incorporate collaboration into their curriculums. As a result, what we see emerge in response to Bruffee is heightened concern about the roles of individual and group agency in collaboration and the conflicts that might arise therein. But the idea of conflict in these discussions is usually limited to concerns about interpersonal conflict, conflicts that result from what David Foster identifies as "the collision of divergent attitudes, values, judgments, and personal temperaments" (1999, 150). Much of the emerging scholarship on collaboration during this period thus dealt with just one primary concern: How do you balance (or manage, plan, evaluate) collaboration while protecting (or prioritizing, acknowledging, respecting) each student's individual autonomy?

Practitioners were thus raising questions about the ideological consequences of collaboration when it gets incorporated into our pedagogies for teaching writing. For example, Donald Stewart acknowledges that while collaborative pedagogies might be able to reinvigorate sterile learning environments, "there is a point beyond which I won't go" (1988, 67). That point is what Stewart sees as a "rather flexible definition of the word *collaboration,* specifically its lack of a clear distinction between *influence* and *collaboration*" (1988, 66). That is, insofar as scholars like Bruffee equate collaboration with conversation aimed at generating consensus, or normal discourse, there is a risk that consensus becomes something around which undue pressure can be directed at those who cannot or do not want to agree with the group. Byron Stay nicely explains this particular concern: "Teachers apply leverage through grades, course expectations, group monitoring, and personal expectations. Peers apply leverage through expectations that all group members be active, responsible, and productive" (1994, 31–32). The result of all this leverage is that "students feel considerable pressure to reach consensus" (31). But Stay's hesitancy also points to the procedural demands of collaboration, especially collaborative writing, and how "the pressure of these demands may in some cases make coauthorship very inefficient" (30). Taken together, Stewart and Stay illustrate the two primary poles around which critiques of consensus as a key concept for understanding collaboration have circulated. On one hand, there is the practice pole where consensus is tricky to qualify because students work for a grade, so they will often do whatever it takes to secure a positive outcome when assigned collaborative work, even if it means feigning agreement with their collaborators to complete a project expeditiously. Then there is the ideology pole where consensus can have more sinister consequences insofar as the contributions of some students might be rejected, ignored, or unfairly challenged by those with whom they are required to work.

The politics of consensus in social turn collaboration theory thus draws attention to how power gets deployed when individuals bring to bear on a collaboration ideologies, subjectivities, personal histories, and educational aims that might be at odds with those of their peers. In "The Sociological Imagination and the Ethics of Collaboration," for instance, John Schilb says that instructors should avoid occasions when requiring students to collaborate might "impinge upon women, people of color, and other historically victimized groups" because in these cases "consensus may amount to compliance with unjust power" (1992, 107). He even goes so far as to remind readers that the term *collaboration* was once exclusively associated with treason—collaboration with the enemy—a point he amplifies to demonstrate how pedagogical renderings of collaboration as a democratic or antiauthoritarian teaching strategy might uphold ideologies that silence minority interests. This critique anticipates the concern Nagar raises about the supposed value of "self-reflexivity" when collaborators, "especially feminist social scientists," avoid or otherwise ignore "the most vexing political questions that lie at the heart of our in/ability to talk across worlds" (2014, 90). But Schilb doesn't reject collaborative pedagogy; in fact, he views it as advantageous insofar as instructors can use the conflicts students experience when negotiating a collaborative assignment "as a catalyst for broader social inquiry" (1992, 112). Schilb's intervention in this debate highlights the neoliberal framework advocates of collaboration had to (and still must, as Nagar shows us) negotiate, especially when it comes to viewing the classroom as a microcosm of an idealized liberal society composed of individual agents who labor alongside one another to reap rewards that supposedly reflect the unique quality of that labor.

The idea of consensus for some critics thus points to tacit institutional and social frameworks tilted in favor of whatever those who already hold privilege want consensus to look like, which is how Greg Myers sees it. In his own critique of Bruffee's collaboration theory, Myers argues that Bruffee's understanding of collaboration assumes consensus is something that can exist separate from the social differences that distinguish individual collaborators from one another (1986, 167). "Having discovered the role of consensus in the production of knowledge," Myers writes, Bruffee "takes this consensus as something that just is, rather than as something that might be good or bad" (1986, 166). Moreover, Myers wonders whether what counts as consensus is what seems most natural within a perceived ideological structure, a point that anticipates Schilb's argument. In other words, consensus for Myers is something that should always be treated with suspicion, if not outright challenged.

To be sure, these criticisms of Bruffee's theory did get pushback of their own. Writing in response to Myers, for example, John Ramage and John Bean question his treatment of consensus as something that always requires the silencing of some interests. "Myers' mistake is his failure to see that collaborative learning is specifically a *process by which one achieves consensus* and not a consensus *per se*" (1987, 210). Consensus is not something that exists in the abstract before individuals reach it, in other words, so to work towards its construction doesn't have to necessarily mean individual identities and values must be subsumed during the process.

This last idea leads to what is perhaps the most direct (and the most anthologized) attempt at coming to terms with the idea of consensus in the field's understanding of collaboration, John Trimbur's "Consensus and Difference in Collaborative Learning." Here, Trimbur qualifies and extends Bruffee's initial theory while acknowledging concerns about the potentially coercive and marginalizing effects of collaboration. In fact, Trimbur suggests that consensus should remain a key concept for understanding the aims of collaboration, but that consensus should not be invoked as a euphemism for benign agreement. Instead, consensus can be understood as a temporary kind of common ground, or stasis, on which collaborators locate differences that make pure, uncomplicated agreement impossible. As he explains, "Consensus can be a powerful instrument for students to generate differences, to identify the systems of authority that organize these students, and to transform the relations of power that determine who may speak and what counts as a meaningful statement" (1989, 603). Conflict is inevitable in collaboration, so teachers should help students recognize the value in negotiating these conflicts as opportunities for exploring their own beliefs and commitments in relation to those of their peers. This view of conflict is Trimbur's primary revision to Bruffee's theory: highlighting the importance of recognizing the differences that distinguish collaborators from one another as central to the democratic principles of participation and inclusion around which our classrooms should be modeled.[11] Collaboration thus becomes meaningful through a group's *attempt* at consensus, an idea that anticipates Miller's (1994) "discourse city" concept for understanding the work of collaboration and one that implies what collaborators should foster with one another is not agreement *per se*, but trust and goodwill.

The qualities of trust and goodwill, however, can't be invoked out of thin air. As David Bleich writes, "Even among culturally homogeneous students and teachers, we know that both sharing and working together are not simply a matter of 'opening up' or 'expressing' ourselves, but above all require the slow, gradual buildup of trust and understanding" (1995, 44). Picking up where Trimbur leaves off, Bleich proposes a "pedagogy of disclosure" for fostering collaboration, one in which both students and teachers are encouraged to share with one another what might at first appear to be sensitive personal information (cultural traditions, political affiliations, religious beliefs, etc.) in such a way as to encourage conversation, even if such conversation might seem incommensurate with or unrelated to the immediate collaborative task at hand. Micciche gets at the potential value of this kind of conversation when she notes that writing, no matter what the occasion, "cannot be bracketed from the moments and events that define us" (2017, 72). The value of disclosure in this framework is as a form of acknowledgment that has the potential for fostering identifications that might otherwise not emerge. As Bleich puts it, "Such teaching can maintain the necessity of understanding the collective *within* the subjective, and the subjective *within* the collective" (1995, 47). This last idea is noteworthy because it underscores a common thread in virtually all the proposals that have tackled the problem of consensus in collaboration: the need to strike a balance accounting for the unique subjectivities collaborators bring to their work and the larger discourse communities that give meaning to these subjectivities in the first place.

As I see it, the takeaway of these proposals is twofold. First, compositionists have come to rely on an understanding of collaboration that largely supports the neoliberal economies in which measurement of individual effort informs the conditions in which most of our educational institutions operate. Second, and related to the first, any attempt to understand what collaborators do ultimately points back to the primacy and autonomy of each individual collaborator as a unique source of influence, or as Trimbur would say, "difference." As a result, the field's debates about collaboration have not gone beyond what is essentially a reshuffling of consensus as the only concern that really matters in articulating the viability of collaboration as a pedagogical utility. Consequently, the idea of an agency collaborators share that defies measurement of individual effort isn't really a thing in our discussions of collaboration.

To be sure, I don't want to minimize the importance of asking questions about how trust develops, authority is negotiated, or conflict gets resolved when collaborators come together. But I agree with Jessica Restaino (2014), who notes that continued resistance to the idea of consensus in Bruffee's theory of collaboration has stalled subsequent theoretical work on the uses of collaboration, especially collaborative writing, in our pedagogies. That coauthors must necessarily always negotiate varying levels of conflict as they work together should be a given, but how might we describe what happens when collaborators work toward the production of writing that cannot, or should not, be dissected into its constituent parts, especially when these parts might then be subjected to valuation in economies in which individual attribution is the ultimate currency? More to the point, what might it look like to encourage cowriters to adopt mindsets that explicitly reject these economies, and to do so before they begin their work? I take on these questions directly in part 2 of this book, but first we must set aside the social turn mindset that presumes what collaborators can achieve together is dependent on how well they can relate to and manage one another. When collaboration is understood as a material practice of mutual intervention and progressive interaction, the discussion shifts toward questions about what happens in the interactions between cowriters *and the various things* with which they are interacting in the material and discursive assemblages that give specific collaborations their exigence.

CULTIVATING COWRITING AGENCY

Even though social turn epistemology rejects romantic notions of the author as an individual, originary genius, the prevailing concern amongst compositionists for understanding the challenges of consensus in collaboration has actually worked to reify a conception of rhetorical agency that, while perhaps socially constructed, is nevertheless individual in its expression.[12] After all, what so much of this scholarship demonstrates is that what ultimately matters in collaboration is how individual subjects work toward a set of common ends while acknowledging and honoring one another's unique identities—and potential contributions—to the project at hand. What might it look like to start with a conception of cowriting agency that doesn't rely on a theoretical model that posits collaboration as simply the combination of individual efforts directed by individual agents working toward a state of consensus?

What I propose is that collaborators consider the nature of their co-constructed agency in terms of *resistance* and *discontinuity*. What collaborators "do" together is confront and acknowledge the resistances posed by the objects of their collaboration and negotiate the discontinuities these resistances engender. If this sounds abstract, what I am drawing attention to is the material, and material effects, that slow down the work of composition when undertaken collaboratively. While collaborators usually produce a lot of talk about their collaboration—talk about what they want to write and how they should write it—there is also much that often goes unspoken, especially when it comes to the myriad fits and starts that mark the work of most writers most of the time. Here I quote at length from a recent article by Andrea Bishop about her experience coming to terms with the material effects of collaborative writing that most of the time go unaccounted for when assessing the labor of coauthorship. In this particular passage she is discussing what she and her coauthor experienced as an unproductive writing session (they intended to draft a conference presentation during this time) that took place in a faculty lounge on their campus:

> Too many people walked by, saw us, and then popped in to talk. The microwave was a popular location that day, and three or four people came in to warm up meals and stay to chat. At one point, a fellow graduate student we'd never met engaged us in conversation for a long 10 minutes about Peter Elbow and Expressivism because she'd heard me mention one or the other and wanted more information. I don't even know her name. I just remember the interruption. We didn't get anything actually written, but we did flesh out an outline . . . of sorts.
>
> We decided what we might cover in our twenty minutes of limelight. We sketched broad strokes and we each took detailed notes. I remember being vaguely disappointed when we gathered our things to head to our respective evening classes. I think I imagined that we would magically produce a collaborative text, that as we talked and planned, something beautiful would happen on the laptop screen and lovely words would appear. She was supposed to finish my sentences. We were supposed to somehow write in perfect harmony. Such a dream.
>
> Collaborative writing is hard. (2018, 35)

What I like about the narrative from which this passage is taken is how Bishop highlights the affective dimensions of collaboration by drawing attention to many of the things *besides* the talk, the planning—the supposedly *instrumental* components of coauthorship—collaborators must negotiate as they try to produce a joint text. For many collaborative writers, these fits and starts are minor and usually momentary, but as Bishop illustrates, they can feel like a small series of failures. But these resistances can expand into and reveal larger points of resistance that affect how the members of a team of coauthors interact with and in turn understand the objects of their writing, not the least of which is an emerging text. But this is what collaborative writers do, interact with objects of discourse and whatever other things populate the ecologies of their collaboration as they mutually intervene in the joint invention of further discourse.

Even though we each carry a unique combination of knowledges, habits, and expectations into the collaborations we enter, what we actually share with others in collaboration is the experience of mutual attunement with the various objects we bring to one another's attention as a collaboration unfolds. And what we come to know about such objects, what we experience, are their resistances. These resistances are in turn manifested in the myriad adjustments we make to our beliefs and expectations about how certain objects exist in particular assemblages. Stephen Yarbrough sketches a similar idea when he explains that for interlocutors to share meaning, they must invent a process "for each to know that the other knows that he or she knows, and so on, that they are communicating about the same thing" (2010, 5). To understand how collaborators co-construct the agency through which they compose together, in other words, we must turn to those actual moments of communicative interaction as the object of analysis. As Yarbrough continues, "The reason the process is necessary for each to know that the other knows, and so on, is that what the interlocutors come to know is the ways the objects resist their intentions toward it . . . [and] these relations, what the object will come to *be* to the interlocutors, is unified by their common relationship with, or attitude toward, the object" (2010, 5). For Yarbrough, discourse is thus a unitary process; as interlocutors identify common objects and sync one another's verbal and nonverbal gestures with those objects, they are also comprehending the relations that exist between these objects and the signs we utilize to talk about them.

In chapter 1, I briefly review Davidson's concept of triangulation, which more or less underscores this interactionist model for explaining how interlocutors must negotiate the resistances of their discourse to successfully communicate. What Davidson's theory does not do, however, is extend the process of triangulation into a more general theory of rhetorical agency as a distributed phenomenon. Marilyn Cooper has proposed a model of rhetorical agency that aligns with the interactional labor triangulation assumes, but she does not turn to Davidson or the tradition of analytic philosophy to explain it. Instead, she draws on complexity theory and neurophenomenology to explain agency as a product of "embodied nonlinear self-organizing systems interacting with the surround" (2011, 421). That's a mouthful, but what this idea suggests is that agency isn't something that exists separate from the material concerns of particular rhetorical situations, nor is rhetorical agency something that can be wielded instrumentally. I can't take up my agency as a writer, carry it into a writing scenario, use it, pack it up, then haul it to the next site of composition. Rather, the agency writers and rhetors expend *emerges* as the result of a multitude of objects and agents—or "actants," as Latour would say—interacting in ways that create feedback loops that reveal possibilities for action. Indeed, Cooper takes a cue from Latour to suggests we forego the use of "agent" in favor of "actor," a rhetorical move that might help us better recognize how things bump up against and communicate with other things in ways that both aid and constrain what actors can do in particular situations.

Cooper employs Latour's notion of a "collective" to signal what compositionists might otherwise call rhetorical situations, another move meant to further nudge us into the discursive assemblage she has constructed to theorize agency as a material phenomenon. You can see from my own choice of diction how keywords in new materialist philosophy (*object, actor, collective, assemblage*) sometimes bleed together. Despite this, I appreciate why Cooper chooses Latour's collective for her theory. A collective, explains Latour, "is not a thing in the world, a being with fixed and definitive borders, but a movement of establishing provisional cohesion that will have to be started all over again every single day" (quoted in Cooper 2011, 425). Situating the emergent quality of agency within collectives therefore speaks to the way writers and rhetors must deliberately identify at least some of the borders that will frame the subject of their discourse (i.e., they must be intentional) but also to how this process will always be provisional and incomplete. More to the point, this process must be started all over again each time. Indeed, experienced writers know the cultivation of rhetorical agency can't be shortcutted.

This gets us to the most relevant aspect of Cooper's theory for the present discussion: how she locates the idea of resistance as a central component in understanding the emergent nature of rhetorical agency. What initiates the generation of rhetorical agency is "perturbation," the actual *sensing* of instability, whether that instability gets manifested as confusion, conflict, misreading, or whatever else might affect the efficacy of one's rhetorical negotiations within a collective. Building from the work of neurophenomenologist Walter Freeman, Cooper explains that "emotions, intentions, actions, meanings, memories, dispositions, and narratives emerge from the complex system of the nervous system through processes of which the agent is mostly not aware," and that result in emotions that indicate "preparations for action." She continues, "[W]e become aware of them (as others do, often before we do) only when they are expressed in publicly observable, and internally felt, adaptations of the body that serve as signals of intent" (2011, 430).[13] Rhetorical agency is thus the felt sense of intention, and these felt intentions denote the genesis of one's emergent recognition of the available means of persuasion in a given context. As Micciche explains, "Cooper's view acknowledges what many of us know in practice—extenuating circumstances mediate agency so that intention and will are only pieces in a process, not determining factors" (2011, 74).

In other words, the objects that nudge us toward rhetorical action can and often do resist our interactions with them, and they do so in what

Cooper memorably describes as "a dance of perturbation and response" (2011, 421). In this way, objects develop meaning as we discover what we can and cannot *do* with them. Put differently, there are always limitations to what we can articulate, especially when we write. These constraints get manifested through such things as our prior experiences with writing, our familiarity with tropes and figures, a situation's decorum, and a writer's felicity with grammar and other rhetorical conventions. Ideas pose resistances, too. If I said this sentence you are reading smells delicious, my statement should trigger a confused response because we normally don't associate the object (or idea) of a sentence with the objects (or ideas) of smell or taste. But we also triangulate around material constraints, such as the presence or absence of things like paper, writing utensils, microphones, internet connections, thesauruses, cell phones, a dexterity for texting. Some of us require word processors to compose, for example, while others prefer to write longhand. When asked, I tell people I prefer to write in the mornings, but the fact is I can *only* write in the mornings because in the afternoon I am usually at home with my kids. And in the evenings?—forget it; my body (or mind?) doesn't allow me to write at night. To borrow one of Hawk's terms, such constraints contribute to the "constellation" of objects and relations that mark the various ecologies writers, especially collaborative writers, negotiate with their discourse (2011, 75).

Like Cooper, Hawk insists that any reliance on understanding the writing process as a kind of linear causation initiated by individual composers (agents) that results in passive texts (objects) should be abandoned for a recognition of how writing gets produced "through the embodied interpretation of complex material assemblages" (2011, 86). But Hawk goes beyond speculation about the materially emergent quality of agency to discuss method, *how* writers engage the materially emergent dimensions of discourse production. "Writing is not the application of simple formalisms to all occasions. It requires a broad-based education and being open to the multiple paths that can emerge out of any given rhetorical situation" (2007, 47). Indeed, I don't think it would be presumptuous to assume the purpose of coauthorship in most situations is to take advantage of "the multiple paths that can emerge" when writers come together, which is to say that built into the work of coauthorship is an impetus to take stock of the different ways a text can develop. Hawk thus helps us recognize that writing—the complex labor that ensues as an author or set of authors invents and inscribes discourse—should not be understood according to methods generated outside the rhetorical assemblages in which writers compose. I might have a plan for completing a piece of writing, in other words, but the various materials in and around which I eventually compose will surely have a say in the process. With that said, collaborative writers especially must recognize the role an emerging *text* has as it acts on them in ways that require taking heed of the resistances at work in their composing.

Here is where an interactionist theory of collaboration can substantially revise the commonplace about how coauthors can sometimes produce a text that neither could have composed alone. What matters in these instances is not necessarily the text itself as a stand-alone object but the awareness collaborators foster about *how* the text developed into such an object in the first place. That is, unless cowriters use explicit signals in their writing to designate the text's genesis and/or qualify "who's writing what," readers will have no point of reference for assessing the quality of the collaboration that produced the text. Claiming a text is better than it could have been because it was coauthored does not change the qualitative experience of readers who approach the work like any other textual object. For the authors of a collaborative text, however, the extent to which such a claim might yield pragmatic knowledge about the quality of the collaboration itself is dependent on their ability to articulate, in terms organic to the collaboration, how and why this is the case, which leads me to the second term I introduce above. The resistances cowriters experience give way to *discontinuities* in their composing, places and moments in which collaborators get stuck and must locate discourse that will resolve these breaks impeding their work.

The extent to which collaborators can resolve the discontinuities in their emerging discourse, especially the discourse they want to articulate into text, is in large part dependent on how thoroughly they can account for the objects posing the most resistance. In very practical terms, this requires taking stock of the language collaborators are using as they work, especially whatever are the terms and concepts most important to the writing underway. The *Collaborative Futures* authors model this practice (or at least offer a snapshot of it) by incorporating the many glossary entries that populate the book. As they explain, "The glossary is a way of elaborating on a number of terms and expressions that, to some degree, form the kernel of the book. A focus is given to the semi-conscious and un-conscious dimension of this glossary (of any glossary?!). While some terms are clearly major threads running through the discussion and throughout the book, others pop up intuitively" (2010, 9). To borrow a term from Mead (1934), collaborators must continuously reappraise the "significant symbols" of their discourse, or what in the idiom of new materialism we might call a collaboration's *discursive superobjects*, those ideas, terms, phrases, and commonplaces most proximate to the work at hand. Such appraisal is necessary because the meaning of our discourse is never stable; as we deploy speech from one situation to the next, the significations of specific words shift as the context for our speech shifts.

What successful collaboration requires, then, is the ability to recognize and anticipate how the meanings of those discursive objects might be a potential source of discontinuity. Mead once defined sociality as "the capacity of being several things at once" (1932, 49). In *Mind, Self, and Society,* he elaborates on this understanding of sociality by explaining how meaning is always an emergent property "of organized sets of responses" to objects in the world (1934, 71). As an example, he points to the word "chair," something that becomes meaningful when the word initiates a similar set of reactions from one individual to the next. Meaning exists not in words themselves, that is, but in the ways "gestures" (another critical term for Mead) provoke common responses among those who use them. As Mead explains in "The Genesis of the Self and Social Control," an essay in *The Philosophy of the Present,*

> If the social object is to appear in his experience, it must be that the stimuli which set free the responses of the others involved in the act should present in his experience, not as stimuli to his response, but as stimuli for the responses of others; and this implies that the social situation which arises after the completion of one phase of the act, which serves as the stimulus for the next participant in the complex procedure, shall in some sense be in the experience of the first actor, tending to call out, not his own response, but that of the succeeding actor. (1932, 181)

Here we see Mead gesturing toward one of the hallmarks of his philosophy of language, which is that the purpose of communication itself is at root the continuation of a common world, one that is "continually breaking down. Problems arise in it and demand solution" (1964, 341). In this way, the evaluation of meaning never stops because we must continually recalibrate our interactions with one another. Like Cooper's understanding of rhetorical agency, meaning is a continually emergent phenomenon that allows individuals to cooperatively share the world in a progressive sense—by doing things, acting in it, and generating change.

According to Mead, we process meaning by amassing sets of common responses directed by whatever "nervous elements" prompt us to make connections between and among objects. By nervous elements, Mead implies phenomenological activity—*perturbation*—the sense of resistance as we interact with things, including others, in an environment. As he puts it (in Mead's typical roundabout idiom), "such an organization of a great group of nervous elements as will lead to conduct with reference to the objects about us is what one would find in the central nervous system answering to what we can call an object" (1934, 70–71). To return to the idea of discontinuity, what Mead suggests is that objects have a say in how we interact with them. When objects resist our actions—say when a chair resists a child's interaction with it as something to stand upon and she falls; or for an example closer to home, when coauthors recognize a particular word or phrase in their work has invoked responses from outside readers that contradict their own understanding of that term—we process the "nervous elements" of these interactions in the construction of future sets of possible responses. To extrapolate this insight into the present discussion of cowriting agency, if we are to successfully resolve the discontinuities that arise when we coauthor, we must anticipate that taking stock of the discursive resistances we can identify in such moments will in turn lead to new possibilities for articulation, ones we might not have considered (or even known were possible) before those moments of discontinuity arose. And it is precisely in this way coauthors come to recognize, when they do, that a text they have written together could not have been composed by either of them individually.

Like most experiences, how collaborators come to identify and name the resistances and discontinuities of their collaboration is contingent on reflection. "Texts that are collaboratively designed and written to integrate perspectives can't help but be qualitatively different from texts designed to express individual perspectives," writes Michael Schrange (1994, 20). What Schrange does not mention is that if a collaborative writing team has produced a stand-alone text, it falls on them to adjudicate its qualitative differences, especially if all an audience will see is the finished text itself. So how should compositionists talk about the benefits collaboration offers to writers who deliberately enter writing projects expecting to produce a text that qualitatively reflects the cowriting agency emergent during its production? Surely such awareness is on display when coauthors say they have composed a text greater than the sum of its parts. Just consider what Sheryl Fontaine and Susan Hunter say in this regard, that the conversation collaborators produce as they write "pushes the generative moments of writing ever further out; it tests the synthetic strength of the text, tests until the synthesis is adequately complex and multidimensional . . . [it] continues until all writers are satisfied and a text exists that the solo writer could not have created" (2006, 47).

By this point it should be clear that this sort of claim, as I've written with John Pell, "has nothing to do with individual ability, inborn talent, or old-fashioned effort; rather it signals the simple fact that one's vision is always partial, which is to say there is always a horizon of insight that limits what one person can see at any given time" (2013, 247). These horizons can and should be thought about in terms of the agency cowriters recognize in themselves at any given moment, agency "manifested in our capacities to intervene in and enhance the ways we read, think, and compose—actions that for many academic writers (as well as for our students) sometimes get entrenched with routine and convention" (247). When cowriters take advantage of the slowdown that so often results when discontinuities disrupt their work—when they learn to see these "stuck places as spaces of beginning" (Van Cleave and Bridges-Rhoads 2013, 679)—they can attune themselves to the rhetorical assemblages of their collaboration in ways that enhance their ability to detect and be directed by the multitude of resistances that are part and parcel of not just collaborative writing but every act of composition undertaken, whether alone or with others.

But what does all this look like in practice?

The preceding discussion is abstract, so I understand if my theoretical sketch of cowriting agency brings to the fore such a straightforward question about practice. But the fact is *what* cowriting agency looks like *in practice* will necessarily be different from one collaboration to the next. Moreover, the only people who can actually name and assess its qualities are those who are privy to it, the collaborators who negotiated this or that particular coauthorship, who produced this or that particular text, or who tried but failed to finish this or that particular project—indeed, we can and should recognize the cowriting agency that gets negotiated even when a collaboration isn't successful. Just because a collaboration may not yield what its members hoped to produce does not mean the collaboration itself was necessarily a failure.

A FEELING FOR AGENCY

When framed in terms of the interactionist theory this book explicates, what collaboration makes possible is the ability of collaborators to draw upon one another's positioning to recognize new connections between and among the various objects relevant to the assemblages within which they are composing. In addition, the writing that emerges from the discourse cowriters produce in these assemblages impacts how an emerging text behaves *as writing* over the course of its development. Assemblages are always in flux, so the act of writing—the material processes writers engage to inscribe their texts—are always being adjusted, often tacitly, to the ebb and flow of the assemblage. That is, as a cowritten text develops, so does its objectivity as a text—as something that becomes another object with which collaborators triangulate.

But this is true of all writing to a certain extent. As a piece of writing starts to develop as an object for its authors, when it starts to exert a certain amount of material force in the assemblage (when a student, for instance, says they really like the introduction to a paper they have written and don't want to change it despite your suggestions to do so), the writing itself starts to have its say with the composers inscribing it. The agency cowriters develop in such moments, to echo Hawk, "is not the universal aspect of a sovereign subject but a matter of what bodies can do, their capacity to affect other bodies by entering into relations with them" (2007, 119). In short, the resistances and discontinuities cowriters navigate as they compose influence the quality as well as the direction of the discourse with which they are triangulating, and as such these resistances and discontinuities are a necessary component of the shared agency that makes collaborative composition possible.

The implications of this theory of cowriting agency can be illustrated by returning to *Collaborative Futures* and looking at how those coauthors literally come to terms with understanding the rhetorical mechanics of collaboration more generally. For instance, there is a moment toward the beginning of the book in which the authors are describing the reason for their book sprint and how it's a continuation of previous book sprints that resulted in manuscripts that went on to be published as well-received FLOSS manuals. They mention how the manual *Introduction to the Command Line*, a guide for Linux programmers, was praised by one well-known software developer for being clearer and more useful than any other similarly focused manual, especially for beginning programmers with little experience (2010, 8). But then the *Collaborative Futures* authors step back and say their book is different. "The difference between the Collaborative Futures and other Book Sprints is that this is the first sprint to make a marked deviation from creating books which are primarily procedural documentation." They continue,

> To ask 5 people who don't know each other to come to Berlin and write a *speculative narrative* in 5 days when all they have is the title is a scary proposition. To clearly define the challenge we did no discussion before everyone entered the room on day 1. Nothing discussed over email, no background reading. Nothing.
>
> Would we succeed? It was hard to consider this question because it was hard to know what might constitute success. What constituted failure was clearer—if those involved thought it was a waste of time at the end of the 5 days this would be clear failure. (9)

I barely took notice of this passage the first time I read it, but as I've subsequently returned to the book, this passage is one that now stands out because of the way it speaks to my own insecurity as a writer who often struggles to *feel* as if I know what I'm doing. This insecurity, this desire for a felt sense of assurance in my intentions as an author, is of course what makes rhetorical agency such a phenomenologically complex quality to understand, let alone control. That the *Collaborative Futures* authors name this struggle so early in their text must therefore be significant. In one sense, this disclaimer partially explains the patchwritten quality of the writing in *Collaborative Futures*. These writers had neither the time nor the advantage of preparation to compose, revise, and edit a more cohesive book. But then again, they admit they were aiming for a kind of text no one in the collaborative could really explain or predict before it was completed. Indeed, how should they have approached the task of writing a handbook about collaboration in a way that doesn't offer, in their own words, "procedural documentation," what some readers might be looking for by way of a how-to guide?

It's clear the book sprint in which *Collaborative Futures* was written functioned as a strategic experiment for its authors. Rather than plan, draft, and revise a handbook on collaboration that can be presented as yet another guide composed of preset strategies and procedures for exploiting collaboration in practice, what its authors actually do is make their handbook *a narrative about making a handbook*. Latour (2005) might describe this project as an extreme version of writing down a risky account, an idea I take up in more detail in the next chapter. Here, though, I wish to underscore how *Collaborative Futures* serves a double function for its authors. On one hand, it is a provisional set of observations about collaboration that has been hacked together by writer-activists passionate about the subject of peer production. On the other hand, the book is an example of those very ideas; it is a material consequence of the kind of collaboration its authors want to promote in a world in which they think the tools of digital culture are too often used to promote cynical iterations of anonymity rather than cultivate forms of collective engagement that expand potentials for identification and relationality.

To the credit of *Collaborative Futures*, not only do its authors name the failure they risked (as seen in the above passage), they also admit their book aims "for a utopia that we can never actually arrive at" (2010, 5). *Collaborative Futures* is thus transparent in its provisional status as an open-ended essay trying to make sense of something much too complex to be clearly articulated in any one particular idiom. In this way, the book exemplifies what Hawk says about the need for "open-ended" methods for composing because whatever method (or methods) writers pursue, they "cannot completely predict the outcome of its application" (2007, 170). It is thus no surprise the *Collaborative Futures* writers end up theorizing collaborative agency using the metaphor of a web, "one that transforms subjectivity" in such ways that "collaboration *produces* subjects—one must submit to the project, become subjected to it—in order to engage" (2010, 43–44; emphasis added).[14] This language might make some of us apprehensive. The idea of *submitting* or being *subjected* to an agency not one's own invokes the poststructuralism of Foucault, especially the figure of the panopticon, which is hardly the kind of ideology one wants to promote in a writing course. But such apprehension speaks directly to the staggering amount of concern for the politics of consensus compositionists have debated over the years when speculating about the value of collaboration in our classrooms.

But by now I hope it is clear that consensus and the various challenges compositionists have linked to this concept might be more productively understood as simply another source of possible resistance that can manifest in a collaboration. Cowriters must talk through the purposes of their collaboration, of course, and they must set goals and eventually develop a sense of what might constitute a finished text. All of this requires reaching provisional agreements of one sort or another; it also requires a certain amount of trust. But it is important to understand that these agreements are but one contingent element in complex rhetorical assemblages that might put forward objects other than anxiety about consensus cowriters will choose to heed.[15] After all, an interactionist theory of collaboration focuses on the discontinuities that result from whatever resistances arise in a collaboration that the writers themselves choose to engage as they negotiate their cowriting agency.

So the idea of submitting to a collaboration, even if all this means is being open to the unexpected insights a collaboration might yield, makes sense if the agency cowriters produce is always at least partially the product of the writing itself. It is something that grows as the writing itself grows. It is in those frustrating moments when the production of a text has been halted, or simply in the felt perception that textual development has ceased, that cowriters are best positioned to recalibrate their shared discourse with whatever objects of concern emerge as viable options with which to continue the work at hand. Heeding the material of cowriting requires the ability to progressively recognize and exploit the moments of complexity when this discursive emergence is recognized, even if only partially. Hence those moments of discontinuity when *the what* or *the why* or *the how* of a text's development gets divorced from our felt senses of intention are precisely those moments when objects in the assemblage push back most, when they most resist. Because of this resistance, the agency cowriters foster is in many ways most powerful when in these moments of discontinuity they can anticipate the resolution of resistance that will allow them to continue writing.

So how might we encourage coauthors to view their agency in these terms? That is, how can cowriters deliberately act on this theoretical orientation of cowriting agency while recognizing such theory cannot be reduced to generic procedures or step-by-step processes? My short answer is that coauthors can assess their cowriting agency by identifying moments of discontinuity in their collaboration—moments when there is a felt uncertainty about what can or should be articulated—and how particular iterations of discourse emerge in relation to the objects of concern generating such discontinuity to reveal an appropriate way forward. Moreover, to the extent cowriters can trace how they adjusted and adapted to those moments, such reflection will point to this agentive capacity they have cultivated. But this answer is still abstract, which is why in the next chapter I offer a more applied discussion of method, namely what coauthors can do when they want to proactively engage the full work of their collaboration, not just in terms of what they are composing but also how they are composing it.

PART 2

Enactments

4

COLLABORATIVE WRITING IN PRACTICE

"So, what do you actually do with your students to promote this approach to collaborative writing?" I recall this question almost verbatim. I was doing a first-round interview over Skype the second time I went on the job market, the search that led to the position I currently hold. At that point this project looked very different from the book you are holding in your hands or reading on a screen. As is often the case for newish PhDs on the job market, I sounded more confident than I actually was about the "book project" I was discussing in my cover letter. In truth, I was frustrated with the project and unsure whether it had a future beyond the summary of it I was marketing in my application materials. I had more than just a summary, of course. I had a dissertation about the history of collaborative writing theory in composition studies, for example, but I wasn't planning to use much of that material in the book. Why not? The simple answer is that I do a lot of throat clearing in that project, which is to say much of that writing (looking at it now in retrospect) is me tracing various lines of inquiry as a method for figuring out what I really want to write about. Still, I had devoted a chapter of my dissertation to collaborative writing pedagogy, so I did have things to say about teaching collaboration.

I also was toying with the idea of a practice-focused journal article about coauthorship in first-year writing courses. And with my writing partner, John, I had a few manuscripts either finished or close to it, one of which was expressly pedagogical, with a focus on cultivating heuristic practices for coauthorship. In other words, when I was asked that question about how I teach collaborative writing, there was no good reason I shouldn't have been able to provide a concise, well-articulated response about the ways I design, instruct, evaluate, and assess coauthorship in my writing courses. But my response to that question was something else entirely, and it too I recall almost verbatim: "I'm still figuring that out."

DOI: 10.7330/9781646420490.c004

That's it. Full stop.

It's not that I didn't have anything to say about collaborative writing in the classroom. In fact, as I note above, I had much to say about it. Nor was I unprepared to discuss how I was experimenting pedagogically with the theoretical concepts about coauthorship I was in the process of developing. For that particular job search, I had even prepared several possible responses for the latter point. For whatever reason, though, I chose to answer that question the way I did, a response that in the moment felt like the only honest one available.

The ensuing exchange was not nearly as dramatic as I've set it up to be. After a few seconds, the person who posed that question asked an innocuous follow-up, which is to say they understood I wasn't trying to be difficult or evasive. I don't remember much about the remainder of that conversation, but I'm sure I explained in a rudimentary way how I was coming to understand that just like all writers, collaborative writers cannot rely on a single process every time they set out to compose, nor can we as instructors "teach" collaborative writing as such because just as composition's early postprocess theorists explained, "When we understand writing as something we learn to do—a series of cognitive steps, or a socially constructed set of internalized conventions, or even a relatively simple pragmatic recursive process of drafting, editing, and redrafting—we imagine that writing may be reduced to a set of necessary and sufficient conditions" (Kent 2011, xvi–xvii). Indeed, if there was one thing I knew for sure about collaboration in the teaching of composition, it was that we should avoid instrumentalizing it as a procedural process.

What I mean by a procedural process gets at my discussion in chapter 2 of instrumentalist conceptions that position collaborative writing as something that can be controlled, but it is also akin to what Ede and Lunsford (1990) term "hierarchical" collaboration, which is collaboration regulated by guidelines and practices a team has agreed to at the start of a project. A process is decided upon before a collaborative team embarks on its work, and each contributor usually has a specific task or set of tasks they are assigned to complete. One of the appeals of hierarchical collaboration is that it operates according to a blueprint, so to speak, one that helps keep everyone on task. The better the blueprint, the logic goes, the better (more efficient, effective, thorough, etc.) the collaboration. This view of collaboration is why pedagogies for collaborative writing usually emphasize planning, including how to anticipate interpersonal conflicts that might arise, as the primary "work" of collaboration. That is, when collaborative writing does get discussed in textbooks and related pedagogical resources, there is usually an abundance of advice on the procedural labor of collaboration while there is a corresponding dearth of advice on the actual work of cowriting. But this lack should not be surprising insofar as pedagogies that stress the procedural work of collaboration are usually operating from the assumption that successful collaborators first and foremost must know how to coordinate the efforts of multiple individuals, so what matters most from an instructional perspective are these procedural concerns focused on the mechanics of teamwork.

To be clear, I have no problem with hierarchical approaches to collaboration. In some cases, collaborative writing is easier when cowriters follow established routines, especially when the texts under production are themselves routine. When I circulate a draft of assessment criteria to fellow faculty in the graduate program for which I serve as coordinator, for example, not only is there a recognizable procedure to this process, but the draft itself adheres to the conventions outlined by the university's Office for Institutional Effectiveness. The work of rhetorical invention required for this writing is therefore minimal because it follows a well-worn path. With that said, when procedure takes precedence in collaborative writing, the emergent quality of a coauthored text as a distinct object with which collaborators interact to invent novel discourse is necessarily limited by whatever are the artificial restrictions of those procedures. Before I elaborate on this argument, however, let me review the terrain I coved in part 1 of this book and how it informs what I do in part 2.

I begin with a conceptual history of collaboration as a critical concept in writing studies, one that largely remains bound up with the precepts of social constructionist epistemology. I then offer what I hope is a compelling argument for defining collaboration as a mutual intervention and progressive interaction with objects of discourse, a kind of noninstrumental technology that facilitates the production of novelty. Finally, I outline a framework for envisioning the material dimensions of the agency cowriters foster when they compose together. Save for a handful of examples and anecdotes, coupled with explication of several coauthored texts that model or otherwise engage the kind of thinking I want to encourage as we consider the work of collaborative composition, I avoid spelling out how this interactionist theory of collaboration does or should work in practice. Thus, I resist buying into the binary that might tempt readers to imagine these ideas can be easily translated into particular strategies for cowriting. In fact, I propose the opposite, that collaborative authorship shouldn't be reduced to a set of procedural activities or generic practices.[1] Nevertheless, some readers might reasonably contest that this book is so far too speculative, that theory by itself always begs for evidence that can in one way or another demonstrate its utility. For coauthors and prospective coauthors, for example, what are the practical implications for this theory? And what about for teachers interested in the pedagogical potential of coauthorship? What can or might we do differently in the classroom if we want our students to gain experience writing collaboratively?

I don't want to write off such questions because they deserve consideration. At the same time, however, I'm interested in how we as practitioners and teachers of writing might develop strategies for pushing back against the authorial economies I discuss in the introduction to this book, those economies that inform the policies and procedures through which many academics come to view coauthorship. And what are those views? At best, these economies position coauthorship as a configuration of autonomous individuals in proximity to a shared piece of writing, which in turn allows assumptions to proliferate about the divisibility of the collective labor of that writing's authors. At worst, these economies position coauthorship as a lesser and less rigorous writing practice compared to solo authorship, which in turn allows for policies that award coauthorship (or rather punish it) by assigning it less credit or requiring coauthors to account for their unique contributions, which returns us to the previous point. One thing these various economies have in common, then, is that they operate under the shadow of a neoliberal push to standardize academic labor in ways that make tracking it easier and more efficient.

I'm not naïve, of course, especially when it comes to the reality that sometimes you just have to "play the game," which is what I grew up hearing my father (a college administrator, no less) tell me anytime I protested a practice I found to be arbitrary. But my father's frequent retort was rarely intended as a defense for passivity or complicity; rather it was more often a pragmatic reminder that sometimes you must work your way into a position where you can better influence the way things get done. What this means for this present discussion is that I'm not interested in promoting coauthorship as something that can be practiced with greater ease and efficiency, which is to say the practices that most interest me as a theorist of collaboration are ones necessarily messy and complex. More to the point, I'm interested in promoting practices that encourage collaborative writers to invent and in turn name their own processes as they negotiate the particular exigence that has brought them together in the first place.

To this end, the primary argument I construct in this chapter is that the best way to teach collaborative writing is also the best way to practice it, and that is to develop methods for enhancing the *experience* of coauthorship by making it, to echo Latour, "as reflexive, articulated, and idiosyncratic as the actors cooperating in its elaboration" (2005, 121). Even for the most seasoned coauthors, collaborative writing can be arduous and demanding, requiring collaborators to constantly recalibrate their efforts while triangulating with one another and the objects of their discourse. As I've said at several points, however, collaborative writing is no different from individual authorship in this regard. Whether we are writing alone or with another person, we must constantly negotiate resistances and discontinuities that make us second-guess what we are doing as writers and how we are doing it. The difference, of course, is that for collaborative writers, these processes usually move slower, so the writing often takes longer. In addition, the effects of these resistances and discontinuities are amplified as they mark the limits and limitations of the collaboration as it progresses—or digresses, as it sometimes can feel.

Writing is hard for most people whether we undertake it alone or together, of course, a point so obvious it almost doesn't need to be said, but this recognition can and often does frustrate coauthors if they attempt to bypass the slowdowns in their work without paying attention to them—without, that is, registering their objections. Collaboration should thus "be as costly as it is necessary to establish connections among the many mediators it finds swarming at every step" (Latour 2005, 121). Indeed, if the daemon of collaborative writing had a refrain, it would surely be this: *I can't be shortcutted.* That's my inner Latour speaking, but for good reason. The line I am quoting comes from Latour's elaboration of actor-network theory, or ANT. What I find attractive about ANT as a way into thinking about the practice of collaborative writing is its emphasis on the slow, mundane work of description. In fact, throughout *Reassembling the Social* (2005), his handbook on ANT, Latour repeatedly highlights the value of serial redescription and the continuous work of paying attention to the various actors contributing to a network.

But paying attention is not a passive activity for Latour. On the contrary, this recursive labor of observing, recording, and describing is at the center of his understanding of sociological inquiry as a construction process, one he equates with engineering. "Learning how to become responsive to the unexpected qualities and virtualities of materials is how engineers will account for the chance encounter with practical solutions" (Latour 2003, 31). "Everywhere," Latour goes on, "building, creating, constructing, laboring means *to learn how to become sensitive* to the contrary requirements, to the exigencies, to the pressures of con-flicting agencies where none of them is really in command" (33). As Cooper reminds us, "Latour insists that his 'compositionist' approach requires attunement, experience, and repeated efforts—work—and that it is not a matter of mastery but a collaborative construction project in which humans and nonhumans participate as actors, or actants" (2015, 185). The "compositionist" moniker is one Latour adopted as part of his efforts to recast the work of critique in a way that explicitly names the constructivism inherent in his political vision for "building a common world," including "the certainty that this common world has to be built from utterly heterogeneous parts that will never make a whole, but at best a fragile, revisable, and diverse composite material" (2010, 474).[2] Whether writing as a political theorist or academic researcher, Latour understands that we construct rather than uncover sites of practice, a conceptual move that flattens the ontological distinctions between observer and observed as a strategy for minimizing our presumptions about the associations that might emerge.

What this means in practice for ANT is not foreclosing processes of observation. As Latour explains, "Instead of taking a reasonable position and imposing some order beforehand, ANT claims to be able to find order much better *after* having let the actors deploy the full range of con-troversies in which they are immersed" (2005, 23). To the extent that the actor-network researcher is capable of recording these deployments, the better positioned they are to construct a narrative about those networks of actors. The same goes for collaborative writing, I believe, especially when cowriters are invested in not just producing a coauthored text but developing an account of the production process itself. To the extent collaborative writers are attuned to the assemblages that constrain and encourage the shape and quality of their collaboration, they are posi-tioned to record the traces of this labor and the deployments that prove most resistant—those that have the most material effect on the progress of the collaboration.

I'm attracted to ANT as a resource for understanding this kind of work because it rejects the philosophical dualism that posits an irrecon-cilable divide between abstraction and materiality. This supposed divide is what motivates some people to reject theory out of hand if it appears inapplicable or otherwise too abstruse. For this reason, I want readers to be clear about the title of this chapter because I can't offer a handbook-style set of instructions for staging collaborative writing as a procedural activity. But this doesn't mean I'm uninterested in discussing how coau-thors might develop methods for conceptualizing collaborative writing *in practice.* Before I continue with this line of inquiry, however, I want to briefly discuss the value of approaching collaborative writing practices from a speculative stance.

TACIT DYSFUNCTIONS

Consider the following two scenarios, each of which paints a different picture of collaborative writing in practice:

Scenario 1

Two colleagues, both of whom are junior faculty in their respective academic departments, have decided to pursue a collaborative writing project. They met for the first time two months ago at a conference where they each delivered papers on a similar topic. They don't know each other very well—in fact, they work at institutions on opposite sides of the country—but they've been exchanging emails almost daily. They also have a pair of documents they are sharing on an online writing platform. In the first document, they each pasted the text from their respective conference papers; in the second document, they have developed an outline and have started to selectively adapt material from those two papers. While they are confident about the viability of the project, the work is nevertheless challenging. Initially, the draft felt like a conglomerate of unconnected parts. These writers, neither of whom have coauthored before now, mostly work on the text asynchronously. Even though they talk to each other on a regular basis through email and the occasional video chat, both have had to learn to interact with each other as writers, which is to say they have had to adjust for the present project what have otherwise been their individual habits of writing. Needless to say, there has been a lot of trial and error. But now their coauthored draft is starting to take shape, and even something of a unified voice is starting to develop in the writing. Moreover, these coauthors have noticed their emerging text is not exactly what they planned to write when they first conceived of the project, which is to say they are a bit surprised by how their writing together has come to direct itself in ways neither of them anticipated. There is still much work to do, but these collaborators are confident about the draft and have even started to discuss another writing project to pursue after they finish this one.

Scenario 2

Two undergraduates in an advanced composition class are collaborating on an ethnography assignment. When their instructor informed the class they would be working collaboratively, these two students self-selected to work with each other. Their instructor provided an outline for managing the project. Using these instructions, the first thing these writers do is break down the project into a series of smaller tasks. From there they divvy up these tasks while also outlining a schedule for completing the work, which includes a weekly brainstorming meeting they will have every Wednesday after class. They write down this plan, and per the assignment instructions, submit a copy to their instructor. Then they get to work. The site for their ethnography is located adjacent to campus, and they've already talked to several of the organization's members and have secured an invitation to study the group for the next six weeks. In sum, there are very few logistical barriers they'll have to manage, at least when it comes to what they've detailed in their work plan. The project is due at the end of semester, which is eight weeks from now. Per their plan, they will start to piece together the final draft of their ethnography two weeks before it's due, which, according to these writers, will leave them with plenty of time to revise the draft and make any final edits before they submit it.

While invented, these scenarios depicting collaborative writing in practice are no doubt fairly common. In the second scenario, an instructor has assigned a collaborative writing project and provided students with what is presumably a detailed set of instructions for completing that assignment. In the first scenario, two academics with similar research interests try their hands at coauthoring an article. We can switch out some of the details in these scenarios to capture a wider range of typical examples. Perhaps in the second scenario, it's a professional writing course, and instead of two students, groups of three or four students are working together and the assignment is a report in which they propose a new student organization on campus. With the first scenario, let's say instead of two faculty it is two graduate students, and what they are working on is not an article manuscript but a seminar paper an instructor has invited them to coauthor. Or perhaps it is a group of three faculty in the same department collaborating on a grant proposal; or maybe it is an instructor who has invited one of his graduate students to coauthor a book chapter for an edited collection. These are the types of scenarios most of us probably imagine when we think about collaborative writing.

But let's focus on the two original scenarios for a moment. In the first scenario, the two coauthors presumably discussed the advantages of working together and are thus invested in the prospect of their collaboration. Neither of them has coauthored before, but they are up for the challenge even though there is a learning curve that must be negotiated; they must push through various fits and starts as they discover how to write together. In the second scenario, the two coauthors are invested in their collaboration as an assignment, so they develop a plan that presumably accounts for whatever are the generic parameters associated with completing the assignment successfully. Besides these scenarios' obvious differences (one involves professionals, the other involves students; one of the collaborations is pursued voluntarily, the other is a course requirement), the biggest difference between the two is that in the first scenario I paint a picture of what the actual work of coauthorship looks like for those two writers, while in the second scenario I describe the students' planning efforts but stop short at speculating on how they will inscribe their coauthored paper.

But most of us can probably imagine how this second scenario will play out. I don't mean to suggest these students won't get the work completed; if they are diligent and stay focused, they most certainly will. But insofar as these students have been encouraged to imagine their collaboration as a series of discrete tasks, they will no doubt have to push through or otherwise ignore the inevitable host of resistances that will threaten to slow down the work once they start inscribing their collaborative text. In fact, the experience of collaborative writing for these students will most likely boil down to the work of project management, including the challenge of fitting together pieces of text they compose individually. Such an experience isn't without value, of course, but the students will not likely be able to take advantage of the slowdowns that would otherwise invite attunement to the complexities of sharing in the production of a piece of writing over which neither writer has complete control.

Let me be clear that I'm not suggesting we should want all academic collaborators to aim for the kind of experience I describe in the first scenario, nor am I suggesting collaborative writing assignments that prescribe a particular process are unproductive, or that the texts resulting from these assignments are less good because they are somehow less authentically collaborative. My point is simply that I imagine most people who are strong supporters of collaborative writing have had experiences similar to the one described in the first scenario, whereas people who dislike collaborative writing or who otherwise might be suspicious of its pedagogical utility have had experiences similar to what is described in the second scenario. While there is nothing about the second scenario that necessarily portends a negative experience for those students, I composed it the way I did to illustrate an example of collaboration structured around procedural requirements.

But as most of us know who have experience with it, collaborative writing is hardly something that can be easily manipulated as a procedural practice. Students know this too. In a 2010 white paper, "The Writing Lives of College Students," the Writing in Digital Environments

Research Center at Michigan State reported that of the over thirteen hundred students from seven different colleges and universities it surveyed, most respondents prefer writing alone to writing with others (Grabel and Pigg 2010).[3] But we don't need empirical data to recognize the ubiquity of this preference. Most college students prefer to write alone because writing with others means they will have to negotiate the instrumental demands of a collaboration.

And what are those demands?

For starters, students aren't always provided with detailed instructions like the ones I discuss in the second scenario above. "All too often, teachers simply tell students to get into groups and work," explain Elizabeth Barkley, Patricia Cross, and Claire Major in *Collaborative Learning Techniques,* their popular handbook for college faculty, when instead "faculty members [should] create intentional learning activities for students . . . by selecting from a range of prestructured activities" (2014, 4). As these instructors see it, three defining features make collaboration effective as a pedagogical tool. First, collaboration must be intentionally designed; second, collaboration requires "co-labor," which means "all participants in the group must engage actively in working toward the stated objectives"; and third, the outcome of collaboration must be "meaningful learning": students, that is, "must increase their knowledge or deepen their understanding" of course material as a result of the collaboration (4). Summarizing these goals in their own definition of the concept, Barkley, Cross, and Major posit collaboration "is two or more people laboring together and sharing the workload equitably as they progress toward intended learning outcomes" (2). As far as a general approach to collaboration in the classroom, this is an admirable one. But the idea of collaboration in this presentation of it is not just as an instrumental process but also a generic practice orchestrated by instructors using the levers of assignment design.

With that said, most of the activities the authors discuss in *Collaborative Learning Techniques* do not involve collaborative writing as such, so I don't want to reject this philosophy of collaboration just because it's at odds with the interactionist theory I've been proposing. Barkley, Cross, and Major (2014) are right to point out that too often instructors assign group work or otherwise ask students to collaborate without putting much thought into the rhyme or reason of such requests. However, when the authors do eventually offer advice on staging collaborative writing assignments, it follows their emphasis on the necessity for designing clear, easy-to-follow procedures that guide students through the generic processes of writing, revising, and editing. That is, collaborative writing is presented as a linear process. And outside of noting collaborative writing can be "challenging" and "particularly difficult," the presumption seems to be that coauthorship requires little more than extra planning.[4] Barkley, Cross, and Major's text is designed for college faculty who want to incorporate collaborative techniques into their teaching, but how do pedagogical texts designed for students address the idea of collaborative writing?

One area of instruction where collaborative writing is common is technical communication, which is why it is no surprise that in standard textbooks like Mike Markel's *Technical Communication* (2014) or his more recent *Practical Strategies for Technical Communication* (2016), entire chapters are devoted to this enterprise. In *Practical Strategies*, the chapter titled "Collaborative Writing" begins with an infographic that juxtaposes the advantages and disadvantages of collaboration. A few of the upsides of collaboration, for example, are that it provides writers with an expanded knowledge base, a wider set of skills to draw upon, and a more accurate picture of how an audience will react to a developing text. However, a few of its downsides are that it takes more time to write collaboratively, it can promote groupthink, and the resulting document might be disjointed (2016, 36). This is a helpful preface about the risks and rewards of coauthorship for potential collaborative writers to consider, but when it comes to the nuts and bolts of writing together, Markel basically equates successful collaboration with effective and efficient teamwork. For example, after illustrating the advantages and disadvantages of collaboration, the next section of the chapter is devoted to managing projects and includes the following set of guidelines: "Break down a large project into several smaller tasks"; "Plan your project"; "Create and maintain an accurate schedule"; "Put your decisions in writing"; "Monitor the project"; "Distribute and act on information quickly"; and "Be flexible regarding schedule and responsibilities" (37). After some advice on how to conduct meetings and what it means to be an effective listener, Markel then stresses the importance of setting a team agenda with this list of requirements: "Define the team's task"; "Choose a team leader"; "Define tasks for each team member"; "Establish working procedures"; "Establish a procedure for resolving conflict productively"; "Create a style sheet"; "Establish a work schedule"; and "Create evaluation materials" (39).

Like Barkley, Cross, and Major's discussion of collaboration, Markel's offers advice for imagining the scope of a collaborative writing project, much of which is helpful in those scenarios when collaborators must compose a document under a set of constraints they might have little control over, which is no doubt the case for many technical and professional writers. Markel's emphasis on project management thus makes sense given that many technical writers occupy a position in workplace cultures resembling "a stage manager, navigating and facilitating the mundane of everyday work that is crucial for teams to be successful" (Lauren and Schreiber 2018, 125). But would it not be more accurate in this regard if Markel had titled this chapter "Project Management" instead of "Writing Collaboratively"? What is important to note is this procedural approach to collaborative writing pedagogy is not an uncommon one, at least insofar as collaboration is frequently figured as the natural consequence of something else, such as various configurations of individuals in proximity to other cultures (e.g., Paretti, McNair, and Holloway-Attaway 2007), project mediums (e.g., Barton and Heiman 2012), workplace environments (e.g., Blakeslee 2001), specific assignments (e.g., Battalio 1993), and assignment outcomes (e.g., Knievel 2008). In this view, collaboration occurs if a proximately configured team of writers can successfully arrange themselves according to a set of artificial guidelines. As long as cowriters can manage a project, set an agenda, listen effectively, and the like, in other words, they will somehow *automatically* collaborate.

While such instrumental engagements are important—a group of cowriters should of course be able to listen effectively, just as they should be able to maintain a schedule—what about the rhetorical and discursive work required to compose a collaborative text? Experienced coauthors understand that many of the resistances collaborative writers encounter can rarely be mitigated by preplanned activity. These tacit dysfunctions, what Andrew Mara and Hawk (2010) might chalk up to the clash of unaccommodating systems, often point not to failures in instrumental design but to their generic limitations. No matter how detailed a team's agenda, collaborative writers always must confront the certain and necessary pushback of objects, including the emerging text, that resist their intentions as cowriters.

As I've been arguing, however, this pushback—this *objec*tive resistance—might be better approached as a resource to exploit rather than an impediment to overcome. For this reason, and following Nathaniel Rivers and Lars Söderlund's recent proposal for a "speculative usability," I suggest that when collaborative writing is understood as a noninstrumental technology that emerges as collaborators engage the shared objects of their writing, it "focuses as much on discovering the multiple relations that an object has as it does on elaborating the specific dysfunctions that a user experiences in his or her encounter with an object" (2016, 127). I introduce this idea of imagining collaboration as a noninstrumental technology in chapter 2, where I also discuss the challenges of figuring collaboration in terms of techne. Using Rivers and Söderlund's speculative usability to further theorize this noninstrumental technology, we can argue that coauthors productively learn *how* to collaborate once they can articulate its "dysfunctions" in relation to their (the coauthors') intentions as composers. Such an approach underscores the value of engaging collaboration as a method for expanding the potential for rhetorical invention, but it does so by insisting that collaboration is not just an activity but a noninstrumental technology coauthors construct through their mutual interventions in the development of a shared text. But how does usability figure in this approach?

A traditional usability study might find a team of technical communicators testing a new website design by observing how easily users locate specific information on the site, manage the navigation process, and respond to the site's interface, those things considered by the website designers to be concerns that necessitated the redesign in the first place. Speculative usability, however, understands "objects not only as tools or aids through which humans exert or extend their own agency, but also as agents themselves, capable of resisting and doing their own thing" (Rivers and Söderlund 2016, 129). Rivers and Söderlund offer a range of examples to illustrate the utility of this concept, from "glitched" images, to a desktop computer that has been turned into a mailbox, to a case in which a car owner successfully installed an electrical outlet in the car's dashboard, all of which speak to the ways a traditional approach to usability would fall short because the objects in question weren't designed to behave in each of these ways. After all, Dell didn't design its computers to be gutted and transformed into mailboxes. But as Rivers and Söderlund contend, the complexity of an object's network can help us "to unlock new forms of usefulness when an object is recontextualized," which is to say speculative usability "attempts to exploit this complexity as potential rather than to control it as error (or noise)" (128–29). In this way, the idea of speculative usability challenges us to consider how the ecologies in which particular objects exist influence our engagement with these same objects. It also encourages us to imagine how the most visible object relations in a usability situation might be hiding other relations we don't notice, or to imagine how particular items might work in different ways if we locate them in different ecological contexts, contexts always marked by the intentions of the object's users, the design of the object itself, the settings in which the object exists, and the relations between and among that object and other objects in this new context.

In sum, speculative usability encourages a more expansive outlook on the idea of instrumentality—how we envision the manipulability of objects as tools. It should not be too much of a stretch to imagine how this concept might be useful as we consider the rhetorical-discursive labor of coauthorship, especially if we follow usability specialist Barbara Mirel's point about the importance of distinguishing between a technology's "ease of use" and its overall "usefulness" (2004, 222). Because collaborative writers often hit those moments of "synergism," to borrow from Ede and Lunsford (1983, 155), when, after all the handwringing and false starts, they hit upon a method for inscribing their coauthored text, I imagine most collaborators would suggest the complexity of these experiences can't be captured through a linear accounting of "how" they wrote what they did. Nor can such complexity be reduced to the generic steps of project management like the ones Markel specifies. Most of all, experienced coauthors would probably say the "ease of use" of collaboration as a noninstrumental technology does not necessarily correspond to its "usefulness" since coauthorship is for many writers harder to pursue than the writing we undertake individually.

At this juncture, I propose the utility of what Latour calls "risky accounts," what in this chapter I describe more specifically as the work of *parallel composition*, the inscription of a text distinct from but related to the primary writing that has brought coauthors together. Through the relatively straightforward work of description, parallel composition offers a method for capturing some of a collaboration's resistances and discontinuities, what we might term "controversies" if using Latour's idiom, but in a way that "attempts to exploit this complexity as potential rather than to control it as error (or noise)," to echo Rivers and Söderlund (2016, 129).

Parallel composition is writing about writing, we might say, but such an account is not the same thing as what compositionists might identify as a *process narrative*, what a writer composes at the conclusion of the drafting process to document how they wrote what they did. The value of parallel composition as a kind of risky account is linked to its coterminous emergence alongside the primary text of the collaboration. That is, a risky account is written *in parallel* with the primary text, not afterward; moreover, such a text isn't inscribed with the same level of deliberation as the primary text, which is to say the parallel composition of risky accounts is best pursued *without deliberation*. This is what makes it risky: it has no preconceived end, no aim its coauthors write toward. We might thus conceive of parallel composition as a methodological practice for enhancing the material dimensions of collaborative writing that results in a text that might function, to borrow language from W. Michelle Simmons, Kristen Moore, and Patricia Sullivan's description of ANT, as "an unstable, uncertain portrait (or palimpsestic map)," one that presents a rhetorical site of composition "more attentive to the ethical urgings to be more inclusive, more in tune to shifting identifications and to what is traditionally hidden" (2015, 277–88).

RISKY ACCOUNTS AND/AS PARALLEL COMPOSITION

Not too long ago when I was working on an earlier version of this chapter, I was rereading Latour's *Reassembling the Social* and came across this passage:

> What we are doing in the field—conducting interviews, passing out questionnaires, taking notes and pictures, shooting films, leafing through the documentation, clumsily loafing around—is unclear to the people with whom we have shared no more than a fleeting moment. What the clients (research centers, state agencies, company boards, NGOs) who have sent us there expect from us remains cloaked in mystery, so circuitous was the road that led to the choice of this investigator, this topic, this method, this site. Even when we are in the midst of things, with our eyes and ears on the lookout, we miss most of what has happened. (2005, 123)

I pulled out my laptop and opened a document filled with notes I wanted to send to my writing partner, John. We had just submitted an article manuscript to a journal, so we were in that in-between time of having finished a piece of writing and waiting for a response to see whether indeed the piece really was finished or reviewer feedback would send us back to the draft with a new set of resistances to consider. I rested Latour's book at the base of my laptop and typed the following:

> What we are doing as coauthors—sketching outlines, meeting for coffee, expanding a paragraph here, adding a comment there, sending another email, revising another section of text—is unclear to the people who know we're writing together but don't see this labor. What our eventual readers (editors, colleagues, family, tenure and promotion committees) who take an interest in this writing assume about its composition is not always clear, so complex are the economies through which our writing must travel. Even as we are in the midst of collaboration, with our eyes and ears attuned to the writing, we no doubt miss most of how it works.

In that moment, my parody of Latour's writing functioned more or less as a cathartic exercise in playful reflection, but I share it here because it speaks to what the experience of coauthorship can so often feel like when we are "in the midst of collaboration," as Latour-me puts it. Even though Latour is writing about the mundane labor of sociological fieldwork, this description about how such labor gets registered by others, including the fieldworkers themselves, speaks to the challenges coauthors often face when prompted to consider how their writing together works. As Latour cautions with what is no doubt a healthy sense of self-awareness, "It is impossible to compose without being firmly attentive to the task at hand" (2010, 487). In a recent essay for *New Literary History* in which he reflects on his experiences as a writer, Latour notes he has always been aware it is not enough "to teach PhD students to 'think' and 'study' without ever directing their attention to the subterranean act of writing," which he says requires "a serious encounter with *textuality*" and "the materiality of writing" (2016, 465). But what is the significance of these ideas for understanding the work of collaborative composition?

The short answer is that coauthors are better positioned to understand the labor of coauthorship the more attuned they are to the "task at hand" of their writing together. But this response amounts to a tautology: the more cowriters pay attention to their work, the more they recognize what they are doing. While this is the basic argument I'm forwarding, it is the *paying attention* part that deserves elaboration because as I discuss in the previous section, most of us are taught that collaboration ultimately boils down to processes of project management. But this focus makes sense when we consider that collaboration often slows down our writing; that is, it makes sense that cowriters would want to push through and find shortcuts to make their collaboration as easy and efficient as possible. Attending to the many resistances and discontinuities that arise in a collaboration can detract from the writing at hand, not to mention the pressures of whatever external constraints, like deadlines, coauthors are up against.

What is needed is a practice that prompts cowriters to register these objections *as they experience them,* but a practice that is conditional insofar as what cowriters register in this regard need not be attended to other than rendering these objections as a line or two of description. Some objections may prompt more description and elaboration, while others might prompt less. What matters is that cowriters *register* these objections in the most conventional sense of this word: as a list or record of something. Here I am suggesting the value of maintaining parallel accounts of coauthorship in practice—not process narratives, not polished texts, but literal accounts, or accounting, of what coauthors experience as they write together.[5] This practice is what I introduce above as *parallel composition,* a kind of "risky account," which is the term Latour uses to describe one of the ways ANT researchers "register the links between unstable and shifting frames of reference," or as he further puts it in his playful idiom, as a space "to float on data, not drown in them" (2005, 24).

So what is a risky account, exactly? According to Latour, it is the bread and butter of social scientific research; it is a textual artifact that reports and in turn shapes research itself. "It is typically a *text*, a small ream of paper a few millimeters thick that has been darkened by a laser beam. It may contain 10,000 words and be read by very few people, often only a few dozen or a few hundred if we are really fortunate" (2005, 122).[6] Risky accounts are the textual products of our research, the narratives that usually contain some combination of literature review, methodological description, data analysis, discussion, and perhaps argument. But what makes them "risky"? This designation is part of Latour's attempt with actor-network theory "to relocate, redistribute, and connect associations in order to flatten their social worlds enough to build a true collective" (Simmons, Moore, and Sullivan 2015, 277). At the heart of Latour's work, in other words, is "his methodological commitment to *symmetry*, the principle that human and nonhuman actants are treated alike when considering how controversies are settled" (Spinuzzi 2015, 23). And where many of these controversies come to a head—where they come into view as objects of concern—is in the finished report, that is, the article, the dissertation, the white paper, and so forth researchers have inscribed.

It is important to remember, however, that Latour views part of the function of actor-network theory as complicating rather than settling these "controversies"—whatever questions about the social that social scientists purport to be in a position to answer. The problem for Latour is the "all-purpose meta-language" of so much of this research, which is why Latour says social scientists need "to learn to feed off uncertainties instead of deciding in advance what the furniture of the world should look like" (2005, 125, 115).[7] In this way, Latour argues "no social scientist can call oneself a *scientist* and abandon the *risk* of writing *a true and complete report* about the topic at hand" (127). He goes on, "Textual accounts are the social scientist's laboratory and if laboratory practice is any guide, it's *because* of the artificial nature of the place that objectivity might be achieved on conditions that artifacts be detected by a continuous and obsessive attention. So, to treat a report of social science as a textual account is not a weakening of its claims to reality, but an extension of the number of precautions that have to be taken onboard and of the skills requested from the enquirers" (127).

As Latour explains, it's the artificiality of textual accounts that gives them significance. And the best accounts reflect the "obsessive attention" of those who inscribed them. As Latour says in one of his reflections on writing, "I could finally follow, step-by-step, how a specific 'action' would be made possible by its 'network' (to use rather poor words). Don't fly, don't jump, pay the price of each connection. And if you are lost, write and write again, describe and describe some more" (2016, 467). This is almost word for word what Latour, speaking through the persona of the "professor," says to the "student" in *Reassembling the Social*: "Not teaching social science doctoral students to *write* their PhDs is like not teaching chemists to do laboratory experiments. That's why I am teaching nothing but writing nowadays. I keep repeating the same mantra: 'describe, write, describe, write'" (2005, 149). What Latour suggests is that the objectivity of a social scientific text is not captured by the style in which it is written or by claiming a particular methodology but instead emerges through the attention with which it is inscribed.[8]

Accordingly, the more "continuous and obsessive attention" coauthors give to the "controversies" of their writing, the more objective becomes the work of cowriting itself, by which I mean the emerging object of the coauthored text assumes more objectivity as its coauthors account for its development. But there is a catch: such accounts may not always work; they may not succeed in rendering observations that prove useful. This danger too is what makes such accounts risky. "Textual accounts can fail like experiments often do" (Latour 2005, 127). No matter how much objectivity coauthors are able to render in a risky account, there is no guarantee it will be useful—that it will make a difference worth the investment. But unless collaborators devote the time and attention required to make visible the objections influencing how they compose a text, the question of its composition *as* a collaboratively composed text will always be up for grabs, especially by other actors wielding generic systems of attribution (like tenure and promotion committees) who may be more than willing to do this accounting work for us.

This possibility leads me to the practice of parallel composition as a method for coauthors to trace the controversies—or the resistances and discontinuities—of their collaboration. As I have developed a picture of this practice, parallel composition involves the maintenance of a shared text (usually one that exists in an open-access, cloud-based platform) in which coauthors inscribe (describe, notate, list) various observations as they experience them in regard to the primary labor of their coauthorship, the work of writing whatever is motivating their coauthorship in the first place.[9] What gives this parallel composition its quality as a risky account is the extent to which coauthors write down all the things, so to speak, accounting for the various objections they register with/in this work. "The simple act of recording anything on paper," writes Latour, "is already an immense transformation that requires as much skill and just as much artifice as painting a landscape or setting up some elaborate biochemical reaction" (2005, 136). While perhaps not quite as complicated as painting a landscape, what the parallel composition of a risky account offers coauthors is a jumping-off point for inquiries into the labor of their coauthorship, including but not limited to the cowriting agency they foster as they write together. In this way, one of the aims of parallel composition should be similar to what Latour says the writing of a good textual account achieves, that "the number of actors might be increased; the range of agencies making the actors act might be expanded; the number of objects active in stabilizing groups and agencies might be multiplied; and the controversies about matters of concern might be mapped" (138). To the extent that what collaborators do when they write together is use their mutual engagements with objects to assemble discourse, parallel composition challenges collaborators to account for some of the details of these engagements.

So a risky account enacted through the work of parallel composition is first and foremost a text in which coauthors might inscribe their questions and observations about their cowriting, things which by the very act of their inscription become potential objects of inquiry that can be traced. As Latour confesses, "If there is one phenomenon I have never stopped wondering at, it's the countless surprises generated by the very material act of writing" (2016, 264). What Latour calls "surprises" I prefer to call *resistances* and *discontinuities*. That is, the material act of notating these resistances and discontinuities makes it easier to assess their influences as such. In other words, once inscribed, these objects become visible and can no longer escape unregistered from the collaboration as intermediaries without consequence or effect.[10]

Parallel composition is thus an empirical act of inquiry insofar as it calls on collaborators to collect and record data, and as Latour reminds us, "*Everything is data*" (2005, 133). Of course, such an inquiry requires commitment, a willingness to be invested in maintaining a risky account as a supplement to the primary work of the collaboration. In this sense it requires more labor, but I wager this labor is not that much more onerous than all the unregistered labor coauthors already do or will exhaust but never inscribe as such. Practically speaking, moreover, such risky accounts can help coauthors literally come to terms with how no *one* person or thing controls the direction and output of the collaboration, or to echo Latour, "*No one* has the answers—this is why they [risky accounts] have to be collectively staged, stabilized, and revised" (138).[11]

At one point in *The Making of Meaning*, Ann Berthoff reflects on how we teach students to be critical readers—that is, how we teach *criticism*—part of which, she argues, should include helping students understand the difference between the "meaning" of a text and whatever might be its "message." Too often teachers focus on the latter, which is to say too often criticism gets presented as a kind of hunting for the important parts in a piece of literature and being able to explain why they are Important with a capital *I*. But to focus on criticism as a kind of meaning making, which is what Berthoff advocates, we must recognize that meanings "are not things, and finding them is not like going on an Easter egg hunt. Meanings are relationships: they are unstable, shifting, dynamic; they do not stay still nor can we prove the authenticity or the validity of one or another meaning that we find" (1981, 42). And one method Berthoff offers for teaching criticism as meaning making is the practice of maintaining what she calls a "double-entry notebook."

Many compositionists and other teachers of writing are no doubt familiar with this practice, which Berthoff describes as follows:

> What makes this notebook different from most, perhaps, is the notion of the double-entry: on the right side [of a page that has been separated into two columns] reading notes, direct quotations, observational notes, fragments, lists, images—verbal and visual—are recorded; on the other (facing) side, notes about those notes, summaries, formulations, aphorisms, editorial suggestions, revisions, comment on comment are written. The reason for the double-entry format is that it provides a way for the student to conduct that "continuous audit of meaning" that is at the heart of learning to read and write critically. The facing pages [or columns] are in dialogue with one another. (1981, 45)

There is an obvious similarity between the practice of parallel composition I am describing in this chapter and Berthoff's notion of a double-entry notebook. Even though my interest in parallel composition is primarily informed by Latour's discussion of risky accounts, both Latour and Berthoff offer compelling arguments for the value of *description* and its role as a necessary component for *analysis*. Even though these discussions are separated by more than two decades and come from otherwise unrelated disciplinary traditions, these scholars offer risky accounts and double-entry notebooks as methodological practices for discovering complexity while coming to terms, quite literally, with the fact that meanings "don't just happen: we make them; we find and form them" (Berthoff 1981, 69).

Obviously, my discussion of parallel composition has been descriptive, focused more on teasing out the implications of this practice in the abstract than on discussing strategies for how coauthors might pursue it *in practice*. To be fair, though, so too are Latour's and Berthoff's respective descriptions of risky accounts and double-entry notebooks. But again, I'm walking a fine line in this chapter insofar as I'm interested in explicating the practical work of collaborative composition without backing myself into a corner through the systematic outline of specific procedures like those found, for example, in Markel's textbook. My approach is especially challenging when it comes to imagining the technicalities of parallel composition because such writing, as far as I see it, should not be intended for an audience beyond the collaborators themselves. That is, even though inscribing risky accounts is a method for making visible the often invisible labor of coauthorship, this rendering is meant to be a resource, one that has value to the extent that coauthors *find value* in it when and if they end up using this risky account to study the terrain of their collaboration. In this way, I've avoided detailed suggestions about how risky accounts should exist *as texts*. However, there's nothing stopping coauthors from transforming risky accounts into public texts, things we might think of in more conventional terms as process narratives, or if not process narratives, something less recognizable, something that speaks more unconventionally to the minor labor of collaboration (an idea I take up in the next chapter), the labor coauthors exert that doesn't get registered by readers who would otherwise only perceive the completed, polished text while perhaps noting more than one name appears in the byline.

TAKING RISKY ACCOUNTS PUBLIC

> *The original un-text was a bit unnerving to me.*
> —Chris Friend, "Episode 7: Collaboration," *HybridPod*

In Episode 7 of the podcast *HybridPod*, Chris Friend facilitates a discussion about collaboration with Maha Bali, Sarah Honeychurch, and Kevin Hodgson, three collaborators who participated in a 2014 MOOC about rhizomatic learning. Bali and Honeychurch are two of the eight named coauthors of the article "Writing the Unreadable Untext: A Collaborative Autoethnography of #rhizo14," published in the journal *Hybrid Pedagogy*, the sponsor of *HybridPod* and the impetus for this particular episode of the podcast. Over the course of their discussion, Friend's interlocutors mostly focus on their experiences participating in the MOOC and what it was like trying to compose a collaborative autoethnography. But as listeners of the podcast discover, the published version of their article is related to but distinct from the collaborative autoethnography that was originally conceived. As Bali tells it, "There was a very, very large group of people contributing to the collaborative autoethnography and so we had several different small projects with different groups of people from there deciding what we wanted to do with it. . . . [It was] one of the craziest things I think I'd ever done" (Friend et al. 2015).

As the authors of the published article describe the origins of their text (going forward I will refer to this group in the in-text citations as the "Untext Collaborative"), their autoethnography began as a Google Doc in mid-February 2014 with thirty-one participants.[12] For the next several months, this cohort engaged one another across various media, including Facebook, Twitter, and personal blogs, to tackle such questions as how to coordinate a thirty-plus-participant writing project, how to discuss rhizomatic learning in ways that are legible but don't betray the nonlinear character of the rhizome, how to frame their writing as scholarly, and how to determine what should be the project's endpoint—its product, so to speak. As these writers admit, however, "We had no definitive answers. We became distracted. Our conversations fell quiet, until the end of October 2014, when Maha Bali and Keith Hamon began jotting words, phrases, and sentences about the CAE [collaborative autoethnography] into a new Google Doc following a conversation via Direct Message on Twitter about our difficulty writing about our nonlinear experiences" (Untext Collaborative 2015). What's important to note is that this newly spun-off autoethnographic writing project, their *Untext* (I'm italicizing the title because this is how the authors refer to the text in their article), was never finished.[13]

What they did publish, their *Hybrid Pedagogy* article "Writing the Unreadable Untext," is about the experience of writing this second attempt at a collaborative autoethnography. To describe it in the terms I've introduced here, "Writing the Unreadable Untext" can be conceived in part as a risky account about their *Untext*, a parallel text these coauthors composed as a way to make sense of this other thing they were trying to write and the many resistances it was posing. I want to discuss the Untext Collaborative because their example points to several useful ideas for imagining and in turn teasing out what a risky account can be and do. As I discuss in more detail below, their example models how such parallel composition can be used as a method for coauthors to develop a context-specific lexicon for their collaboration, assess and interrogate the objective dimensions of their writing, and determine what aspects of their coauthorship can and should be legible to outside audiences and what such translations require.

As the above epigraph shows, Friend found the Untext Collaborative's autoethnography to be "unnerving," which is only a step or two removed from Baha's comment about how it was one of the "craziest" things she has experienced as a writer. For Friend's part, he is talking about serving as a peer reviewer for the piece published in *Hybrid Pedagogy*, a piece which, just to be clear, is not the *Untext* even though the *Untext* is what he is referencing in this comment. This is because the Untext Collaborative includes a link to the *Untext* in the body of their article, which as of this writing still exists as an open Google Doc on which any-one can comment. If someone visits this document and scrolls through its seventeen pages, they'll see a messy, comment-filled playground of text. Mixed within and between blocks of exposition are comics, screen-shots, and GIFs; there are random shifts in font, strings of highlighted text; and then there are the marginal comments, well over a hundred of them, the last of which is attributed to Hamon and simply says "This is being Deleuze."

So what is going on in this document? Indeed, what's going on in either of these documents, both the *Untext* and the published "Untext" article? To a certain extent, the Untext Collaborative's Google Doc resembles the *Collaborative Futures* text I discuss in chapter 3, except the former is messier and less legible to outside audiences. But comparing these two documents is problematic insofar as the *Collaborative Futures* writers published what is an otherwise polished text despite their hur-ried timeline composing the book. The *Untext*, however, is not a published text, at least not in the same way the *Hybrid Pedagogy* article is published (edited, peer reviewed, formatted for digital publication), despite the fact that the *Untext* is a public text by virtue of being connected, via hyperlink, to the "Untext" article. But there is also the question of the original collaborative autoethnography, the one that had more than thirty participants and about which the authors say the "conversation fell quiet."[14] It is not easy to keep this information organized, linearly or chronologically, but this is one of the points the Untext Collaborative is encouraging their readers to consider: collaboration as rhizome.

As the Untext Collaborative writes about their attempt at inscribing the *Untext*, it was "a document that none of us planned to write but that seemed to write itself" (2015). This observation speaks to what I see as one of the advantages of parallel composition, which is that it helps coauthors recognize how their shared text develops objectivity. Even though the *Untext* was an indispensable site for the Untext Collaborative to articulate their ideas and experiences, they say in the "Untext" article that they "are not considering *The Untext* as data to be mined, to be appropriated, to be sculpted" (2015) because the *Untext* functions more as a "map" or a "handprint" of what capturing a rhizomatic experience, no matter how partial the attempt, looks like. The Untext Collaborative borrows heavily from and writes out of concepts originated by Deleuze and Guattari, specifically the pair's notions of cartography and decalcomania, as they try to make sense of what the *Untext* is doing as an assemblage.[15] These concepts, the Untext Collaborative writes, help them "describe in part how engagement of reality (what we tried to do in *The Untext*) differs from analysis of reality (what other ethnographies do)" (2015). Insofar as these writers view their *Untext* as a kind of "engagement" rather than "analysis," this too speaks to the kind of perspective parallel composition opens to cowriters interested in understanding the mechanics of their coauthorship, especially when it comes to how the Untext Collaborative constructed a set of critical terms for explaining what the experience of their collaboration produced and what this experience, in turn, made possible.

The metaphor of mapping, for example, emerges as an important analytic term for making the Untext Collaborative's collaboration legible. But consider a longer excerpt from the "Untext" and notice the ways these writers assemble other key terms to explain their collaboration:

> Something about *The Untext* strikes us as more scholarly, more insightful, and more in touch with the real than the traditional scholarly document we could have written and have written. We believe that *The Untext* is an accurate expression of rhizomatic learning as we experienced it in #rhizo14, and we invite readers to look through it, in all its chaotic messiness, multimedia-ness, and important marginalia. It is a glimpse into the process of rhizomatic collaborative writing, what might be called swarm writing. It might be considered illegible. Or it may have all the legibility of a swarm of bees or a murmuration of starlings. We are writing here in *Hybrid Pedagogy* to make our thoughts and ideas about rhizomatic collaborative writing more legible, but at the risk of distorting "the chaotic, nonlinear, lived experiences" of *The Untext*. (2015)

There is a distinct idiom at work in this passage, one that communicates its own ethos even though the Untext Collaborative insists its article is not a piece of "traditional scholarship," in part because "the lack of a unified voice is problematic. Where is the authority? What position is taken?" (2015). Here their "swarm" metaphor and the related idea of "swarm writing" assume significance. There is a logic to these terms despite the complexity out of which the Untext Collaborative writes. I don't mean to suggest they have specific meanings that can be abstracted and applied elsewhere by other sets of coauthors. On the contrary, says the Untext Collaborative, "We frame the swarm for clarity, but that always leaves something out, something important" (2015).

What is left out that is so important?

As a reader of the "Untext" and the *Untext*, I'm not sure, but my position is that of an outsider looking in rather than a participant of the collective looking out. "The swarm doesn't focus while writing, so don't focus while reading," these writers suggest. "Absorb the hum coming from all angles and washing over you, and listen for the pockets of resonance. Triangulate to find something similar to the truth in the emergence of repetitive patterns" (2015). "Swarm," "murmuration," "hum," "pockets of resonance," "triangulate"—this language is the language of the Untext Collaborative; it is the critical vocabulary these writers have invented to articulate the critical dimensions of their collaboration, to explain as legibly as possible this writing and how they managed to compose it. But just as this terminology constructs a language for understanding the labor of this group's collaboration, this terminology can just as easily be used against the group *un*critically, or *mis*critically, to marginalize the value of this risky account. That is, this writing could be (and perhaps has been) dismissed as too performative, too abstract, too disjointed, too self-indulgent. Perhaps this possibility is why the Untext Collaborative says the knowledge generated by the "swarm" of their writing is incomplete: "We need a rhetoric for this, an ethic, a logic, something to calm our anxiety about not knowing enough" (2015). Accounting for coauthorship is a risky business. Not only can our accounts fail, as Latour would remind us, they can also be ignored.

But this illegibility is what I most appreciate about the Untext Collaborative's work: that whatever might be considered legible in it no doubt obscures more than it reveals. Bali says as much in the *HybridPod* interview. "When you try to make anything legible, which we do in any kind of social science or any kind of science," the reality is that "it is chaotic and messy. You try to represent it in a more organized way and you lose what it really is" (Friend et al. 2015). This statement reminds me of a line from Jacques Rancière: "To explain something to someone is first of all to show him he cannot understand it by himself" (1991, 6). The "Untext" article, as well as the *Untext* itself, is the Untext Collaborative's invitation to not give up on the idea of leaning into the complexity of collaborative authorship while owning up to the impossibility of representing with any accuracy what this complexity entails.

This uncertainty might sound interesting to those of us who are already invested in collaborative writing or who may wish to experiment with how we coauthor, but I will be the first to admit that the ideas suggested by the Untext Collaborative would be at best intimidating, if not downright confusing, to our students. So, in the next section I transition into an explicitly pedagogical discussion, one that might help us to imagine ways for students to experience the complexities of collaboration without, or rather without being overwhelmed by, the procedural demands collaborative work often presents.

TEACHING COLLABORATIVE WRITING IN PRACTICE

Teachers of English-language learners sometimes use the concepts of writing fluency and writing accuracy to distinguish between two types of skills students cultivate as they learn to write in a nonnative language. The first one, writing fluency, concerns a student's ability to write in a nonnative language without stopping or otherwise pausing to consider "how" to write whatever it is they are composing. Writing accuracy, as you can probably infer, concerns a student's ability to edit their writing according to whatever technical conventions related to grammar and usage are appropriate for the situation. Distinguishing between the ability to get words down on the page and the ability to revise those words so as to conform to a generic set of standards probably makes sense to most compositionists who have been trained in process pedagogy and other approaches that encourage teachers to differentiate between higher-order and lower-order concerns in the assessment of student writing. In fact, the concept of writing fluency is obviously related to the practice of freewriting, inscribing a text without stopping no matter what writers finds themselves writing about. Theories of freewriting are rooted in the value of what Peter Elbow calls "unfocused exploring," writing about an idea in ways that "build mental momentum . . . so that more ideas come" (2000, 118). Accordingly, most of our conceptions of freewriting view it as a technique for invention, for discovering ideas.

The concept of writing fluency, however, has more to do with a writer's ability to "naturally" compose in a nonnative language. Writing instructors who teach English-language learners might ask their students to engage in practices that resemble freewriting, but the goal is not to discover an idea but instead to inscribe a progressively increasing number of words. If at the beginning of a course a nonnative speaker can compose a passage only 30 or 40 words in length during a set duration of time, but at the end of that term this writer can compose a passage 150 words in length during that same amount of time, their writing fluency—their ability *to use* the written language—has increased. When it comes to the idea of teaching collaborative writing, I find these concepts useful for talking about the work coauthorship requires and how this work corresponds to the capacities students must develop to be effective collaborators.

Specifically, I believe in most cases it is more useful to focus on helping coauthors develop writing fluency rather than writing accuracy. In my experience, what novice coauthors often struggle with is getting words on the page. Indeed, simply figuring out *how* to inscribe a shared text is often one of the most challenging problems collaborators can face. For many coauthors, in other words, writer's block is not something they might have to eventually worry about; it's there from the start. Should coauthors write separately and then shoehorn their respective pieces together? Should they create a shared, online document and compose in that space? If so, is it easier to write together synchronously or asynchronously? These questions get us into the weeds of technique, which I'd like to avoid because, as I already say at several points in this book, like all writers, coauthors must invent their own processes as they write.[16] But just because I'm not interested in discussing specific processes doesn't mean I don't have advice on ways to help coauthors get started.

First, I have found the most useful method for helping collaborative writers get comfortable with the idea of sharing words is to avoid artificially separating the planning phases of a collaboration from the drafting phases. I invoke these categories for heuristic purposes to distinguish between the work of *talking* about what to write and the work of *writing* it. As experienced collaborators know, we almost always spend more time talking about what to write than we do actually writing. All this talking becomes problematic, of course, when it starts to get in the way of the writing.

To anticipate this challenge, and to start building a corpus of written prose about whatever it is coauthors will eventually inscribe, I sometimes invite students to "talk" about their planning using the space of a Google Doc. For example, an instructor might give coauthors time in class to discuss their initial ideas about a project, then instruct these teams of writers to come up with a set of questions related to the project that must be worked out before they start drafting and post these questions on a shared digital document. For homework, the coauthors respond to these questions through a written conversation in that document. The next time the class meets, the instructor might then ask these teams to use their inscribed conversation to identify a jumping-off point for the next phase of their planning. This process, such as it is, could be adapted according to any number of variations and time frames, but the benefits of such an activity are twofold: first, it helps students get comfortable with sharing a document that doesn't belong to any writer individually; second, it helps students recognize that once they start inscribing their talk, the writing becomes material that can potentially be used in the primary text they will compose together. That is, this inscribed conversation becomes a kind of *surplus composition*, a term I use to name one of three strategies I often suggest to coauthors who are eager to experiment with different methods for getting words on the page. The other two I call *nonattribution composing* and *turnaround writing*. These are strategies I teach to students, on both the undergraduate and graduate level, but I must emphasize I don't believe we can "teach" students to write collaboratively in general any more than we can teach them to write individually in general. What I can and try to do is to help writers discover methods for getting comfortable with inscribing a text with coauthors. Additionally, I want to help them discover the importance of recognizing the objective dimensions of an emerging text and learn how to ask questions about and engage the resistances it poses.

I'll say a bit more about each of these strategies.

Surplus Composition

Surplus composition is all the writing one does that is related to but not the primary writing of a particular project. When I write by myself, for example, I typically develop three to four texts simultaneously as I research and write: (1) a document that contains various notes, ideas, and relevant lines from secondary research; (2) an outline document in which I'm experimenting with, well, outlines and other organizing strategies for my writing; (3) a document in which I store all my writing "compost," freewriting and other text I've written that I'm not using in the primary draft but that might eventually be useful; and (4) the primary draft itself. Using surplus composition as a method for coauthorship means turning to all this "extra" text outside the developing draft as material with and around which to invent.

For example, two coauthors might give each other an assignment to collect and read a certain number of sources related to the topic about which they are writing. As part of this task, they challenge each other to use these sources to answer in writing a handful of questions they come up with about their topic. The writing they each produce becomes surplus composition, material that can be mined or otherwise turned to as a resource. The primary idea is to get coauthors to recognize how their informal writing about or related to a particular writing task can be developed as a common resource for the collaboration.

Turnaround Writing

One of my earliest memories of writing collaboratively was in a graduate seminar. The instructor asked us to partner with another student and engage in some turnaround writing, although the instructor didn't use that term. The basic conceit of turnaround around is to treat collaborative composition like a dialogue or informal correspondence. I write a bit, then give the text to my writing partner, who then writes a bit, they give the text back to me, and so forth. This isn't a particularly novel strategy for coauthorship, but it can be an effective practice for getting comfortable writing with another person.

I find that turnaround writing lends itself well to informal or otherwise preparatory activities that can be pursued during class time. For instance, an instructor might give a collaborative writing team a topic-specific prompt and invite one of the collaborators to devote five minutes to an initial response, after which the writer hands off the text to their collaborator, who then gets five minutes to continue the composition. Depending on the frequency and length of these turnaround sessions, it is interesting to observe how students slowly come to invent ideas and observations "separately together," so to speak, which is to say the products of turnaround writing can be used as objects coauthors analyze to identify where and how their "individual" contributions relied on the ideas of their collaborator.

Turnaround writing can also be adapted by more experienced writers in ways significantly less generic than the practice I describe above. In fact, I've advised graduate students who are coauthoring to experiment with an extended kind of turnaround writing in which they sketch an outline of the paper they intend to write and then pass their shared draft back and forth until they have a working manuscript. From there, they continue this back-and-forth turnaround writing to revise and eventually edit the essay. I imagine most experienced coauthors follow a similar practice, especially if they are geographically separated from one another or otherwise have little time to work on their writing synchronously.

Nonattribution Composing

The practice of nonattribution composing is one method for showing students what textual resistance can entail in contexts of coauthorship. Nonattribution composing involves two or more writers contributing to a text anonymously. This is of course the basic structure of wikis, but the practice itself speaks to the ways a text can grow into something that eludes the expectations of individual contribution. The point of nonattribution composing, at least from a pedagogical perspective, is to foster that sense of strangeness that can occur when our writing slips out from under our control to reveal new possibilities for itself.

In terms of classroom practice, I like to use the website PiratePad for this type of composing. For the sake of space, I won't elaborate on how PiratePad works, but it's an online collaborative-writing utility that is easy (and free) to use. In an upcoming course, I plan to use nonattribution composing to engage students in some low-stakes collaborative writing in order to get them thinking about the concepts of agency and control as features of the writing process. Specifically, I will randomly distribute numbers to each student and instruct them to use this number as their avatar when they register as a PiratePad user. I will then create a series of blank documents and send those links to pairs of students. Using this process, coauthor teams will be established. From there, I will ask students to coauthor short responses to a number of different prompts over the course of several weeks as a method for showing them how a piece of writing can develop objectivity.

Even if the attribution tracker is turned off, you might wonder whether students can still monitor who wrote what since they are only working in pairs. Yes, initially they can, and they no doubt will. But my later prompts will ask them to go back and take lines from one another's contributions to their responses and rework them in various ways, thus turning the activity into a kind of turnaround writing. Importantly, the point is not to create a set of responses that cannot be traced back to the individual collaborators—in some cases I expect they could be; the point instead is to get students engaged with a shared text that can exist as an object unto itself. Will I be able to prevent these coauthor teams from revealing their identities to each other? No. Will every coauthor team embrace the challenges that come with this kind of semianonymous activity? I doubt it. But this activity is an example of collaborative writing students can experiment with in ways that likely differ from their previous experiences with collaboration. The bigger point is that this kind of activity can be used in just about any undergraduate classroom without asking students to compose entire papers or other labor-intensive projects together.

What these three strategies share in common, and why I've offered them as examples, is how they each can be started with relatively little effort. That is, these activities are not difficult to imagine as practices that can be initiated via procedural instruction. They can be easily adapted into a prompt or set of directions, in other words, which I realize may sound like I'm going against my position on not framing collaborative writing as a procedural process. However, most novice collaborators spend too much time in the planning stages of a project when they should be experimenting with methods for getting words on the page. As such, generic prompts that might help a team of coauthors initiate some of these writing practices certainly have value, especially if the prompt leaves room for them to experiment with the process if the collaboration continues beyond that initial activity.

CONCLUSION: WHERE COAUTHORSHIP BEGINS

The above practices, including my earlier explication of risky accounts, can be imagined not only as specific activities collaborative writers might take up and adapt but also as a conceptual vocabulary for collaboration. Another thing all these practices have in common is that they presuppose collaborative writing requires coauthors to engage the limits of their individual perceptions as writers. Insofar as these practices can be said to reflect the interactionist theory of collaboration I explicate in this book, they are at best what Ralph Waldo Emerson calls "imperfect theories" (1909, 73), since, as Hephzibah Roskelly and Kate Ronald explain, "they derive from the active mind, always questioning, leaning toward, searching for, seeing beyond," that is, "those ideas that are unfinished but whose very tentativeness give them the potential for truth and useful action" (1998, 79). Moreover, and more important, these practices also share in common the imperative for inscribing text as a central component of their deployment. That is, these practices don't require preparation, at least not in the sense that coauthors must first know the details of what they are going to write.

In fact, these practices point to ways coauthors *can begin writing* as a way *to begin their coauthorship*. As Casey Boyle reminds us, "*We write so that we may compose*" (2015, 203). Rather than rely on instrumental staging to provide an opening for when coauthors can begin their writing "for real," these practices emphasize the ways writing one's way into a collaboration can not only establish the footholds necessary to imagine how coauthorship can work but also offer cowriters some initial material that can be used to help navigate their way through the project.

These practices can also be used to imagine methods for recognizing the concrete differences that result when coauthors experiment with the "risky" work of collaboration. In this way, I want to highlight how an interactionist approach to collaboration is pragmatic through and through because it rests on an understanding of the way things matter for and in experience. For the American pragmatists, there is an empirical claim on experience to understand it as the concrete ground on which action is made meaningful. As John Dewey explains in "The Postulate of Immediate Empiricism," we cognize experience in the moment, which is to say what we experience "as" experience is always in passing. "I should define cognitive experience," he writes, "as one that has certain bearings or implications which induce and fulfill themselves in a subsequent experience in which the relevant thing is experienced *as* cognized" (2000, 457). In Dewey's theory, experience is heightened—that is, made all the more material—if a person is ready for and sensitive to the various pressures and perturbations that bear upon a context (Rogers 2007, 94). For Dewey, to name an experience is to name some "thing" specifically, and what collaborators might learn to name are the qualities of the discursive interaction fostered in and through their work, hence the potential use-value for coauthors of maintaining risky accounts.

If collaboration implies, at least in part, the anticipation of resistances and discontinuities that slow down the work, to account for these qualities is part of the work collaborators can undertake to make whatever concepts they use to explain or justify their collaboration in the first place pragmatically viable. As Dewey states, "It is in the *concrete* thing *as experienced* that all the grounds and clues to its own intellectual or logical rectification are contained" (2000, 458). What our theories of collaboration should do is provide material to start this process of "intellectual or logical rectification" that yields the knowledge of experience needed to imagine and navigate collaboration *in this* or *that moment*, that is, to empirically ground it as something that grows out of a particular assemblage of objects and actions, not as an abstract set of practices that can be applied *to* a collaboration before it begins.

To return to my discussion of collaboration as a noninstrumental technology, the technical capacity of a collaborative writing team is determined by the writers' ability to anticipate the potentiality for discursive interaction, for what they determine, that is, to be discursively possible because they are writing together. What collaborators foster for their shared work is thus a unique, context-specific techne that resists identification with normative subjects and "deductive postulates" (Atwill 1998). Already this understanding renders insufficient any attempt to reduce collaboration to certain tactical configurations or step-by-step processes. In other words, this interactionist orientation to collaboration renders attempts at defining collaboration too closely inadequate because what collaboration is at any given point should be determined by the degrees of interaction that allow collaborators to share the discourse they inscribe. Therefore we cannot point to collaboration as such because collaboration speaks to the reasoned capacity for developing the know-how collaborators foster to mutually intervene in and progressively interact with discourse.

So let me summarize what I see as the pedagogical value of this discussion. First and foremost, I don't believe these methods should replace or disqualify the kinds of team writing we sometimes assign to students, especially in professional and technical writing courses. At the root of my interest in rhetoric and composition theory is a concern for how writing works as an object that can and often does elude our control, and because of this concern, I understand rhetorical invention as a perennially speculative endeavor, one that, to echo Berthoff, "is a matter of learning to tolerate ambiguity," "to think about thinking," and to "interpret our interpretations" (1981, 71, 72). In fact, for speculative usability, as Rivers and Söderlund point out, what is required is an openness to the "increased inventional capacity" of objects when they resist our interactions with them, a disposition that invites ambiguity and uncertainty (2016, 127). Consequently, I view the practices I discuss in this chapter as opportunities that allow students to recognize how writing can have agency apart from the intentions with which it gets inscribed. And trying to make sense of this hybrid agency at work in our writing is one way to foster the dispositions needed to be effective writers more generally. In the spirit of concluding this chapter with the voice of another, I end with part of Michael Carter's understanding of where writing, and I would add cowriting, begins:

> When writing is defined by the initiating act of recognizing and analyzing a dissonance, it becomes, as its advocates claim, an act of inquiry. This definition of writing is significantly different from seeing writing as a goal-directed act. Writing that begins by identifying a purpose for the writing is circumscribed by that sense of purpose; though the purpose may shift during the writing, the act of writing is understood in terms of achieving a goal. Writing that begins with an "uneasy feeling," however, is not initially defined by a goal state; the dissonance becomes a motivating force for exploration, and writing itself becomes an act of wondering. (2003, 19–20)

5

(POST)QUALIFYING COAUTHORSHIP

In *Repurposing Composition: Feminist Interventions for a Neoliberal Age*, Shari Stenberg juxtaposes what has become a standard, neoliberal understanding of agency with one that grows out of and claims marginalized locations as sites of authority. "In the neoliberal model," Stenberg writes, "self-commodification and acclimation—belonging in and to the dominant structure—serve as pathways to agency"; but the latter model "insists upon illuminating traits obscured by neoliberalism: embodiment, location, and responsibility to and connection with one another" (2015, 99). Even though she does not focus explicitly on practices of authorship, Stenberg's interest in disrupting the "standard mode of being and doing" in neoliberal discourses can certainly be extended to critique the logics of attribution coauthors must negotiate within these discourses, especially because "neoliberal conceptions of whom to be, how that mode is enacted, and what is desired are so commonly repeated, adhering to them becomes not only the norm but the only 'rational' option" (102).

Indeed, such critique can be pushed to problematize notions of authorship that remain entrenched in the kinds of representational thinking that lead us to believe not only that writers are autonomous but also that we can draw straight lines of attribution that connect these autonomous writers to what are equally autonomous texts. In cases of coauthorship, such representational thinking prompts us to assume we can account for the contributions of each coauthor in a way that positions the piece of writing in question as something that can be unambiguously broken down into its constituent parts.[1] Feminist interventions into debates about authorship as well as agency more generally, like Stenberg's, thus remind us we can and should challenge these dominant value systems that continue to circulate in the neoliberal academy.

But deciding on ways to best represent coauthorship will not necessarily lead us to better conceptualizations of coauthorship in practice. After all, "Invisibility undermines agency, we cannot alter that which we cannot see," writes Aimee Carillo Rowe (quoted in Stenberg 2015, 107).

DOI: 10.7330/9781646420490.c005

As I discuss in this book's introduction, we should not conflate generic systems of attribution with the labor coauthorship requires. But if we can talk about this labor in ways that highlight its complexity, especially as it concerns the discursive ecologies collaborators are invented by just as much as they invent—something I start to do in the chapters that compose the first part of this book—the question of attribution becomes all the more problematic. But it also becomes a springboard for more creative and potentially more disruptive inquiry into the economies of authorship that inform how many of us have been trained to understand collaboration.

The stakes of such an inquiry are illustrated by Bill Hart-Davidson in a recent interview he gave on the podcast *Rhetoricity*. A technical writing scholar whose work also crosses into the digital humanities, Hart-Davidson (2018) is asked to account for his propensity for collaborative writing. The interviewer, Jennifer Juszkiewicz, reminds Hart-Davidson that he has coauthored over forty journal articles and book chapters—many more than he's written individually—and invokes her own experience with coauthorship to note its challenges. Without missing a beat, Hart-Davidson explains that for him the most valuable aspect of collaborative writing is in how it changes the writers themselves: "I will say yes to doing a project because I want the experience of doing it as much as I want the outcome." In fact, he confesses that after receiving tenure, he "made a conscious decision that [he] didn't care if [he] ever wrote alone again." An ethic of reciprocity is evident in his understanding of collaborative writing, but Hart-Davidson cautions that he works in an academic department that values collaboration, which leads him to make a comment with which many collaborative writers, especially in the humanities, would probably agree: "We have it exactly backward in most English departments; it's much harder and much more valuable overall to write collaboratively because then you are helping someone else. So we should give more credit, not less, if you do it that way."

Turning to an explanation of how he approaches the work of coauthorship, Hart-Davidson explains that instead of divvying up a project and completing the parts individually, he likes to have a "kick-off meeting [with his coauthors] where we can co-own the shape of the line of argument." This "line of argument then shows us where we can each add our bits of expertise, where they are most needed." Aware of how collaborative writing gets positioned in economies of authorship that ascribe more value to writing done alone than to writing done with others, Hart-Davidson underscores why it is important for collaborators to "co-own" not just the text they might produce but also the experience of producing it. The value of collaborative authorship, in other words, has just as much to do with the process as it does the product.

Hart-Davidson's notion of a "line of argument" shares both grammatical and conceptual similarities to Liza Mazzei's notion of "lines of articulation," which grow out of "collective assemblages of enunciation," language Mazzei borrows from Deleuze and Guattari. A collective assemblage of enunciation, she explains, is "how a writer is invented by an assemblage at the very moment when, in the moment of originality, he or she is inventing and being invented" (2017, 683, 682).[2] Lines of articulation are the concepts writers use to write, we might say, akin to what Richards calls (via Berthoff, who really gives the concept legs) "speculative instruments."[3] But lines of articulation shouldn't be imagined simply as ideas we have, ideas we invent *ex nihilo* as autonomous subjects. Instead, they constitute the amorphous but nonetheless material forces that delimit and determine what writers can inscribe at any given moment. "Lines of articulation are presented as a form of writing that goes beyond the matter of any livable or lived experience of a singular subject, unbounded by the constraints of a body, a place, a time, an utterance, a voice"; moreover, while "there is no beginning or origin, a beginning or attunement is presented, prompted, or provoked" (Mazzei 2017, 683). Like lines of argument for Hart-Davidson, lines of articulation are for Mazzei what initiate writing, what mark the conceptual beginning points of the writing act; they are what signal an opening—disjunctions, discontinuities, ruptures of possibility—that emerge and "are spoken from our bodies, our histories, our communities, our materialities" (682).

This language is speculative and hard to pin down, but it reflects a particular way of thinking about writing that has been attracting a fair amount of interest as it relates to what in the social sciences has been dubbed *postqualitative inquiry*. Alecia Jackson, who frequently coauthors with Mazzei, describes postqualitative inquiry as a kind of "thinking without method," which, she explains, "relieves qualitative inquiry from the twin forms of epistemological imperatives of knowledge production and a conventional dependency on procedural method" (2017, 666). Gesturing to Deleuze, Elizabeth Adams St. Pierre, who is credited with coining the *postqualitative* moniker, explains "that research training (repetition) can stifle invention (difference)"; and more to the point, "The assumptions and practices of pre-existing, formalized, systematic, methods-driven social science research methodologies invented to answer questions we can already think" should be supplemented, if not replaced, with ones that seem "peculiar, odd, unnatural" (2016, 8).

St. Pierre wants to see social science research, especially its qualitative methodologies, become less instrumentalized and more open-ended. In short, postqualitative theorists reject the ontological and epistemological assumptions inherent in traditional qualitative research, and they propose alternative methods—many of which are steeped in the language of poststructuralism—for reimagining qualitative inquiry itself.

While I won't label Hart-Davidson a postqualitative thinker, his discussion of collaborative authorship is in line with how this latter group of theorists and researchers approach the topic. Indeed, many of these scholars have taken up postqualitative methods to not just better understand but to also promote collaborative writing, especially in academic contexts. Ken Gale and Jonathan Wyatt are perhaps the most prolific in this regard. In a special issue of the *International Journal of Qualitative Research* focused on collaborative writing, they pose a seemingly straightforward question: "How do co-authors write together?" As they put it, for most people without much collaborative writing experience, "this process is hidden and assumed to be innocent, even magical" (2012, 474).

But as I've been explaining it, collaboration is not magic. Successful collaborative writers don't conjure invisible forces from the ether, nor do they divine elusive capacities that come and go without explanation. Gale and Wyatt agree. Like other postqualitative theorists, moreover, they resist the instrumentalist imperative to reduce coauthorship to procedural methods legible to and dependent on the shibboleths of reliability, validity, and generalizability. They also recognize what Hart-Davidson and many other collaborative writers know to be true, that coauthorship very often requires *more*, not *less* work than single authorship.

But the available language for talking about coauthorship in this way is limited. For example, my use of the term *work* just now invokes what in most economies of authorship is a Marxian notion of labor that in this case depends upon the recognition of a particular kind of commodity, a written text that reflects this labor and gives it value. So when a set of coauthors suggests it is harder to write together than it is to write alone, we assume they are saying such labor—the labor of coauthorship—is qualitatively more demanding. If such a claim is accurate, it makes sense that the product of their labor, the commodity of a coauthored text, should "count" more in the economic terms that dictate how authorial labor is ascribed institutional value.

Since I've already discussed these institutional economies to show how their logics inform the debates academics have (when they have them) about the risks and rewards of collaboration, my goal with this chapter is to argue for why and how collaborative writers might resist labor theories of value for understanding and in turn advocating for what Judith Entes asks in her appropriately titled "The Right to Write a Co-authored Manuscript": "If a refereed publication assumes that multiple readers achieve a 'better' reading, might not multiple authors achieve a 'better' writing?" (1994, 47). One of the motivations of postqualitative inquiry is to dismantle the logical structures that make this type of question necessary in the first place, such as the belief that a coauthored text can be understood as the sum total of individual efforts. As Ede and Lunsford put it, "While we cannot dismantle these structures, we can make our students [and colleagues] increasingly aware of them and engage them in constructive critique as acts of resistance where possible" (2011, 204). But postqualitative researchers seem to think otherwise, that these authorial economies can be altered, and they are pursuing these changes in part by reinventing the language of qualitative methodology.

It is important to note that postqualitative inquiry is rooted in a materialist ontology, one that "challenges the status of qualitative research *per se*, since boundaries between qualitative and quantitative cannot stand" (MacClure 2013, 659). Postqualitative methods embrace what DeLanda (2002) terms a "flat ontology" between human and nonhuman actors, or as Latour once put it, "Nothing is, by itself, either reducible or irreducible to anything else" (1988, 158), which is another way of saying an object shouldn't be understood as the singular effect or cause of another object, which is to say even further that any*thing* that poses resistance is by necessity implicated in an assemblage of many other objects that pose their own resistances. Postqualitative inquiry thus operates from the premise that within assemblages "there are no singulars, only connectives" (Mazzei 2017, 678).

So what does postqualitative inquiry offer to an interactionist theory of collaboration? If we agree, as I have argued, that collaboration allows writers to produce discourse that exceeds the agencies of each individual collaborator, we need language capable of transgressing the divide between process and product collaborative writers are often forced to account for in their attempts to render coauthorship not only beneficial but also worthy of the same recognitions and rewards ascribed to single authors. Yet in most contexts, these ends depend on the ability of collaborative writers to represent their labor *as coauthors* in terms equitable to the work we expect from single authors. This is where the enterprise of postqualitative inquiry becomes important because it forces us to reassess the conceptual structures that limit the available responses to questions like the following: What are the differences that make a difference for collaborative writers? Can these qualities be named, studied, and pursued in and as forms of practice? Should collaborative writing be undertaken for its own sake?

My answer to these questions begins with the suggestion that we should follow in the footsteps of our colleagues in the social sciences who have been theorizing postqualitative methodologies. Specifically, I propose we recognize what I call here *minor literatures of collaboration*, scholarship that performs the complexities of authorship it theorizes or otherwise takes as its subject, a practice that celebrates what Jacqueline Preston asserts is the value "in recognizing writing as a complex and dynamic gathering of 'things' and pieces of 'things'—ideas, people, memories, events, and experiences" (2015, 37). As I elaborate in this chapter, such minor literatures cannot be easily classified in authorial economies that account for collaboration as a zero-sum undertaking. But insofar as such minor literatures are produced in these economies and circulated using the infrastructure that supports them, these minor literatures provoke—to degrees that can only be anticipated but not predicted, and in ways that resonate differently from one location to the next—perturbations that can frustrate these economies, potentially leading to their reform.

WRITING (INTO) THE POSTQUALITATIVE

Since the 1970s, compositionists have theorized writing as a mode of inquiry, as a practice for learning and discovery. Writing is not just a representational medium for recording thought; it is a tool for thinking. Janet Emig's "Writing as a Mode of Learning" (1977) is one of the most canonical texts to make this argument. Citing work from a variety of educational researchers and philosophers, Emig summarizes what were then the commonplace assumptions about the relationship between writing and the "languaging processes" of listening, talking, and reading; she argues, "If the most efficacious learning occurs when learning is re-inforced, then writing through its inherent reinforcing cycle involving hand, eye, and brain marks a uniquely powerful multi-representational mode for learning" (122, 124–25). Emig thus makes an argument for the educational value of writing by explaining how it activates the cognitive processes that stimulate learning.[4]

A few years before Emig's article appeared, a debate played out in the pages of *College Composition and Communication* about the definition of problem solving and the utility of heuristics. In 1970, Janice Lauer published "Heuristics and Composition," an essay that argued for teachers of writing taking up research in psychology to reinvigorate rhetoric as a science of invention. Among other claims, Lauer suggested composition was stuck in an intellectual rut, weighted down in particular by its association as a subdiscipline of English in service of literature. In response, Ann Berthoff criticized Lauer's apparent failure to recognize the intellectual tools of creativity already available to teachers of writing. She also criticized Lauer's willingness to cede to psychology, as the title of Berthoff's article reads, "The Problem of Problem-Solving" (1971).[5] In support of the latter claim, Berthoff criticized the field of psychology for reducing the idea of problem solving to a series of mental operations that can be tested as such, which "requires a view of language as signal-code, a notion that converts meaning to 'information,' form to 'medium,' interpretation to 'decoding,' etc." (238). Berthoff summarized the stakes of this argument the following year:

> If we make use of the knowledge we have as teachers of English, we can pursue such speculation fruitfully, without guidance of psychologists who are studying the "area" of "creativity." For creativity is not an *area*; it is the heart of the matter and the matter is using the mind by means of language. The "creative problem solving" we develop as we learn to compose is called *thinking*, and thinking is something other than "effective guessing," which is what Janice Lauer tells us the psychologists mean by *heuristics*. Anything pedagogically useful that can be said about thinking . . . will also be true of the process of composing. (1972, 415)

Lauer suggested her and Berthoff's divergent opinions about the mechanics of invention were more semantic than conceptual and that psychologists researching heuristics were still "experimenting to find methodology better suited to the study of creativity" (1972, 209). But Berthoff wasn't having it. The problem, she explained, is that creativity is a complex activity of mind that cannot and should not be fragmented into separate categories like *thinking* and *composing*, which, as she pointed out, are one in the same.

I review this episode in the history of rhetoric and composition studies because the development of postqualitative inquiry in educational research and psychology has followed a set of arguments similar to those invoked in the Lauer/Berthoff debate, but in a kind of reverse order. As the social and cultural turns swept through various academic fields in the 1980s and 1990s, qualitative researchers largely came to embrace postmodernism and its method of deconstruction. As discussions of these theories proliferated, they of course brought into question the processes through which social scientists assumed knowledge is created and circulated. But as St. Pierre notes, "We were more comfortable with the posts' [postmodernism, poststructuralism, etc.] epistemological critiques than we were with their possibilities for rethinking ontology" (2014, 2). It is one thing to question how we understand and represent knowledge claims, while it is something else to change the practices these epistemologies support. In other words, qualitative research had on the surface come to accept the epistemological critiques of postmodernism, but in practice researchers still relied on methodologies rooted in processes that qualitatively mirrored the linearity of positivist social science.[6]

For some social scientists, the real problem started to arise when pernicious policies like the 2002 No Child Left Behind Act, for example, were being justified using so-called scientifically based research rooted in these positivist methodologies. Qualitative researchers in the field of education found themselves in an increasingly untenable position. Something had to change, and for St. Pierre and the many researchers who followed her example, that something was the idea of methodology itself and the habitualized practices that had become solidified as the only practices available to qualitative researchers. As noted above, St. Pierre is credited as one of the intellectual originators of postqualitative inquiry, which is perhaps best described as a philosophy of method that embraces poststructuralist critique with the added element of a materialist's attention to objects and assemblages. To a certain extent it is an antimethod in that it questions many of the assumptions that propel qualitative research in general.

> If we cease to privilege knowing over being; if we refuse positivist and phenomenological assumptions about the nature of lived experience and the world; if we give up representational and binary logics; if we see language, the human, and the material not as separate entities mixed together but as completely imbricated "on the surface"—if we do all that and the "more" it will open up—will qualitative inquiry as we know it be possible? Perhaps not. (Lather and St. Pierre 2013, 629–30)

While Lather and St. Pierre are hesitant to define postqualitative inquiry too closely, what most of its practitioners have in common is a desire to give up the representational logic that gives qualitative research its supposed rigor. Postqualitative inquiry is in this way a speculative methodology, which leads me back to the Lauer/Berthoff debate. Just as Lauer advised taking up the procedural methods of the social sciences to study problem solving, postqualitative researchers suggest turning away from these procedures in favor of inquiry that resists standardization—what is at the heart of Berthoff's disdain for heuristics—and instead embrace the creative potential of more speculative practices like writing as a mode for learning and discovery.

Indeed, postqualitative theories that engage the relationship among language, writing, and inquiry echo points Berthoff made decades earlier. Calling on qualitative researchers to consider the materiality of language to better conceptualize "where discourse and matter are mutually implicated in the unfolding emergence of the world," for example, Maggie MacLure speculates about how a sense for the rich ambiguity of language can "trigger action in the face of the unknown" (2013, 659–60, 662). Writing more than thirty years earlier, Berthoff argued that meanings "don't just happen: we make them; we find and form them"; she then invokes the idea of "chaos" to name the material from which we form such concepts, concepts which in turn we use to compose and generate meaning (1981, 69). "Now, chaos is scary," says Berthoff, "the meanings that can emerge from it, which can be discerned taking shape within it, can be discovered only if students who are learning to write can learn to tolerate ambiguity" (70). The ambiguity of meaning is what interests MacLure, and she argues that things like "humour, mockery, disgust, fascination, unease or resistance" should be embraced in qualitative research instead of treated "as obstacles to the production of good data, clear ideas, or trustworthy accounts" (2013, 664). Accordingly, Berthoff and MacLure are similarly invested in the ways language functions as the source of meaning, not just its handmaiden. While MacLure draws on concepts from Deleuze, DeLanda, and feminist theorist Karen Barad to direct her inquiry, and Berthoff draws on concepts from Freire, Richards, and the philosopher Gaston Bachelard, both scholars are probing what Berthoff would say is "this critical, reflexive character of language that allows us to think about thinking" (1981, 72).

Berthoff's general critique of social science is that its researchers often let "behavioral objectives" dictate how they approach research itself. What's needed first, she says, is a commitment to theoretical inquiry, a searching for concepts with which to think about the research before doing it. "The trouble with behavioral objectives is that they are not meant to be modified by our practice," she writes, so "the primary use of theory should be to define what our purposes and aims are and thereby how to evaluate our efforts in reaching them" (1981, 32). Compare this idea to Mazzei's proposal for tracing "the contour of concepts" as a way into the research process. Referencing the cultural theorist and Deleuze explicator Claire Colebook, Mazzei explains that concepts are not words but the starting points for ways of thinking that emerge as inquiry plays out, so to follow a contour means "thought moves on its own, not according to a given trajectory, fundamentally changing the shape of inquiry as the contour of concepts allow connections to flow and bend"

(2017, 676). In this way, "concepts vibrate, resonate with other concepts, perhaps with existing concepts, establishing relations with others, thus laying out the plane on which they converge" (676). This resonance is essentially what Berthoff recognizes as the function of what Richards calls "the audit of meaning," the practice of reflecting on reflections and "the gathering of sense organs, reality, remembered experience, and so forth" to interrogate experience and "comprehend more comprehensively by finding ways of letting recognition serve recognition" (1982, 68, 76). Researchers don't just need methodology, Berthoff stipulates, they need a theory of imagination.

This patchwork pile of quotation atop quotation, this back-and-forth construction of a dialogue between Berthoff and a handful of postqualitative theorists, is more than anything a way for me to write into a discussion of the role of writing in postqualitative inquiry. I'm not pursuing comparison for comparison's sake, that is, nor am I simply carving out a conceptual path that links Berthoff's pragmatism to Mazzei's thinking with theory to MacLure's interest in the materiality of language. I am forming (one of Berthoff's favorite metaphors) a structure of thought meant to resonate with compositionists probably already familiar with Berthoff but who might be skeptical that this group of education researchers has anything to say about writing as inquiry that we ourselves don't already know. Not only do I believe they do—that postqualitative thinkers have something to teach us about writing—but I also believe they can teach us more specifically about collaborative writing because so many of these thinkers are themselves coauthors who are continuously qualifying coauthorship as a complex practice. In this way, I'm following in the footsteps of Lauer in that I'm suggesting we turn to the social sciences to consider ideas about methodology, although the postqualitative theory I take up is more in line with the spirit of what Berthoff is after—to harness *thinking* and by default *writing* as a method for studying what she calls the "concrete particulars" of experience (1999, 6).

My introduction to postqualitative inquiry came about because of my initial fascination with a handful of coauthored texts about collaborative writing that, to be honest, baffled me in how they were operating as texts—in their concrete particularity, so to speak, as artifacts of coauthored scholarship. These texts were from special issues of the journals *Cultural Studies ↔ Critical Methodologies* and the *International Journal of Qualitative Research* (the latter I mention at the beginning of this chapter), both edited by Ken Gale and Jonathan Wyatt. Nearly all the articles across these two issues blend personal narrative with qualitative analysis; many are multivocal and structured as dialogues, or to be more precise, call-and-response pastiches of text; and a good number of them experiment with form insofar as they depart from the linear structure most of us associate with academic prose. As I read (or in some cases *tried* to read) these articles, my responses to them vacillated between curiosity and disdain because they were at once invigorating and frustrating. At one point I would be engrossed in how a set of coauthors had constructed a process narrative of their writing while simultaneously using that narrative to demonstrate how that process could never be replicated, while at another point I would be rolling my eyes at the off-the-cuff poetry another set of coauthors slipped into a section of scholarly explication. In sum, I was intrigued by the way these texts embodied the complexities of collaboration, but I was also challenged by what at times felt like self-indulgent ambiguity insofar as these coauthors seemed to be, at least some of the time, only writing for themselves.

To illustrate what I mean, I'll describe one of Gale and Wyatt's more popular coauthored works, a monograph titled *Between the Two: A Nomadic Inquiry in Collaborative Writing and Subjectivity*, a book that performs just as much as it theorizes, and one many of the articles in those two special issues reference. In most of the book, Gale and Wyatt blend scholarly explication with personal correspondence, sometimes in ways that make telling the difference difficult, if not impossible. In one chapter, Gale and Wyatt offer an autoethnographic introduction to themselves and discuss each of their backgrounds, including how they became collaborators. They include textual artifacts, like transcriptions of the emails they sent to one another as graduate students, to illustrate how they constructed a shared voice before they knew that was what they were doing. But in the chapter following that one, their writing shifts into and is formatted as a polished narrative in which Ken and Jonathan appear as characters in a dialogue, one that could be staged by actors. These characters discuss a range of ideas about subjectivity while managing to reference the work of Bourdieu, Foucault, Butler, Cixous, De Beauvoir, Kerouac, and Ginsberg, among others, including the various scholars they call their "elders" in qualitative research methodology, including Laurel Richardson and St. Pierre (Gale and Wyatt 2009, 27).

Like other postqualitative thinkers, Gale and Wyatt draw heavily from the work of Deleuze and Guattari—the title of their book is taken from one of Deleuze's descriptions of how he writes with Guattari: "You know how we work—I repeat it because it seems to me to be important—we do not work together, we work between the two" (quoted in Gale and Wyatt 2009, 2). Here is how Gale and Wyatt riff on the meaning of this idea for themselves as coauthors: "As the living, breathing heart, our 'between the two' is also elusive and mercurial. We are still trying to search it out, our epistemological sensibilities creating our intrigue, our intellectual wonder, at what this is. We search for its logos and trouble ourselves with the use of elaborated codes, plying our trade as writers and applying words from our lexicon . . . we give it a meaning; we make it a thing" (3).

What stands out to me is how this pair of collaborative writers understand their collaboration as a kind of materialization of the abstract. Their "between the two" is "elusive and mercurial"—I read this as the two of them saying their collaboration is marked by resistances and discontinuities that elude their control. Yet it is, or at least becomes, "a thing"; it develops an objectivity, but an objectivity that can only be partially accounted for via the "elaborated codes" and "lexicon" they developed to understand it. "We have sense of what this writing is but we are unsure of what it means. This 'between the two' that we have worked within has provided a space in which our writing is becoming" (Gale and Wyatt 2009, 3).

Like Gale and Wyatt, Mazzei and Jackson imagine their writing together as an in-between practice, "a thinking between-the-two that produces new thought, new connectives, new affects, new beginnings" (2012, 451). Extending the idea of collaboration as something that transpires "between the two," they offer the concept of a threshold to describe the spaces in which their collaborative agency develops, a concept Mazzei and Jackson connect to the digital spaces in which they compose.

> For the practical aspects of writing—of putting words on a document that we could easily access and share—we used Buzzword, a software program that allows document sharing and collaboration and is most likely nothing new to readers by way of online collaboration. Yet what we have come to imagine is the digital space as part of our threshold experience in that it allows us to map materiality and embodiment even as we work at a physical and temporal distance. Part of what we have learned . . . is that writing between-the-two in the threshold is not a process of working individually to contribute to the whole but is a process of producing thinking not possible outside the space of the threshold where the "two" produce thinking not possible otherwise. (451)

Notice how even though Mazzei and Jackson explain *how* they write together (they use an online word-processing program), such procedural details are not what is important for how they account for what their writing together *is* and *does*. The same goes for Gale and Wyatt, which is to say the procedural details of how these coauthors write together (they mainly compose over email using a version of what in the previous chapter I call *turnaround writing*) are not what matters in terms of what these coauthors perceive themselves doing as collaborators. There is so much *more*, so much *excess* that cannot be accurately identified, let alone represented, in the language these coauthors develop for their work. "So in the threshold, the text, with its magnetic force, draws us in and produces affect," write Mazzei and Jackson, and "the material force of the text also induces frustrations when we get stuck in thought-places; our passing through the threshold is mutually constituting in that as we make matter, matter makes us" (2012, 453).

To do this, to make collaborative writing a thing, a kind of *matter*, we must develop methods that recognize and account for the full range of practices that in all their excess constitute the work of coauthorship for any given team of writers. "As we reflect upon our 'method,'" Gale and Wyatt write, "it seems that we are working with a desire to be productive, to think differently and to create concepts that are new" (2009, 37). In a more recent piece, they pose the goal of their writing together more explicitly: "How might collaborative writing take us—and the academy—somewhere different? Where might we as a scholarly community take collaborative writing?" (2017, 355–56). As I've been suggesting, to get "somewhere different" may require promoting methods to describe and subsequently take stock of the *excesses* of collaboration in specific cases, excesses that would otherwise go unexamined, perhaps even unnoticed, which, to echo St. Pierre, involves "attending to the surprises that point to difference" (2018, 605). This means developing practices that attend to the discontinuities that stymie the progress of writing and to what the experience of coauthorship is in those moments as the work progresses, stalls, stops, lurches forward, backtracks, and, with hope, finally finds a way.

If nothing else, critiquing the rationality of the institutions in and through which our practices of coauthorship transpire has proven insufficient because lines of critique, as Latour has famously demonstrated, rarely dismantle institutions.[7] Put another way, the register of critique *is* the register of academia's authorial economies. A different register might therefore be required.

MAJOR AND MINOR LABOR

The search for such a register, one that privileges the minor labor of collaboration as a site from which to advocate for and experiment with coauthorship, is what has led me to embrace the value of what I'm calling here *minor literatures of collaboration*. It is with and through minor literatures of collaboration that I believe postqualitative inquiry shows us how to imagine methods that can challenge authorship economies that continue to limit how collaborative writing is understood, recognized, and even practiced. Minor literatures of collaboration offer a lens through which to consider the different ways collaborative writers, to echo Mirka Koro-Ljungberg and Jasmine Ulmer, "write alone and together at the same time; they exist within the same space as many writing one" (2016, 104). As I continue, I consider a few examples of this postqualitative inquiry in action to speculate in somewhat broad terms about what minor literatures of collaboration do, but first let me explain how I arrived at the name for this emerging body of work.

The term "minor literature" comes from Deleuze and Guattari and is often discussed alongside the idea of a "major language," concepts first explicated in their 1975 work *Kafka: Toward a Minor Literature* and adapted five years later in *A Thousand Plateaus*, both of which were translated into English in 1986 and 1987, respectively. A major language refers to dominant modes or registers for analyzing and categorizing, modes that exist prior to the emergence of the object of inquiry under investigation. Minor literatures, however, are works that elude or otherwise resist the homogenizing efforts of a major language. "A minor literature doesn't come from a minor language," write Deleuze and Guattari, "it is rather that which a minority constructs within a major language" (1986, 16). They offer three characteristics of minor literatures: "the deterritorialization of language, the connection to a political immediacy, and the collective assemblage of enunciation" (18). As with most of their writing to and with "assemblages," a term they use in *Kafka* to explain their interpretive methodology, what these three characteristics underscore is how minor literatures are necessarily performative.

So what do Deleuze and Guattari mean by the deterritorialization of language? As Mazzei explains, "Within language, deterritorialization unsettles habitual uses of language and sedimented thought. A major language is hegemonic, thereby reterritorializing by exerting a gravitational pull of sameness" (2017, 677). To deterritorialize language means to trouble not just its meaning but also the way it functions, to make it, in a word, uncomfortable.[8] Rhetoricians and compositionists may be reminded of the distinction Victor Vitanza makes between so-called "philosophical rhetoric" and his preferred "antibody rhetoric," the latter of which he says "is a Rhetoric that not only *is without* the philosophical pretensions of adjudicating 'philosophical knowledge claims' but also (and more importantly) *is without the philosophical-Rhetorical pretensions of adjudicating 'hermeneutical understandings.'* It is, in other words, not concerned either with attempting to resolve rhetorical, interpretative differences or with even accounting for them" (1987, 42). Vitanza's anti-body rhetoric is one that doesn't just invite but also celebrates practices that deterritorialize language; moreover, it does not just question the utility of critical-analytical discourse, it challenges its viability.

That a minor literature is connected to a political immediacy means there is something at stake in and for this minor literature, which is to further say minor literatures are always political in that they seek to provoke some kind of change even though such literatures are always up against the pressures of a major language. Minor literatures cannot help but borrow from and reference back to a major language, in other words, because a minor literature's "cramped space forces each individual intrigue to connect immediately to politics" because "commercial, economic, bureaucratic, juridical" standards of a major language will always be used to critique minor literatures and annex such works into the dominant register (Deleuze and Guattari 1986, 17).

Third, a minor literature points to a collective assemblage of enunciation, which means no one single agent or subject can be credited for the production of that literature. As Deleuze and Guattari write in *A Thousand Plateaus*, "Every statement is the product of a machinic assemblage, in other words, of collective agents of enunciation (take 'collective agents' to mean not peoples or societies but multiplicities)" (1987, 37). Utterances in a major language can always be traced back to or otherwise credited to distinct subjects, but in a minor literature the individual voice, such as it is, has no stability because a "voice" within a minor literature "cannot be thought as existing separately from the milieu in which it exists" (Mazzei 2013, 734).

In sum, even though minor literatures grow out of a major language, the assemblages through which they are enunciated cannot be registered in that language even as these assemblages work to unsettle it. "The major and minor mode are two different treatments of language, one which consists in extracting constants from it, the other in placing it in continuous variation" (Deleuze and Guattari 1987, 106). Deleuze and Guattari thus suggest a minor literature always exceeds the economies of a major language. When viewed from or in the terms of a major language, that is, a minor literature is always *in excess*.

When it comes to coauthorship, I see postqualitative thinkers exploring what for lack of a better term we might call the *minor labor* of collaboration, the excesses that don't easily translate into a major language or otherwise are not recognized or valued in situations when what ultimately matters is the *major labor* of collaboration. The major labor of collaboration can be imagined as its finished products, the things like a coauthored text that can be evaluated alongside other commodities and the extent to which this commodity can be accounted for in terms the major language provides. This major labor is thus embodied in what those outside the collaboration see and can in turn register *as a specific kind* of labor. As I detail in the introduction of this book, disciplines have developed systems that translate the work of collaboration into major labor, labor that can be accounted for using standardized schemes.

But as all writers know, not just coauthors, the thing itself—in this case the finished text—represents only a fraction of the labor often devoted to its production. For example, there is always a trail of notes, outlines, drafts, and other writerly detritus, material that didn't make it into the final draft. And of course there is all the talk—the conversation—that went into this work, talk between coauthors, with colleagues, with interview subjects, with students, with anyone and everyone with whom coauthors bounce around ideas, seek advice, or otherwise produce discourse that contributes to the rhetorical ecology of that particular collaboration. There is the body of research that has been read or consulted and the scribbled marginalia therein; there are the diagrams and flowcharts, emails and text messages, fieldnotes and interview transcripts. And these are just the textual artifacts. There are also what Jackson and Mazzei point out as "previously unthought 'data',," whatever constitutes the "*something else*" a major language (in Jackson and Mazzei's case, what they see as "humanistic qualitative inquiry") cannot capture, let alone recognize (2013, 262). This something else might be what Hellevi Lenz Taguchi (2016) understands as sense making; or what Susan Nordstrom calls "object-interviews" (2013, 2018); or what Elyse Pineau describes as "an attitude of hospitality toward the complex, superfluous, and 'ghostly' qualities of the other emergent in interaction" (2012, 460). Just like the textual compost that accumulates over the course of a writing project, these latter things speak to the minor labor of collaboration, the excesses that can't be pinned down *as labor*, at least not in ways that align with what we understand to be major iterations of authorial labor.

In sum, minor labor is invisible next to what registers as major labor, which is why I believe there is value in how postqualitative researchers have attempted to render this labor in ways that are more visible using the tools and resources—published journal articles, for instance—of the major language. The result of this laboring to make the minor labor of collaboration more visible is what I am calling *minor literatures of collaboration*, an emerging literature—or a body of scholarship—that as a whole can be recognized not just for the ways it challenges the authorial conventions of the academy's major languages in the sense that it presents alternative arguments to them, but also for the ways it *performs these arguments* through practices of inscription, attribution, and information design that challenge how we read, interpret, or otherwise account for this literature.[9] Put another way, and to echo a phrase I use quite a bit in this book, these minor literatures force writers and readers to *slow down*.

As I am coming to understand the ways minor labor can and cannot be assessed alongside major labor, to render a minor literature of collaboration requires approaching data not as a source or material that needs interpretation but as a body of experiences that requires description. As Taguchi writes, "Sometimes we are so deeply embedded and inscribed in the dominant discourses of our own research field as qualitative researchers, that everything we think we can see in the data is what we already know" (2010, 50). What does this observation mean for collaborative writers? "Each time we think together, we must make sense of our writing relationship, productions of the author, and citational practices anew," write Jessica Van Cleave and Sarah Bridges-Rhoads; "Each new text simultaneously enables different ways of *being* with writing and requires that we keep writing to think what we cannot yet imagine to be thought" (2013, 682). For this pair of writers, taking stock of their minor labor means resisting the urge to write up what another pair of postqualitative researchers call "transparent narratives that do little to critique the complexities of social life" (Jackson and Mazzei 2013, 261). That is, coauthors should not presume to know what method will best produce the experience of coauthorship they desire before they actually invent such a method in practice. Coauthors must thus develop habits for navigating the rhetorical ecologies they construct alongside the uncountable body of objects that inform and are taken up in those ecologies, and while doing so they must try to avoid reducing all this minor labor to indecipherable background noise, noise that eventually disappears altogether once coauthors have reached the conclusion of their work together.

To bring this discussion full circle, what *is* a minor literature of collaboration? Other than how I have attempted to describe the concept here, I don't think it can be defined using language that might prescribe its features because by definition minor literatures depend on processes of deterritorialization, or what Mazzei describes as "uncoding habitual relations, experiences, and ordinary usages of language to separate the constructs of a major language that orients dogmatic thought and thereby method in a specific manner" (2017, 678). What I do feel comfortable saying about minor literatures of collaboration, however, is that extolling the virtues of collaboration is not enough. We can talk all day about how valuable it is, how collaboration, and coauthorship in particular, promotes the ethics articulated in feminist and poststructuralist theory, and how writing with others enacts the knowledge virtually every academic discipline has come to accept in theory thanks to social constructionist epistemology, which is that writing, especially academic writing, is rarely if ever something one does in isolation. But none of this really matters unless the minor labor of collaboration is made more visible, rendered into and as experience encountered alongside the products of collaboration accounted for in the major languages with which we discourse about our teaching, research, and writing.

(ON NOT) SURVEYING MINOR LITERATURES OF COLLABORATION

I've offered the figurations of major and minor labor to situate the work of coauthorship in ways that might lead to new questions about the methodologies coauthors invent to write together. In many cases, these methods are ad hoc, invented as coauthors go, and this is what makes the potential for minor literatures of collaboration all the more viable as a rhetorical practice. They grow out of and reflect grounded experiences of collaboration while giving voice to the labor of coauthorship in all its idiosyncratic, complex, and often illegible qualities. When read as a body of literature, in other words, they offer readers a way into thinking about what, to borrow from Deleuze, is the "multiplicity of relations between forces" that coauthors navigate, forces—what I've been calling *resistances* and *discontinuities*—that can't be accounted for *from the outside* of a collaboration because "things are no longer perceived or propositions articulated in the same way" (1988, 83, 87). But this accounting is one of the aims of postqualitative inquiry more generally.

In "This Is Not a Collaborative Writing," a text that incorporates photography, unconventional (broken?) syntax, mixed use of first- and third-person pronouns, and multiple section headings simply labeled "AND," Koro-Ljungberg and Ulmer explain that growing interest in postqualitative inquiry "calls for different forms and conceptualizations of writing that are responsive to diverse ways of knowing and practicing critical social science" (2016, 112). In this rethinking of the work of writing in social science, they ask, "How can we write collaboratively in the absence of individual self and negotiated authorship?" (112). Such a question springs from a collection of observations they offer about the nature of collaborative writing itself, such as how it "occurs at the intersections of the accidental and theoretical," or how collaborative writing "could be as much an issue of multiplication as it is its inverse operation:

division," or how coauthors "write alone and together at the same time; they exist within the same space as many writing one" (103, 104). Turning to a reflection on new materialist ontology, these coauthors ask how we might imagine collaborative writing if deciding who is responsible for it is always already a flawed line of inquiry. These collaborators believe the agency at work in their writing, and in particular the voice that comes through in their text, is an emergent quality neither coauthor can claim, let alone account for in ways that might make their individual selves more visible in the text. "By naming this text as not a collaborative writing," they explain, "we create an illusive separation of the image of writing/writing experience from itself" (110).

To a certain extent, Koro-Ljungberg and Ulmer are asking questions about collaboration—and experimenting with the form through which these questions get articulated—in a way that echoes what we see the *Collaborative Futures* writers doing, but Koro-Ljungberg and Ulmer are also problematizing notions of process in and with collaborative writing to question whether collaboration can actually be navigated *as* a process, which is what Hanna Guttorm, Teija Löytönen, Eeva Anttila, and Anita Valkeemäki do, but in a register at first more traditionally autobiographical. In what they call a "process/article" that considers their own embodied research practices as collaborators, they speculate about "how our collaboration through various embodied/artistic/experimental practices makes a difference in how we work, think, write, and move in the academic spaces of research" (Guttorm et al. 2016, 418). One of the first observations they make about the consequences of their collaboration is how it "keeps pushing us off our habitual trails," whether they are meeting together in person or collaborating virtually (417). "So this (ad)venture is an ongoing and open-ended process whether we four (or more) move, talk, and write toward the next presentation in an academic conference, always toward something not-yet-known. We move toward unexpectedness, incidents, and encounters, which are not pre-designed. With these encounters and becomings, we later assemble an article, a map on where we've been" (418). As their article progresses, the form it takes becomes less legible in critical-analytical terms. Like Koro-Ljungberg and Ulmer, these authors complicate representations of their voice, incorporate strings of personal narrative that read more like stream-of-consciousness freewriting, and, to echo one of the article's section titles, turn a description of research methodology "on its head" through the textual performance their writing delivers.

For many postqualitative researchers, in fact, collaborative writing provides the mechanism (for lack of a better word) to rethink the more common, if not mundane, practices of scholarly research. Dagmar Alexander and Jonathan Wyatt created what they term "a writing cocoon" around one of their kitchen tables, for example, and for several months experimented with collaborative writing as they considered "the ontological, epistemological, and methodological difficulties with the qualitative research interview" (2018, 101). The research project they were writing up was, not coincidentally, about the viability of collaborative writing in the development of graduate students as academic writers. In this particular article, a piece that is focused more on their own collaboration than the results of their research on collaboration—and that thus functions as an iteration of a minor literature of collaboration—these coauthors narrate the development of the lexicon they used to understand their writing together, in particular the portmanteau "in(tra)fusion," which they present as an open-ended method defined by what it's not.

But here's the thing: these texts I'm trying to explicate as iterations of a minor literature of collaboration are indescribable in the register of a major research language, or at least in one of its major conventions: the literature survey. To be more accurate, they *can be* registered in such a major language—this is what I have been doing for several paragraphs—but such a pursuit misses the point of this minor literature insofar as the authors of these experimental texts aren't attempting to situate them within chronologically organized "traditions" of research practices.

As I write these words, there are easily a dozen more texts like these on the desk in front of me that enact and in turn complicate, through their performance as texts, experiments about the work of collaboration and the processes, subjectivities, epistemologies, and ontologies it calls into question. But to weave a survey of these works in a register that aligns with how I've been writing this book seems at best reductive, especially insofar as what matters for these teams of coauthors is the *matter* of their coauthorship in all its varied manifestations. Indeed, one of the challenges these minor literatures pose is in how they depict the materiality of coauthorship in ways that resist categorization. Another way to think about this challenge is to suggest that the value of these minor literatures is found not just in what they say about their subject but also in how they say it. If the differences collaborative writing affords are worth the labor required to pursue them, and if this labor exceeds the economies of authorship that dictate the value of such collaboration, then perhaps these differences must be rendered differently, that is, made visible and enacted in and as a kind of excess that eludes these economies.

Here, then, is why I don't want to and why I really can't "survey" these minor literatures of collaboration because the point of my speculating on such a literature is to suggest their potential as actants in assemblages of scholarship about qualitative research, collaborative writing, subjectivity, and whatever other matters of concern these writers take up in their attempts to do such work differently.[10] As actants, these works can be imagined as contributions to collective assemblages of enunciation that invoke the political immediacies of authorship as they deterritorialize the discourses we bring to them as "scholarly" participant-observers. My riffing off Deleuze and Guattari aside, these minor literatures compose passages in the material sense of bodies of articulated discourse, ones that do not ignore the excess of collaboration—the perpetual *and* in such labor, "the too much of inquiry" (St. Pierre 2018, 607). Minor literatures of collaboration thus reflect and grow out of the realization that minor labor is always an emergent phenomenon organic to rhetorical ecologies that must be navigated piecemeal as they are experienced, which is also true for readers of these minor literatures, a point I wish to elaborate by turning to work that comes not from postqualitative inquiry but from rhetoric and composition.

More than a decade before Gale and Wyatt started writing together, Michael Spooner and Kathleen Blake Yancey were exploring similar questions about subjectivity, textuality, and collaboration in essays and articles that troubled the major conventions of published academic discourse. The first paragraph of their 1996 "Postings on a Genre of Email," a twenty-seven-page essay published in *College Composition and Communication*, is bifurcated by white space that resembles an ascending staircase with half the paragraph italicized and written in the first person and the second half not italicized and written in the second person. As they explain at the beginning of this first paragraph (or is it really two paragraphs?), "This text takes the form of a dialogue and is a dialogue" (253).[11] Except it is and it isn't. On the one hand, there is a clear back-and-forth quality in the form of the voices that come through in the article, at least until those points in the article where that form stops and new forms emerge, such as lists and vignettes. Moreover, for most of the dialogue, it is neither clear who is speaking nor whether the dialogue as presented follows the actual dialogue Spooner and Yancey engaged over email as they were preparing their article. That is, the product of their writing is more essay than dialogue in the sense that it has been arranged, formatted, and edited for delivery in *College Composition and Communication* even though the mechanics of this delivery depart from those readers of the journal would expect to see in its usual offerings. To be sure, readers of Spooner and Yancey's article did take notice.

Here is how Carolyn Miller begins a response to Spooner and Yancey, which I quote at length because of how well she captures what I imagine was the general sentiment of most readers after first encountering the piece:

> Does a text that appears in *CCC*—a text that was composed by academics, addresses disciplinarily determined intellectual issues, draws on prior academic texts, has been subjected to peer review by other academics, seems destined for indexing in ERIC and for citation by graduate students—does such a text necessarily take the identity of a particular genre? Is this particular text by Spooner and Yancey an essay, an essay/dialogue, a refereed journal article, something else? Do the dialogue form, the typographic novelty, the smiley faces, the lack of a univocal claim make it a different genre from other texts in *CCC*? Is it a genre on the move? How much latitude do Spooner and Yancey have? Why are they addressing us, the readers of *CCC*? Why are we the readers taking them up? (1996, 28)

In his own response, James Sosnoski begins by meditating on how his initial attempts at composing a response to Spooner and Yancey stalled because he found himself thinking he had to write in the register of a counterargument. As he explains, however, "Since 'Postings' is not focused upon definitive answers to the questions raised in it and since the postings included in it are taken from an unfinished debate/conversation—what could a counter-argument accomplish?" (1996, 289). Indeed, in their essay, Spooner and Yancey don't forward arguments about the email genre so much as they speculate on its affordances and constraints while trying to represent for readers the experience of writing in this medium.

Two years later, Yancey and Spooner again published an article in *College Composition and Communication*, but this time the idea of collaboration itself was the focus of their writing. Keep in mind that even in 1998, the only practical way to write collaboratively using the internet was over email, so the form and voices in this second article resemble those in "Postings"; however, there is a greater cut-and-paste quality to the arrangement of this 1998 writing, which is to say it is practically impossible to describe the arrangement of this essay using conventional terminology for the genre of a scholarly article. But while the layout and delivery of this article is discordant and even a bit unsettling, the questions about collaboration Yancey and Spooner take up are quite conventional and include speculations about how to define it, what is or should be the status of the collaborative author, who "owns" such texts, and whether as teachers and scholars we are experimenting with collaborative writing as much as we should be.

But my personal favorite of Yancey and Spooner's works is an essay titled "*Petals on a Wet Black Bough*: Textuality, Collaboration, and the New Essay," published under their open pseudonym, Myka Vielstimmig.[12] Like their other collaborations, this essay disrupts the textual conventions of published academic discourse, but this piece is exceptional for the theory it proposes as the writing plays out, which is to say it most resembles a protoexample of postqualitative inquiry before postqualitative inquiry was a thing, at least as it exists now as a distinct site of scholarly inquiry in the social sciences. Extending their inquiry into the idea of collaborative writing, Yancey and Spooner, or Vielstimmig, more explicitly consider how genres influence who or what counts as an author within those spaces and conventions, but they push this inquiry to also consider what counts as writing itself. "*The assumption seems pretty much conventional and universal: that writing will continue to be writing: the old genres will suffice to contain it,*" they explain, but "*that's part of the problem: the old genres contain it. In other words, it seems pretty obvious that if we want traces and resonances of these collaborative processes—this collective intelligence?—represented textually, we might have to invent new genres that wouldn't contain it*" (Vielstimmig 1999, 91). Similar in scope to the ways postqualitative theorists have challenged fundamental assumptions about the nature of qualitative research, Yancey and Spooner question what it means to write and be a writer, in this case what it means to write and be a writer of "the essay." Exploring what digital technologies afford in this regard, they note how "elements like multivocality, association, disruption, the unpredicated assertion, not to mention the graphical highjinks now available to writers, require academic readers to apprehend by more wholistic, more intuitive logic"; and readers of these "new" essays thus "need a bit of the verbal artist's instinct for pattern, contrast, unity, and balance, and a bit of the poet's ability to posit and to juxta/pose" (108–9).

If I had to assess the significance of their collective work, what Yancey and Spooner theorize is how to anticipate textual novelty and the opportunities *qua* disruptions manifested therein, especially those opportunities for reimagining the work of collaborative authorship. Indeed, at the end of "A Single Good Mind," Yancey and Spooner summarize the value of producing texts like theirs: "*This method of collaboration—which we are arguing is one in a panoply of others—is best represented by a text's replicating it. This text speaks to its author/s' collective intelligence, attempts to give it some definition by reference to the claims made here and the ways these claims were developed. The text, we might say, embodies collective intelligence and some of the ways, at least, that such intelligence is created*" (1998, 61). Such a claim, one now more than twenty years old, is as good a justification for minor literatures of collaboration as any I have forwarded.

Through the delivery of their arguments, Yancey and Spooner deterritorialize academic discourse, respond to the political exigence of digital technology and its impact on academic research, and pursue these efforts through the delivery of collective enunciations they developed over the then-emergent medium of email. Of course, Yancey and Spooner do not use any of this language, nor do they cite Deleuze and Guattari in any of their coauthored work, but in this way—especially when it comes to how they are building a minor literature of collaboration using the resources of composition theory, especially theories of genre—Yancey and Spooner evidence that compositionists have much to offer postqualitative theorists of collaboration, just as these postqualitative theorists have much to offer us.

Pursuing minor literatures of collaboration encourages coauthors to name the experience of collaboration in their own terms, which is to say in the postqualitative work of constructing a minor literature of collaboration, "gone is the compulsion to represent the experience of individual participants that traditional research patterned by method in a major language" (Mazzei 2017, 676). As I've tried to explain, such a project is failed from the start insofar as it is impossible to capture, let alone survey, all this excess—all this minor labor—in a conventionally academic sense. As George Landow writes in *Hypertext 2.0*, "We must abandon systems founded upon ideas of center, margin, hierarchy, and linearity and replace them with ones of multilinearity, nodes, links, and networks" (1997, 2). Attempting to postqualify coauthorship means coauthors must be attuned to what "is unintelligible and unrecognizable within existing categories and practices" (St. Pierre 2017, 604), and they must cultivate methods for bringing these things into view. That is, to change the economies in which coauthorship is evaluated, we must make the ecologies in which coauthorship transpires more visible, but not to create better "standards" or to even find ways to mathematically qualify coauthorship as something that can be evaluated alongside single authorship. Instead, the goal can simply be to make the dissonances of this or that coauthorship's minor labor something that can be heeded, even welcomed, as practices we celebrate as teachers and scholars of writing.

But this change is easier said than done, and not just because the kinds of texts Yancey and Spooner have written are uncommon enough that they get labeled "experimental"[13] but also because coauthors aren't usually prompted to deliberately interrogate the excesses of their work together. "As co-writers explore their processes of collaboration," write Spooner and Yancey, "it may be the our/self that they have to [first] discover and acknowledge" (Vielstimmig 1999, 97). Indeed, what I haven't considered in this discussion of collaboration in terms of major and minor labor is the sometimes impossible challenge of discovering a method for writing with someone else and how every time we sit down to write with another person, either figuratively or literally, we must invent a process for doing so, and very often that work can feel like we must start from scratch each time. But this is how all writing works; we always must start from scratch. Even though I take up the question of practice more explicitly in the previous chapter, I've counterbalanced that discussion with this foray into the work of postqualitative inquiry to suggest that what a method of cowriting is and can be as a distinct practice may not be translatable as a process that can be taken up by others, at least not by others who think the experience can be easily replicated.

Nevertheless, the point of this discussion has not been to present models for how minor literatures of collaboration operate or how they should be read, not that such considerations aren't worth exploring. Instead, and what I hope readers will consider, is how works like these can exist alongside scholarship on collaboration that isn't written in the minor key. To this point, and if there was any question about it, this book of mine you are reading is decidedly *not* an example of such a minor literature because it is written as a traditional monograph that enacts a geography common for such a work: I review literature, offer close readings of exemplary texts, historicize disciplinary commonplaces, and outline some new theoretical terrain for mapping collaborative writing in practice. In this way I'm not suggesting minor literatures are more important than work produced in a major language, just as I'm not suggesting the latter are worthy of closer attention than the former. But they *are* different, and these differences have value that warrants attention from those of us who are committed to influencing the authorial economies that shape how we understand and approach collaborative composition.

In the next and final chapter, I take up this question of value—specifically what it can mean for cowriters to value the minor labor of their work—but I do so by pursuing this inquiry with my frequent collaborator, John Pell, as we reflect on our work together and speculate about the ongoing direction of our collaboration. This last chapter is different. It is multivocal. It is written alone and then together and in part relies on the voices of another pair of collaborative writers who have influenced how we write alone and together.

6

WRITING ALONE AND TOGETHER

Coauthored with John Pell

2019

I am not the author of this book. At least, I do not remember writing this book. Yet, as I read, something is familiar. Reading a sentence for the first time is an act of memory. I know these words; I remember these ideas.

I am not the author of this book, but I hear my voice.

2015

The idea for the interview project wasn't ours, but Will was the only one who would be at the conference, so it fell on his shoulders to conduct the first of what we imagined would be two or three conversations with Kate Ronald and Hephzibah Roskelly, conversations that would then be transformed into the digital text that had been pitched to and provisionally accepted by the journal our friend suggested. Hepsie was not only Will's dissertation director but John's as well, and we had both gotten to know Kate through Hepsie. Hepsie and Kate started writing together as graduate students at the University of Louisville and continued to collaborate when Kate went to the University of Nebraska in 1984 and Hepsie to the University of Massachusetts–Boston in 1985. They eventually landed at Miami University and the University of North Carolina–Greensboro, respectively, and were now both about to retire. This was the exigence for the interview project, a kind of retrospective on feminism, pragmatism, and collaboration, which was the title we were thinking about for the piece.[1]

Will, Kate, and Hepsie were sitting in a booth in one of the restaurants in the Tampa Marriott, where that year's Conference on College Composition and Communication was being held.

"Our first paper as collaborators was at Cs. That was in 1983," Hepsie mentioned.

DOI: 10.7330/9781646420490.c006

"We walked to the podium together and people were confused," Kate added.

"We had been codirectors of a writing center and the paper was about this work," Hepsie explained. "So we both talked, and the way we did it was Kate would talk for awhile then I would talk. Because the podium was little and there was just one microphone, Kate would step back and I would step forward, then I would step back and Kate would step forward. And honest to goodness, the people in the audience didn't know what to make of this. After it was over a lot of the conversation was not about what we said but the fact that we were up there together."

Kate smirked.

"A few years later after that first Cs experience, Hepsie and I gave a keynote together at a graduate conference at the University of Nebraska, and we got to the place and they had put two podiums up there on separate sides of the stage. They assumed we were giving a point-counterpoint speech. We ended up pushing the podiums together."

2006

I walked into Hepsie's office and told her I had a problem. On a whim I had submitted an abstract for a proposed edited collection that was advertised on a listserv. Even though I was only in my first year as a doctoral student, I was eager to professionalize and was particularly curious about the publication process. How exactly did it work? When editors advertise CFPs, like the one in question, could anyone respond? I decided to test the waters and submitted something. To my complete and utter shock, the editors of this particular collection were interested in my proposal.

That's why I was in Hepsie's office. I didn't know what to do.

I explained to her that I only submitted a proposal because I wanted to see what the process was like and that I wasn't expecting to get a positive response. My academic writing experience up to that point had consisted of seminar papers and a handful of conference presentations, but that's it. For this project, the only thing I had written was the abstract, and I couldn't imagine the prospect of writing a fully fleshed-out chapter. I wanted her advice on how to pull out of the project. I could do that, right?

After explaining it was okay to not pursue the project, Hepsie suggested that perhaps I could ask my friend John to write the chapter with me. We were interested in the same things, she pointed out, and writing together might relieve some of the pressure I was feeling.

2006

There are no mountains, not really, in North Carolina. I moved to Greensboro, North Carolina, from Bellingham, Washington. I grew up in the Pacific Northwest, and moving to the southeast for graduate school forced us to confront loneliness in new ways. It's ironic, of course, that while I had the privilege of moving across the country with my partner, we still felt moments of severe loneliness. We missed seeing Mt. Baker and Mt. Rainier towering in the distance. We missed knowing the streets and the best places to find cheap food. While I would never say it out loud, it was hard to imagine how I would complete my program of study if these feelings remained.

Despite my second-guessing, the first year of doctoral study went smoothly. I enjoyed my cohort and found the students in my first-year writing courses to be engaging, thoughtful, and funny. However, I struggled to find my way as a scholar. I enjoyed my courses and adored my faculty mentors, but I couldn't find my voice as a scholarly writer. I was much too attracted to complicated, esoteric ideas and grand notions of articulating a unifying theory of rhetoric.

I desperately needed collaborators, especially ones who could help ground me from flights of fancy but who weren't afraid of wrestling with big ideas. I remember on many occasions speaking with Hepsie and Elizabeth Chiseri-Strater, another professor in the program, about my desire to work with others. I wanted a relationship like the one Hepsie had with Kate, or the one Elizabeth had with Bonnie Sunstein and Donna Qualley, two of Elizabeth's longtime collaborators. They reminded me to be patient, to keep my eyes open, that I would no doubt find someone with whom to collaborate. One afternoon Elizabeth stopped me in the hallway and asked if I'd ever spoken to Will.

"You two think the same way," she said.

Sometimes we need a push from another to get things rolling.

2015

We learned early on from Kate and Hepsie about their belief that collaboration has made them better individual writers. Based on our experiences, this is something we can now relate to. But when we were discussing the interview project, we wanted to know whether and how collaboration makes us better collaborators—whether and how, that is, the experience of writing with one person is transferable to the experience of writing with a different person.

During their conversation in Tampa, Will asked Kate and Hepsie how their work together prepared them for the collaborations they have pursued with others.

"First of all, it makes you willing to take the leap," Kate answered.

"Secondly, it makes you look for the skill or the experience that the other person has," added Hepsie. "And the third thing is you realize that not everybody has the same experiences. It also makes you realize that the best collaboration is the one that you engage in over and over again. For example, I would say that my work with David Jollife has been a really great collaboration. But we had to learn how we were going to do it; and I realized it wasn't going to be the same as how I work with Kate."[2]

Kate said the same thing about her work with Joy Ritchie, that they had to invent a method for writing with each other that was different from the one she shared with Hepsie.[3]

2006

John and I had no method. The draft was due in a month and we needed to start writing. We had an outline, and we had started to give each other small assignments—I'd read this article and he'd read that one; I'd fill in the outline this way, he'd fill it in that way—but we had nothing close to resembling a draft. We ended up huddled over our computers in John's home office.

After several afternoons of this, we had some words we liked. The next few weeks are a blur in my memory, but I remember at some point we split up what was still left to write and each of us composed by ourselves for a day or two. Just before the essay was due, we pieced our parts together and revised what we had already written, then we sat side by side and edited the draft. We were unsure of how, but we had finished. We emailed the editors our draft.

It didn't take long to get a response. Maybe a week at most.

The email was brief and polite. The editors thanked us for letting them consider our work, but they wouldn't be able to include our essay in their collection. John and I were disappointed but not necessarily upset. We were proud of this essay and confident it could be published somewhere else.

2019

Yes, our first few attempts at writing were exercises in futility. We did not have a method, and usually we didn't even have an occasion—we just had ideas. We had animated conversations about something we read in our coursework, or something one of our professors said to us, or about a comment made by a fellow grad student. We talked early in the morning over coffee while watching my daughter, Emma, play on the living room rug, or late at night over beer once Emma had gone to bed. Then, when an idea or a line of inquiry reached its zenith, we sought an outlet. A conference proposal or a call for papers served as the site for our exuberance; we needed to share our ideas. We wanted to share our ideas, to bring others into our conversations.

2015

Hepsie and Kate weren't the only collaborative writers that influenced us. Elizabeth Chiseri-Strater had an ongoing collaboration with Bonnie Sunstein she talked about quite often. Then there were the more well-known collaborative partnerships, like that between Andrea Lunsford and Lisa Ede, that also influenced us.

Sitting with Kate and Hepsie, Will commented on how his own education in collaboration seemed to have come primarily from women whose commitment to coauthorship couldn't be untangled from their commitment to feminism, ethnography, pragmatism, and other philosophical and methodological commitments that relied on inductive practices of knowledge production. He then pointed out how he had never heard Kate or Hepsie say much about the field's predominant theories of collaboration, rooted as they are in social constructionist epistemology. Why was that?

Kate jumped at this question. "Actually, I wouldn't call a lot of that work scholarship on collaboration."

Hepsie nodded in agreement, noting that other than the work Lunsford and Ede were doing, there wasn't a lot of theory on collaboration as such when they started writing together in the 1980s.

"Well, let me go back to what I just said," explained Kate. "I wouldn't call a lot of what we're talking about scholarship on collaboration because the overarching interest was in exploring the concept that knowledge and discourse are socially constructed. That's great and all, but *duh*! We knew that! We had all read Piaget and Vygotsky. But saying that knowledge is constructed is not the same thing as talking about collaboration. It seems the difference between us and many of the scholars writing about so-called collaboration at that point was their focus on conflict. And that arose out of another sort of history, namely that of the first-year writing class as a place to train docile workers for the system. It was reaction against that. So, theory prescribed that to teach collaboration required the teaching of conflict."

Hepsie followed this up by pointing to the assumptions about authorship that informed much of this theory.

"I think the emphasis of a lot of this scholarship on the tensions between the ideas of consensus and conflict in relation to collaboration is at its deepest level built on the premise of the primacy of the borders that separate us. So, you either agree with another individual or you fight with another individual. In other words, there's only this dyad for understanding what happens in collaboration. And I think what Kate and I are saying is that conflict and consensus were really not part of the game. For us collaboration has always been about, well, we got this thing we're working on, and we're both really interested in it, and we're coming at it from all these directions, so let's go with it and see what happens."

2004

I wasn't sure what to make of the laughing, but I was positive it was bad. Donna Qualley, my first real academic mentor, had just listened to my list of potential PhD programs. I had completed my MA the previous spring at Western Washington University and was now taking the year to work on graduate applications while teaching some adjunct sections at WWU. I had a list of about eight schools with rhetoric and composition programs that appealed to me.

As I read through the list and gave my two-sentence rationale for each, Donna nodded her head, as if carefully considering each institution I named. I read the name of the last school on my list: University of North Carolina at Greensboro. I was interested in the idea of working with Hephzibah Roskelly, whose coauthored book with Kate Ronald, *Reason to Believe: Romanticism, Pragmatism, and the Teaching of Writing* (1998), spoke to many of my own academic interests with its focus on exploring the relationship between writing and pragmatism.

It was at this point that Donna began to laugh. Before I could ask her why she was laughing, she stood up, darted to her office, then returned quickly with a copy of *Academic Literacies* by Elizabeth Chiseri-Strater.

Donna flipped open the book to the chapter we had read a year earlier in her course on social class and literacy. I could remember reading the chapter, but it was in the form of a PDF, so I had never seen the entire book.

Over the next few but spirited minutes, Donna explained the reason for her laughter. *Academic Literacies* was an ethnographic study of first-year writing, and the bulk of Elizabeth's fieldwork occurred in Donna's first-year writing course while they were both graduate students at the University of New Hampshire. It was there they had developed a deep and lasting friendship; indeed, they continued to collaborate as scholars. And then, bringing this aside full circle, Donna said that Elizabeth was the current director of first-year writing at UNCG.

"Yes," Donna concluded, "I think UNCG would be a good fit."

2010

The second time something we wrote together was turned down for publication came after we revised a coauthored conference paper into an article for a journal whose editor we had met at that particular conference. By that point, John and I had more experience as collaborators. We'd gotten into the habit of cowriting seminar papers, for instance, and we had also presented together at a number of conferences and had even coauthored an essay about collaboration for our university's first-year writing textbook.

I was working on a dissertation about the history of collaborative writing theory and was surprised by how much of it focused on conflict and consensus as perpetual problems in collaboration. Because all our work together had been pursued voluntarily, John and I couldn't relate to these issues as problems. Writing together was hard, for sure, but it was also rewarding. Its benefits far outweighed its costs, the latter of which manifested in the stress and anxiety that came with always having to figure out what exactly we were writing once we started something.

In his response, this editor provided some useful feedback. He had read our essay closely but decided not to send it out for review. He said that even though it needed a lot of work, it definitely had a future. John and I were a little embarrassed because we should have anticipated some of the shortcomings in the manuscript this editor drew our attention to, but we were nonetheless appreciative of the feedback.

"Keep writing together," this editor noted to us in closing, "'Pell and Duffy' has a nice ring to it."

2019

When I think about our time in graduate school, I cannot remember when we began writing together—it seems like we always wrote together. But I know that is not true. In fact, we didn't begin graduate school at the same time, nor did we graduate at the same time. I know this because I can look at transcripts and dates. But that's not exactly true either. The truth is that my life as a professional scholar began when we started working together. When we started collaborating, I began to see myself, to see us, as writers. Yes, our first collaborative attempts were unsuccessful insofar as the finished products did not hold up to the scrutiny of peer review. But our collaboration, the work of forming ideas and arguments with another, improved with each iteration. We spent less and less time trying to fit our individual ideas with each other's and more time allowing our ideas to grow together. Our ideas became our ideas.

2015

Even though Hepsie and Kate have been writing together for over thirty years—and encouraging their students to write together for nearly as long—they are disappointed academic coauthorship in the humanities is still considered less rigorous and thus less worthy of reward than single authorship.

Will asked if they had to defend their collaborative work when they each went through the tenure process.

"Yes, we had to argue for ourselves," Hepsie answered. "When Kate was asked to comment on my tenure, she was asked how much of our work she was responsible for. Kate said 'every word,' as did I. We were both responsible for all of it."

"I remember when I had to write that letter for Hepsie," says Kate. "I wrote a fake one first and sent it to her. It said, 'I have done none of this research. I simply pay her a monthly stipend to put my name on things.'"

Hepsie laughed. "I wanted to give that letter to the chair! I didn't, but I wanted to!"

She continued, "But this is still an issue of course. To me it's particularly paradoxical that collaborators still have to defend their work, especially given that scholars have continually reinforced and supported social constructionism. We are always interacting with the things around us and people around us; we are always in fact collaborating. So, at the very same time we're saying all of this, and in the classroom we're talking about how we're creating cooperative learning environments, on the other side there is still a persistence that collaborative work is somehow less valuable."

Will commented on how when he was a grad student Hepsie never wallowed in discussions about the way collaboration gets treated in some institutional cultures. Instead she always talked about its benefits. Will asked Kate if she did the same.

"When I encourage graduate students to collaborate, I talk about the benefit of becoming more aware of how your own sentences work. You develop an awareness of your own style. Writing with someone, and I don't mean collaboration by juxtaposition, I mean actually working on sentences together, shows you so much in this regard."

"That's one thing," added Hepsie, "but you also have to understand the benefit of deepening your own experience with the experience of others. You might say, 'Here's what I think,' and the other person says, 'Well, based on my experience here's what I think.' Then you have to find a third way that brings together what we are thinking together. But maybe you can't. Maybe you need to say something is an anomaly for now and go on and talk about something else. This is a pragmatist idea—and I don't think we always think about collaboration as an act of pragmatism—it is the principle of continually widening and deepening experience. So, collaboration is about systematizing that widening by recognizing how your experience and my experience can be combined to build something."

But Will pointed out that this also seems to be why people are resistant to collaboration; the combination of different styles and different sets of experiences can make it difficult to write in a way that feels authentic.

"Yes, and this is something we discuss in 'Learning to Take it Personally,' namely this need to create a third voice."

"This is why both of us claim our collaborative work as wholly original," Kate added, "because this third voice belongs to neither of us in isolation of the other."

Hepsie chimed back in. "And the more you work together, the more quickly you get to a point where you can immediately harness this voice that you know is the voice of you two together."

"Right," said Kate, "and that gets to a second point I always want to emphasize to graduate students. The first point is how collaboration teaches you about style. The second point is that if you want to stay together you better write together."

"That would be a good title," Hepsie laughed.

"I'm really serious," said Kate. "It's hard enough being a professor with all those responsibilities. But you're also in different places, and you have families, and in some cases you might even feel isolated in your department."

After a moment, Hepsie nodded her head and added, "It's not just the personal side that collaboration helps to keep intact. If you build the collaboration you also have somebody who knows what and how you think. And now your collaborator is like what Hawthorn says about a trusted friend, that person who can help me think. And I know I always go to the most abstract place when talking about collaboration, but it reminds you of the principle of how people learn, how people get ideas, and how they imagine: not in isolation. It reminds you the entire time you're writing together, *this is how you imagine.* When Kate and I are working on something, I get fired up. We talked this morning about a paper we're giving together later, and I'm fired up to write this essay now. Collaboration is the acting out of the principle of how the imagination works."

2014

There are scholarly rhythms to the year. In the spring I find myself, for example, writing papers for conferences and workshops and then, just as soon as those events conclude, I'm writing proposals for papers for the next set of conferences and workshops the following year.

Now it was spring, and Will and I were once again writing a proposal for a paper we wanted to deliver together. Will was publishing his work and pursuing in earnest his monograph on collaboration and theories of coauthorship. As the WPA at my institution, I was in the midst of writing accreditation reports. We were both busy, but there were moments I wished for the days of leaning over a keyboard together with no defined time frame and no professional commitments pulling at us.

Opening the Google Doc, what has become our preferred writing medium, I looked at our developing proposal, and the geographic separation between us felt more palpable. We no longer had long brainstorming sessions in our living rooms. We no longer lived across the street from each other. We didn't share the same adjunct office. I longed for the energy of proximity and castigated myself for having sometimes taken it for granted.

Yet, here is this proposal we are writing and it contains our voice. As I read and then reread the draft, my imagination is piqued. My fingers furiously move across the keys for a few moments. I sit back and start reading again from the beginning of the document.

I love where this is going. And I know that once the proposal is finished, the traces of what I just typed will be all but invisible, dissolved into this draft we have written alone and together.

2011

The third time something we submitted for publication was rejected, we had already revised the draft two times based on reviewer feedback.

In our resubmission letter, we noted this third revision would be our last because the voice represented in this piece no longer felt like our own. After we submitted the first version of the draft, the feedback we received seemed reasonable. When we got a request for a second revision, we noticed the feedback this time around was asking for changes that contradicted the first round of feedback. Did the editors recognize this discrepancy? We have since learned this kind of experience is not uncommon—getting conflicting signals from editors or reviewers—but we were nevertheless wary of going through with a third revision. At what point does our writing stop being ours? We nevertheless revised the essay once more, and we tactfully explained to the editors that if they still thought changes needed to be made, we would prefer to pull the essay.

After reading this latest draft, however, the editors still weren't satisfied. "It was a hard decision for us at this stage because everyone has invested so much time and work in this piece," they noted in an email just after telling us they were passing on our work. I pointed out how this message made it sound as if it was their decision not to move forward. "It's like they're trying to break up with us after we've already broken up with them," John joked.

2010

This was one of those moments. We sat around a table at a Thai restaurant after a long day of conference sessions, and one of our mentors leaned toward us. If you did not know him, you would have guessed from his body language that he wanted us to know he was going to say something important. But that was not him. Usually if he wanted to say something important, he would lean away from the table, exasperated that he should have to explain something so obvious.

No, leaning in and making eye contact was something different. Such movement betrayed the persona he had cultivated as the disinterested stoic, suspicious of sentimental gestures.

"Don't be like me. I can be a jerk and don't play nice with others. It's a lonely way to go through your career."

We were taken aback by his honesty. His work had deeply informed our own theoretical commitments, but his personal style made it difficult to feel at ease with the relationship we shared with him. In many ways this relationship was a well-worn academic cliché: the brilliant scholar, a lion in winter, passing on his hard-earned wisdom to his eager, but naïve, students—students always feeling insecure about their standing with him, wanting nothing more than to be recognized by him as colleagues.

But this was one of those moments. He was letting us in, taking us into his confidence.

"Keep writing together. It doesn't have to be the way I did it. You don't have to be like me."

2019

What if we did show up in the book? Something like an epilogue? A collaborative piece, but one that isn't really a piece of writing that could exist elsewhere as a stand-alone object. We could organize it around vignettes and memories. We could even use the interview material with Kate and Hepsie.

I like that idea.

A piece that makes clear our third way, the voice that emerges from this kind of dipping into the resonances of all this minor labor.

Like a way of modeling collaboration, making it clear how collaboration informs even those moments when we write alone.

Yes.

Yes.

And it doesn't have to be the way anyone else would do it.

Okay, so how should we begin?

2006-2019

None of the pieces we wrote together that we discuss here were ever published. And we haven't mentioned the many more drafts of things we started but never completed.

While those rejections and unfinished drafts are examples of discontinuities that brought our work on those particular projects to a halt, viewed in the developing arc of our ongoing collaboration these rejections were simply occasions of resistance, ones we were able to consider retrospectively as we pursued other projects together, and in some cases separately. Indeed, each of us has experience collaborating with others we have met as we have pursued our respective careers. And similar to Kate and Hepsie's experiences, we have had to adjust what we think we know about coauthorship for these other collaborations.

During Will's conversation with Hepsie and Kate, he asked about their affection for Ann Berthoff, with whom Hepsie worked when she joined the faculty at UMass–Boston. They explained it was through Berthoff that they discovered C. S. Peirce, one of the founding philosophers of American pragmatism, whom they discuss at several points in their book *Reason to Believe*. "But in particular," Hepsie went on to say, "what Berthoff has taught us, and I've passed this curse on to most of the graduate students I've taught, is to be interested in the people who are philosophers of what we study, people who want to think about not just how to do something but what such work means in the world."

We were reminded of this idea not too long ago when Will came across an essay by the linguist James Paul Gee (2016) in which he says the following to his readers: "Your job as an academic is to have ideas and to put them together with other people's ideas to make better ones with potential for real impact." But such an idea takes us back to something Berthoff says in *The Making of Meaning* when she introduces the idea of double-entry notebooks: "If we are all continuously discovering, recognizing what it is we are doing, we'll have many more ways of finding out how to do it" (1981, 41). As we put the finishing touches on this piece of writing, what we're left thinking about is how to strive to be continuously discovering what it means to be a coauthor, what it means *to* coauthor, to experiment with the many ways we can inscribe words together.

2019

Even though I have written this book "alone" as a single author, the motivation for this book and nearly every claim I have made in it have been directly informed by my experiences as a collaborative writer trained by other collaborative writers. As far as the specifics go as to why I have written this book as a single author, it mainly boils down to the mundane logistics of navigating an academic career—schedules, family obligations, tenure and promotion requirements, administrative responsibilities. None of this stopped John and I from writing together, though, the continued experience of which provided the laboratory for these ideas.

When I started writing this book, I wanted to better understand this thing I've become passionate about, and I wanted to put voice to some of the ideas that have grown out of my experiences as a collaborative writer, ideas I also wanted to put into conversation with postqualitative inquiry, new materialist philosophy, interactionist rhetorical theory, and the many explicators of these things that show up in these pages. Yes, I've written it alone, but anything of value found in these pages is the result of those others who have showed me how and why these ideas deserve articulation.

I am and am not the author of this book.

NOTES

INTRODUCTION: ACCOUNTING FOR COAUTHORSHIP

1. My discussion of collaboration throughout this book primarily concerns collaborative writing, or, more generally, the joint production of discourse intended to be inscribed. For stylistic reasons, I vary the terms I use (*collaboration, collaborative writing, coauthorship, cowriting, collaborative composition*), but when I invoke these terms I mean to reference the complex of interactions cowriters negotiate to compose texts.

2. There is no simple definition of rhetorical invention that doesn't inevitably limit its meaning. For this reason, I appreciate the thoroughness of Janice Lauer's description when she explains that invention in the study of rhetoric "has historically encompassed strategic acts that provide the discourser with direction, multiple ideas, subject matter, arguments, insights to probable judgments, and understanding of the rhetorical situation. Such acts include initiating discourse, exploring alternatives, framing and testing judgments, interpreting texts, and analyzing audiences" (2004, 2). I believe all these concerns inform the work of rhetorical invention in collaborative writing.

3. I discuss Mead in more detail in chapter 2, but it's worth noting that LeFevre's use of Mead in her continuum of social perspectives on rhetorical invention doesn't accurately reflect his philosophy of language because she leaves out what for Mead was a critical component of communicative interaction: the objects to which gestures are always in reference. I make this point not to nitpick but because my interactionist approach to theorizing collaboration is partially indebted to Mead.

4. In her review of the book, Elizabeth Ervin observes how the aim of Clark's project "lies in his curious insistence that dialogue, dialectic, and conversation *are not the same things*, and that tendencies to equate them are facile and oversimplified," an aim Ervin questions by way of its utility (1991, 368). I appreciate Ervin's criticism because it illustrates that when social constructionism is plumbed, we find premises that rely on equivocation.

5. This understanding is partially informed by Stephen Yarbrough's definition of novelty as "the beliefs that a discourse produces that could not have been implied from the concepts governing the beliefs that previously the interlocutors held individually" (2006, 124).

6. Davidson put her money where her mouth is and with David Theo Goldberg founded in 2002 the online network HASTAC (Humanities, Arts, Sciences, and Technology Advanced Collaboratory). According to its website, the idea for HASTAC grew out of a coauthored article Davidson and Goldberg wrote that argues "today's new, global forms of communication and online learning are so complex that they demand a new alliance of humanists, artists, social scientists, natural scientists, and engineers, working collaboratively to think and make creatively and critically, including about equity, access, privacy, security, and other social dimensions of technology and learning" (Humanities n.d.).

7. These questions come to a head in the interesting scenario Cecile Janssens (2014) discusses in the *Chronicle of Higher Education*. When doing a database search for

information with which she was going to update her CV, she discovered a citation for "[her] third publication that [she] did not write." As she explains, "I contacted the lead author and learned that I had been acknowledged because the study was based on data collected by a consortium of which I was once a member. I was reassured that I am not responsible for the contents of the paper because I am credited as a collaborator, not as an author." This scenario highlights the shortcomings of "authorial" terminology—descriptors like *author, collaborator, contributor*, and the like don't mean the same thing in the same way to the same people; it also highlights the conceptual overlap between what it means to author and to authorize.

8.   I should also add media coverage to this list. "Writing a book is a big deal. Being invited to discuss that book on National Public Radio is an occasion for joy, too. But you know what sucks? When these two realities converge and you, the co-author of said book, receive no credit" (Fessler 2018). So begins an article on the website *Quartz* about a June 30, 2018, segment on NPR's *All Things Considered* about a new book written by Silke-Maria Weineck and Stefan Szymanski about the sport of soccer. Not only did the journalist who narrated the story fail to mention Weineck as a coauthor, the day before the story aired, Weineck and Szymanski got an email from the segment's producers saying they decided to only use Szymanski's voice in the piece even though both authors were interviewed. NPR put out a retraction on the version of the segment that appears on its website, but I mention this example because the conventions of radio and television interviews put constraints on how coauthors get represented in those mediums. In this particular case, however, the controversy centered on the obvious gender bias, and rightly so.

9.   Rhetoricians and compositionists have for quite some time been troubling these assumptions, especially the idea that writers are capable of creating wholly "original" works. Beginning in the mid-2000s, moreover, the concept of remix started gaining ground as a metaphor for the inventional dimension of writing (see Davis et al. 2010; Logie 2009; Palmeri 2012; Rife and DeVoss 2012; Yancey 2009). Fitzpatrick (2011) also considers remix in *Planned Obsolescence* (see 76–80).

10.   This is not the only criticism that gets directed at author-metric tools. One shortcoming of the h-index, for example, is that it fails to account for the quantitative impact of individual publications. A researcher with three publications, one of which has been cited seventy-five times while his others have only been cited twice, would have the same h-index score as a researcher who has published three articles that have each only been cited three times. Moreover, the score doesn't consider the quality of the venues in which publications appear (even though journals themselves can be given h-index scores).

11.   At the time of this writing, *JAMA* articles list authors' names and affiliations on the first page. But a section titled "Article Information" that describes the individual roles of each collaborator appears immediately after an article's conclusion. For instance, I just reviewed one example of an article with fifteen listed contributors, and each of their roles is broken into the following categories (and in this order): "concept and design"; "acquisition, analysis, and interpretation of data"; "drafting of the manuscript"; "critical revision of the manuscript for important intellectual content"; "statistical analysis;" and "obtained funding" (Kim et al. 2018).

12.   That there is not a more well-defined statement on the assessment of collaborative work in rhetoric and composition, or writing studies, is frequently questioned in some of the discipline's more informal venues for conversation and debate. For instance, a discussion thread with the title message "Authorship Guidelines/ Position Statements?" was initiated in March 2015 on the Writing Program Administrators listserv and garnered close to a dozen responses. Just over a year later, in September 2016, another discussion was initiated on that same listserv with the title

message "Collaborative Authorship: Position Statement?" It could be argued that organizations like NCTE, CCCC, and CWPA are hesitant to devise "official" guidelines regarding collaborative work because they don't want to put artificial limits on how collaborators should be credited for their work. Of course, by not suggesting more specific guidelines, these organizations make it easier for institutions to apply standards developed by other disciplines.

CHAPTER 1: IS WRITING INHERENTLY COLLABORATIVE?

1. According to Google Scholar, at the time of this writing, Bruffee's article has been cited nearly eighteen hundred times. By comparison, *Singular Texts, Plural Authors*, Lisa Ede and Andrea Lunsford's landmark study of collaborative writing, has been cited just over nine hundred times.

2. To be fair, Bruffee does outline such pedagogy in his textbook *A Short Course in Writing*, originally published in 1972. The third edition was published in 1985, a year after "Collaborative Learning and the 'Conversation of Mankind.'" A fourth edition was published by Pearson in 2007.

3. Mason is credited with coining the term "collaborative learning," but the idea of collaborative learning has a rich history in the development of American progressive education, specifically the work of John Dewey. Mara Holt's recent study concisely outlines the high points of this history, including the links between collaborative learning and the development of American pragmatist philosophy. Indeed, Holt asserts, "Pragmatism remains the best guide to collaborative practice" (2018, 6). Coterminous with this history of collaborative learning in the United States, the Soviet psychologist Lev Vygotsky was developing his protoconstructivist theory of human development with its emphasis on the social nature of learning. One of Vygotsky's better-known concepts, his theory of the zone of proximal development (ZPD), lends itself especially well to contemporary theories of collaborative learning. For a brief overview of the overlaps between Dewey's and Vygotsky's respective theories of social learning, see Michael Glassman (2001). For an interesting discussion of how both these thinkers' theories of language align more with Davidson's externalist language philosophy than with the Cartesian dualism at work in most iterations of social constructionist epistemology, see David Russell (1993).

4. If you recall from the introduction, this is the same logic at work in LeFevre's theory of rhetorical invention as a social process, "one in which individuals interact with society and culture" (1987, 121). We might say, that is, that what LeFevre calls "society and culture" is functionally the same thing as what Herzberg identifies as "discourse communities" insofar as each of these things "constitute" the processes of invention through which we come to know things.

5. While this might be a bit of an overgeneralization, Bruffee's interest has nonetheless always focused on explicating the pedagogical implications of social constructionist epistemology. Even when he does parse the term *collaboration*, he does so in the context of the overall learning situation, as he does in his 1995 article for the magazine *Change*, "Sharing Our Toys: Cooperative Learning versus Collaborative Learning."

6. For example, Irene Clark parses the beginnings of a taxonomy that distinguishes "legitimate" acts of collaboration from "illegitimate" ones (1993, 519–21), which is similar to what Muriel Harris (1992) does in her aptly titled article "Collaboration Is Not Collaboration Is Not Collaboration." More recently, Peter Kittle and Troy Hicks have observed how "people can contribute to a project or cooperate in a group without truly collaborating"; they then describe "genuine" collaboration with

a long list of discrete activities that make a writing group collaborative (2009, 527). In these instances, what counts as collaboration is determined by certain logistic configurations, but a third party actually delineates these logistics beforehand and in ways that render "collaboration" a generic moniker for specific activities.

7. Interestingly, Donald Stewart made a similar claim a few years after Bruffee published "Collaborative Learning and the 'Conversation of Mankind.'" In his critique, Stewart outlines why "neither collaborative learning nor the social constructionist epistemology that supports it is the educational panacea which its advocates imply" (1988, 64).

8. My objections to social turn epistemology are ones that have already been clearly explicated by a wide array of rhetoric and composition scholars. For examples, see Reed Dasenbrock (1991), Kent (1991), Yarbrough (1999), Roberts-Miller (2001), and Rhodes and Robinson (2013–14).

9. Much of this work has centered on the import of consensus as a defining characteristic of collaboration, an idea I take up in chapter 3.

10. Despite how I've framed it, Clark isn't directly responding to Harris. He is instead responding to arguments like Kent's (1991) that challenge not just the metaphoric value of community but also the entire program of social turn epistemology that underwrites it. With that said, Harris's and Clark's respective arguments can certainly be read as a kind of debate over the terminology that should define how compositionists frame their work in the wake of the field's social turn.

11. In this article (Anderson et al. 1990), the authors consider how the literacy training they received in their first-year writing course prepared them for the reading and writing scenarios they encountered in other courses across the curriculum.

12. I should add that compositionists still approach collaboration as a means to democratize learning, which isn't a bad thing, of course, but it does reveal how much social turn epistemology has influenced the ways we envision collaboration as a pedagogical resource. For example, see Julia Voss's (2018) recent argument for pursuing collaborative digital projects in writing courses.

13. Latour (2009) explains the idea of missing masses in "Where Are the Missing Masses? The Sociology of a Few Mundane Artifacts." The list of examples I offer follows Latour's style of stringing together lists of seemingly random objects that are ultimately related, what Ian Bogost has dubbed "Latour litanies" (2012, 38).

14. For an experience to be rendered a trial, there must be "differences" or "transformations" that proceed from those encounters because "without differences, without transformation in some state of affairs, there is no meaningful argument to be made about a given agency, no detectable frame of reference" (Latour 2005, 53).

15. Kevin Porter (2001) nicely situates Davidson's language philosophy in the context of a composition classroom, as does Matthew Heard (2008). Also see Kent (1991) and Yarbrough (2005).

16. Even though I argue against the value of social turn epistemology for understanding and in turn promoting collaborative composition, I don't believe this epistemological school is without value. For example, in their introduction to a special issue of *College English* themed around "Reimagining the Social Turn," Jacqueline Rhodes and Jonathan Alexander note how "the initial assumptions and theoretical bases upon which the 'social turn' in composition studies emerged have shifted," but this shift has not been away from social turn theory itself; it is a shift toward more nuanced inquiries that "interrogate notions of identity-based politics and ask instead how writing might move the articulation of difference to address questions of social inequality and social justice from more systemic and intersectional standpoints" (2014, 481). What Rhodes and Alexander show us, along with the other contributors to this special issue, is that social turn epistemology was never meant

to be a static theoretical framework and that we can and should "turn" toward the social in new and more nuanced ways as questions about identity, economic inequality, and social justice prompt us toward such inquiry.

CHAPTER 2: THE TECHNOLOGY OF TALK

1. I'm essentially suggesting that we consider collaborative composition as a joint enactment of what Pierre Bourdieu would call a *habitus*, which he defines as a "system of structured, structuring dispositions" that develop with experience to orient the relations among objects we can (and cannot) perceive in a given context (1990, 52). As Yarbrough qualifies, however, "Bourdieu emphasizes the individual's passive relation to *habitus*, stressing the function of maintaining the continuity of human interaction" (2011, 146). In interactionist terms, we might say the *habitus* collaborators share points to the relations between objects of discourse that inform the dispositions collaborators (tacitly) draw upon to maintain the continuity of their interaction.

2. Johnson would also support this claim. In an article about the ethical demands technical communicators must recognize, he criticizes those who seek to limit technical communication to a purely instrumental endeavor and notes that "until humans activate technologies, they are for most intents and purposes inert objects. A knife on the table, an automobile in a showroom, a vacuum cleaner on the department store shelf. These all can be 'read' and deconstructed, but they have little if any ethical value until they are used" (1998b). In other words, such technologies only exist as such once they are taken up by users and become an active force in the ends to which they are applied. But I don't see Johnson reducing technology to mere instrumentality here. He is instead pointing to the way the value of specific technologies is actualized in the spaces of their use, spaces that bring with them demands that will influence what users of these technologies can "do" with them. On a related note, I appreciate how Johnson and Frances Ranney qualify one meaning of techne as "an inventively systematic knowledge . . . aimed toward previously thought-out, but not pre-determined, ends" (2002, 239).

3. Even though I don't name it as such, I'm persuaded by what scholars like Poulakos (1984) identify as a Sophistic understanding of dynamis. I'm still working through this aspect of linking collaboration and techne, so I expect my ideas here will change. While I am not prepared to elaborate on its significance, I'm fascinated by Nicolai Hartmann's treatment of dynamis and how it both aligns with and departs from the Sophistic understanding Poulakos forwards (see Hartmann, Tremblay, and Peterson 2017).

4. As Freire sees it, limit-situations can only be surmounted once oppressed groups develop a vision for their flourishing, which in turn implies the creative use of language to describe the conditions under which they have been oppressed (thus the importance of naming in Freirian pedagogy). However, Freire also believes in cultivating awareness of the "meaningful thematics" (1970, 102) that inform how we recognize and in turn engage limit-situations. Such investigation is at the heart of problem-posing education and relies on cultivating "generative themes" that make possible "a new, critical attitude towards the limit-situations" (104). Thus, the role of hope in Freirian pedagogy is not a kind of wishful thinking but a generative disposition needed to anticipate the possibility of transgressing such limit-situations in the first place.

5. John Pell and I discuss this idea in "Freire in the Agora: Critical Pedagogy and Civil Discourse" (2015).

CHAPTER 3: COWRITING AGENCY

1. The book is available as a 188-page PDF file on the *Collaborative Futures* website, and it's published under a Creative Commons Attribution-ShareAlike license.

2. In Tarsa's "Upvoting the Exordium," she considers how digital interface design eases "the transition from consumption to production" when it comes to how users of certain websites become participants therein (2015, 13), an idea that builds on arguments initially articulated in works like Cynthia Selfe and Richard Selfe's (1994) "Politics of the Interface" and Sarah Arroyo's (2013) *Participatory Composition*.

3. Lunsford recently raised a similar concern in a November 11, 2014, *Bedford Bits* blog post.

4. The 2012 documentary *We Are Legion* examines the contradictions that surround Anonymous, especially the group's extralegal mission to target organizations that obviously cause significant harm. But it's a double-edged sword, says cybersecurity specialist Joshua Corman: "Individual, young, nameless, faceless folks are having geopolitical impact, [and] it's both exhilarating to realize that and terrifying to realize that. It kind of depends on how that power is wielded" (Knappenberger 2012).

5. For one of the more succinct overviews of such criticism, see Woodmansee's (1994) "On the Author Effect"; Patricia Sullivan's (1994) "Revising the Myth of the Independent Scholar" is also useful for situating this history within composition studies.

6. On a related note, Belenky insists scholars "have to learn, and we have to find, forms for naming collective authors or collaboration is not going to become routine" (Ashton-Jones and Thomas 1990, 281). The *et al.* abbreviation is a case in point.

7. I bring this up because new materialist philosophies (especially object-oriented ontology, which shouldn't be conflated with new materialism) have been met with criticism by some feminist philosophers, as well as scholars of indigenous studies. For example, Micciche explains such objections focus on new materialism's interest in bringing attention to the agency of nonhuman objects, which is problematic "because of women's longstanding vexed relation to Nature" (2017, 44). Much critical feminist work has focused on restoring and empowering women's agency and unobjectifying, so to speak, historical constructs of women as passive objects.

8. Because I focus on a new materialist approach to understanding the agency cowriters negotiate when they compose, I'm reminded of what Jane Bennett describes as the incalculability of the vital forces that propel human (and nonhuman) agents, which she explores in relationship to the vitalist philosophies of Kant, Blumenback, Driesch, and Bergson, who all believe, to one degree or another, that "the formative drive can be known only indirectly, only by examining its effects"; moreover, what we can learn about these formative drives can only ever be partial and incomplete (2010, 67).

9. It is in *Philosophy and the Mirror of Nature* that Bruffee strikes upon Richard Rorty's "language" of social constructionism as a resource for articulating the work of collaborative learning. As Peter Hawkes notes, "Bruffee marks the reading of this book as the beginning of a new way of thinking and talking in groups" (2008, 29–30). I put quotes around the term *language* here because despite the fact that Bruffee's explication of social constructionism *is* theoretical, he says it's not. In a response to an interview Rorty did for the *Journal of Advanced Composition*, Bruffee says, "Rorty is not a 'theorist.' Neither am I. Social construction is not a theory. It is a way of talking, a language, a vernacular" (1990, 145).

10. As Bruffee explicates Rorty's "socially justified belief," he highlights how all three of these terms are operative. We hold beliefs, many of which are personal, but these

personal beliefs don't constitute real knowledge unless they have been justified, proven true by the fact that our peers also believe these things. Such justification is arrived at socially through talk, or as Bruffee puts it, "To justify a belief is to establish a certain kind of relationship among ourselves and among the things we say" (1982, 104–5).

11.   Trimbur does say that the extent to which collaborators can map their differences "represents the potentiality of social agency in group life" (1989, 603). But he is vague on this point and doesn't elaborate on what this "social agency" is comprised of or might amount to.

12.   Such concern is on display in Christine Martorana's recent *Composition Studies* article in which she uses the concept of "figured worlds" to outline a heuristic for collaborative assignments. A figured world, Martorana explains, "produces and is produced by specific identities, discourses, and values," and "these socially constructed worlds inform our every thought, action, and interaction to such an extent that we often fail to recognize their constructedness" (2017, 60). While certainly useful for helping students locate and articulate how their various beliefs and commitments might conflict with those of their peers, this focus on figured worlds continues to position collaboration as something that requires the management of sovereign subjects who wield autonomous agencies.

13.   Yarbrough (2006) articulates a similar understanding of the relationship between emotion and rhetorical agency in *Inventive Intercourse* (see especially chapter 5).

14.   The metaphor of a web is also the image Cooper (1986) uses in "The Ecology of Writing," one of her earliest attempts at sketching an ecological theory of rhetorical agency.

15.   Day and Eodice note that not all the collaborative writing teams they interviewed for their study expressed concern about the challenge of consensus. In fact, "several [teams] claimed they had never thought explicitly about it" (2001, 139). But Day and Eodice are careful to note that their interviewees all self-selected their collaborators and willingly entered those academic partnerships. That is, we should not assume the experience of professional academics who choose to collaborate is indicative of that of students who might be forced to as part of an assignment.

CHAPTER 4: COLLABORATIVE WRITING IN PRACTICE

1.   This is hardly an original position. In *Singular Texts/Plural Authors*, Ede and Lunsford note that some of their readers might be disappointed that they seemingly privilege "abstruse" theory over pedagogy. But as they explain, this is not the case: "Our reluctance to detail specific, concrete guidelines reflects instead our growing appreciation for the complexity of our rhetorical situation as teachers and our awareness of the profound ways that explorations of collaborative writing challenge not only many traditional classroom practices in English studies but our entire curriculum" (1990, 122, 123). In my case, I'm not offering "concrete guidelines" because I don't believe something called *theory* can be translated into something else called *practice*. In fact, I believe the reverse is true, that what becomes a "theory" for us is always contingent on the experiences that have made possible its recognition, an idea I credit to Lynch (2013) in *After Pedagogy* for helping me to understand.

2.   In a recent profile of Latour, Ava Kofman notes how Latour is pushing back against those who have used his work to question the legitimacy of global warming and climate science. As she writes, "Latour believes that if scientists were transparent about how science really functions—as a process in which people, politics, institutions,

peer review and so forth all play their parts—they would be in a stronger position to convince people of their claims" (2018).

3. The report doesn't specify how the survey explicitly or implicitly defined collaboration or what is the meaning of "writing with others," although in the section of the white paper where these data are discussed, it does mention that only 245 respondents (about 19 percent) "report collaborating with writing center consultants" (Grabel and Pigg 2010, 11). Also, the name of this research center has changed since the publication of this white paper; it is now called the Writing, Information, and Digital Experience (WIDE) Research Center.

4. While I don't find their presentation of collaborative writing useful, in the chapter "Techniques Focusing on Writing," Barkley, Cross, and Major (2014) elaborate on various other activities using things like "dialogue journals" and "dyadic essays," which I think are helpful illustrations of low-stake methods for getting students to write together, or at least in close proximity to one another.

5. The double significance of the term *account* in this context deserves to be underscored; it points to the idea of a narrative or chronicle but also to the literal work of accounting: the recording of expenditures, income, balances, and so forth. Latour draws attention to this latter significance in *Reassembling the Social* (2005, 126).

6. Latour discusses the limitations of the term "textual accounts" for figuring the work of such risky texts, noting how the social sciences, especially the sociology of science, is sometimes critiqued for trafficking in "just stories" (2005, 126).

7. Clay Spinuzzi offers a nice analogy for understanding the significance of actor-network theory in this regard: "Suppose that as you walk home, you spot your neighbor on the roof. Do you think to yourself, 'I am amazed that my neighbor can jump so high'? Or do you look for a ladder? Analogically speaking, *Latour always looks for the ladder*" (2015, 30).

8. This sentiment is captured by Latour when he acknowledges his "distrust of critical distance and [his] preference for what [he calls] *critical proximity*, a situation where you let your own interpretation be chemically dissolved by the 'object' of your study" (2016, 469).

9. The "informal, collaborative journal" Anson, Brady, and Larson (1993) discuss in their essay, which I detail in the opening of chapter 2, can certainly be imagined as a kind of parallel composition. Indeed, one could easily argue these cowriters use their published essay to draw on their experiences to outline a persuasive argument for maintaining a risky account of their collaboration, although they don't use that term, of course.

10. In the lexicon Latour creates, an intermediary "is what transports meaning or force without transformation: defining its inputs is enough to define its outputs. For all practical purposes, an intermediary can be taken not only as a black box, but also as a black box counting for one, even if it is internally made of many parts" (2005, 39). "Black box" is a term he uses to explain what happens when the workings of a technology or scientific process are invisible. Black boxes are thus problematic to the extent we fail to appreciate the artificiality of their constructions.

11. While not necessarily an example of parallel composition as I've been discussing here, we might nonetheless chalk up as a risky account Bishop's (2018) recent reflection on the value of actor-network theory for exploring collaborative composition. I also consider this essay one that leans toward a minor literature of collaboration, which I discuss in chapter 5.

12. Even though I use "Untext Collaborative" in the internal citations to name this group of writers, the citation for this article in the reference list begins with Hamon's name and includes the other seven named coauthors.

13. This is one of the initial concerns raised by that first group of MOOC participants: What would it even mean to "finish" their autoethnographic inquiry?

14. Since the *Hybrid Pedagogy* publication, there have been at least four additional publications that appear to have grown out of or been inspired by the #RHIZO14 MOOC collaborative (see Bali and Sharma 2017; Bali et al. 2016; Honeychurch et al. 2016; Koutropoulos 2017) and composed by a range of different writing teams, which might mean the conversation that "fell quiet" was only inaudible for a spell before being taken up again by various configurations of those MOOC participants. But these publications also evidence how sustained inquiry into the processes through which a collaboration works often spurs what Anne O'Meara and Nancy MacKenzie dub "offshoot projects," ones that allow coauthors to consider how "substantive talk on the newer projects enriches, and at times modifies, the conclusions we reached on our earlier projects" (1998, 214).

15. As the Untext Collaborative explains, "Decalcomania is perhaps best known in the handprints that children make when they put wet paint on their hands and press them helter-skelter onto paper. The deterritorialization of the children's palms and their reterritorialization onto the paper is evocative and convenient, but not precise" (Hamon et al. 2015).

16. Even though I am skeptical of the conceptual value of procedurally focused "how-to" guides for collaborative writers, there is no shortage of resources along these lines that could be usefully taken up by students as guides to help orient or otherwise experiment with process strategies. Some of these I've used myself, including the following: Rebecca Ingalls (2011), Matt Barton and Karl Klint (2011), Karen Weingarten and Corey Frost (2011), Joanna Wolfe (2010), and Kittle and Hicks (2009).

CHAPTER 5: (POST)QUALIFYING COAUTHORSHIP

1. Here I am reminded of how Yarbrough uses the image of a car to propose that we understand discourse as a unitary process that can't be broken down and reassembled. Specifically, he prompts us to conceive of the rhetorical appeals (ethos, logos, and pathos) as phases through which all discourse passes. As he explains, "The assumption seems to be that the associations among thought, emotion, and ethics are merely coincidental—much as one might assume that a car's color, shape, and material are coincidental—and that one might well alter an argument's ethical appeal without affecting its rational or emotional appeal—just as one might alter a car's color without affecting its shape or material" (2005, 491). But as Yarbrough contends, "Discourse is not some thing that can be broken into parts and put together again like a car. Discourse is an intervention in an ongoing, complex, but normally habitual process. Writing is more like driving a car than building one" (508–9). This thinking can be applied to the textual products of coauthorship insofar as we can talk about the process—the "driving" of the car—but to reduce coauthored texts to a series of parts that add up to a whole not only undervalues the labor of coauthorship but also misrepresents how discourse works in general, whether one is producing a piece of writing as a single author or writing collaboratively.

2. Here I should also mention Deleuze and Guattari's concept of "lines of flight," which, like collective assemblages of enunciation, they develop in *A Thousand Plateaus* (1987). "Lines of flight" are in contrast to "lines of consistency" in that rhizomatic thinking relies on the interplay between the two, that is, one cannot exist without the other. Lines of flight work as a destabilizing force that can multiply

unanticipated connections and allow for novelty. Whereas lines of consistency might stand in for organized systems, lines of flight disrupt those systems.

3. Berthoff (1981) develops this concept in *The Making of Meaning* (see especially chapter 3).

4. Emig's essay remains a staple in anthologies such as Victor Villanueva and Kristin Arola's *Cross-Talk in Comp Theory* (2011). For one of the clearest summaries of the essay, including a discussion of why it should continue to be read, see Ede and Lunsford (2002).

5. In his recovery of philosophical vitalism, Hawk suggests the Lauer/Berthoff debate also propagated disputes about the definition of rhetoric, specifically whether rhetoric is more science than art, an argument that in Hawk's estimation limited how rhetoricians approached theories of invention in subsequent years (2007, 37–41).

6. For instance, St. Pierre offers the hypothetical example of a researcher who might want to use Foucault's notion of archaeology in her analysis of interview data even though in *The Archaeology of Knowledge*, Foucault rejects the idea of "speaking subjects" (2014, 3).

7. See Latour's "Why Has Critique Run out of Steam?" (2004).

8. Even though the contexts are very different, studying this notion of deterritorialization has helped me better understand what in a previous work I explain as the transformation of decorum, a way rhetors intentionally unsettle the contexts that make particular iterations of language acceptable (Duffy 2015). In particular, I look at the example of prophetic language and how it demands acknowledgment even if its meanings are uncertain. While I don't want to equate these two concepts, I do see some overlap.

9. Nordstrom, a postqualitative researcher and one of my colleagues at the University of Memphis, was recently attacked in right-wing media outlets because she published an essay, one she terms "a multispecies narrative," that considers the ontology of human/animal "naturecultures," or the ways humans and animals live together and are thus entwined. What some of these anti-intellectual, right-wing commentators decided to mock was that Nordstrom listed as coauthors two of her cats. But setting aside these baseless and unfair attacks, Nordstrom's, or rather, Nordstrom, Nordstrom, and Nordstrom's (2018) essay, enacts the kind of thinking it undertakes, enactments that challenge how we account for the piece as a scholarly narrative with two nonhuman coauthors; with that said, and as you'll see in the reference list, I'm citing the piece as I would any other coauthored work. For instructors interested in leading a discussion about human-animal relations and the question of authorship, Nordstrom's piece would pair well with the chapter "Acknowledging Animal Companions" in Micciche's (2017) *Acknowledging Writing Partners*.

10. On a practical note, readers interested in reading these texts or learning more about them can easily find their bibliographic information in my reference list. From there, each of these articles, including the various works I cite earlier in the chapter (like those from Gale and Wyatt), themselves include citations that point to other works we might qualify as minor literatures of collaboration.

11. In a footnote corresponding to this statement, Spooner and Yancey offer readers a key of sorts that explains how they use "emoticons," abbreviations like "imho," and what certain textual features mean (Spooner and Yancey 1996, 253). For some context: I didn't have a personal email account until my first year of college, which was 1999. So as quaint a textual feature as this key might appear to some younger readers, Spooner and Yancey were treading in waters I imagine were very new for the vast majority of this journal's readership at the time.

12. I call this an *open pseudonym* because in the pieces for which they use this name in the byline, they include a note explaining its significance. In *"Petals,"* for example, they point out "vielstimmig" is the German word for "many-voiced" (Vielstimmig 1999, 114).

13. As Yancey and Spooner observe, "'Experimental' writing too easily becomes obscure writing" (Vielstimmig 1999, 92), which for me means that once writing gets labeled *experimental* it becomes sanitized and made palatable for a major language. Yancey and Spooner frequently refer to the "experiments" their writing together undertakes, but to experiment with writing—and to call one's own writing an experiment—is not the same thing as outside readers labeling such writing *experimental*. Having said this, I want to note that Yancey and Spooner are not the only compositionists who have written texts that might fall under the banner of a minor literature. One of my favorite pieces to give students when we are discussing the idea of literacy is Anne Wysocki and Johndan Johnson-Eilola's (1999) chapter that plays with form, voice, and layout to problematize how notions of literacy rely on assumptions about time and space that get disrupted as new technologies influence the skills and capacities needed to effectively navigate literate environments that have been altered by such technological change. I focus on Yancey and Spooner's work because it most engages and presupposes, through its various forms, the concerns postqualitative theorists have been raising about the nature of collaboration. With that said, "The *experimentation* required for post qualitative inquiry cannot be accomplished within the methodological enclosure. This experimental work is risky, creative, surprising, and remarkable. It cannot be measured, predicted, controlled, systematized, formalized, described in a textbook, or called forth by preexisting, approved methodological processes, methods, and practices" (St. Pierre 2018, 604).

CHAPTER 6: WRITING ALONE AND TOGETHER

1. This interview project was never completed. The person with whom John and I were working, the one with the tech savvy who was going to build the webtext, had to pull out of the project. I'm nevertheless happy to be able to share parts of that conversation here.

2. Roskelly and David Jollife collaborated on several editions of a popular textbook, *Everyday Use: Rhetoric at Work in Reading and Writing* (2008).

3. Ronald and Joy Ritchie collaborated on two edited collections, *Available Means: An Anthology of Women's Rhetoric(s)* (2001) and *Teaching Rhetorica: Theory, Pedagogy, Practice* (2006).

REFERENCES

Abercrombie, M.L.J. 1960. *The Anatomy of Judgment: An Investigation into the Processes of Perception and Reasoning.* New York: Basic.

Alexander, Dagmar, and Jonathan Wyatt. 2018. "In(tra)fusion: Kitchen Research Practices, Collaborative Writing, and Re-conceptualising the Interview." *Qualitative Inquiry* 24 (2): 101–8.

American Psychological Association. 2001. *Publication Manual of the American Psychological Association.* 5th ed. Washington, DC: American Psychological Association.

American Psychological Association. 2017. "Ethical Principles of Psychologists and Code of Conduct." www.apa.org/ethics/code/.

Anderson, Worth, Cynthia Best, Alycia Black, John Hurst, Brandt Miller, and Susan Miller. 1990. "Cross-Curricular Underlife: A Collaborative Report on Ways with Academic Words." *College Composition and Communication* 41 (1): 11–36.

Anson, Chris, Laura Brady, and Marion Larson. 1993. "Collaboration in Practice." *Writing on the Edge* 4 (2): 80–96.

Arac, Jonathan. 1977. "Shop Window or Laboratory: Connection, Collaboration, and the Humanities." In *The Politics of Research,* edited by E. Ann Kaplan and George Levine, 116–26. New Brunswick: Rutgers University Press.

Arroyo, Sarah J. 2013. *Participatory Composition: Video Culture, Writing, and Electracy.* Carbondale: Southern Illinois University Press.

Ashton-Jones, Evelyn, and Dene Kay Thomas. 1990. "Composition, Collaboration, and Women's Ways of Knowing: A Conversation with Mary Belenky." *Journal of Advanced Composition* 10 (2): 275–92.

Atwill, Janet M. 1998. *Rhetoric Reclaimed: Aristotle and the Liberal Arts Tradition.* Ithaca, NY: Cornell University Press.

Atwill, Janet, and Janice Lauer. 1995. "Refiguring Rhetoric as an Art: Aristotle's Concept of Techne." In *Discourse Studies in Honor of James L. Kinneavy,* edited by Rosalind Gabin, 25–40. Potomac, MD: Scripta Humanistica.

Austin, Ann E., and Roger G. Baldwin. 1991. *Faculty Collaboration: Enhancing the Quality of Scholarship and Teaching.* ASHE-ERIC Higher Education Report No. 7. Washington, DC: George Washington University, School of Education and Human Development.

Bali, Maha, and Shyam Sharma. 2017. "Envisioning Postcolonial MOOCs: Critiques and Ways Forward." In *MOOCs and Higher Education: What Went Right, What Went Wrong and Where to Next?,* edited by Rebecca Bennett and Mike Kent, 26–44. New York: Routledge.

Bali, Maha, Sarah Honeychurch, Keith Hamon, Rebecca J. Hogue, Apostolos Koutropoulos, Scott Johnson, Ronald Leunissen, and Lenandlar Singh. 2016. "What Is It Like to Learn and Participate in Rhizomatic MOOCs? A Collaborative Autoethnography of #RHIZO14." *Current Issues in Emerging eLearning* 3 (1): 41–59.

Barkley, Elizabeth, K., Patricia Cross, and Claire Howell Major. 2014. *Collaborative Learning Techniques.* 2nd ed. San Francisco: Jossey-Bass.

Baron, Dennis. 2001. "From Pencils to Pixels: The Stages of Literacy Technologies." In *Literacy: A Critical Sourcebook,* edited by Ellen Cushman, Eugene R. Kintgen, Barry M. Kroll, and Mike Rose, 70–84. Boston: Bedford/St. Martin's.

Barthes, Roland. 1977. *Image, Music, Text.* Translated by Stephen Heath. New York: Hill and Wang.

DOI: 10.7330/9781646420490.c007

Bartholomae, David. 1985. "Inventing the University." In *When a Writer Can't Write*, edited by Mike Rose, 134–65. New York: Guilford Press.

Barton, Matt, and Karl Klint. 2011. "A Student's Guide to Collaborative Writing Technologies." In *Writing Spaces: Readings on Writing*, vol. 2, edited by Drew Lowe and Pavel Zemleansky, 320–32. Anderson, SC: Parlor.

Barton, Matthew D., and James R. Heiman. 2012. "Process, Product, and Potential: The Archaeological Assessment of Collaborative, Wiki-Based Student Projects in the Technical Communication Classroom." *Technical Communication Quarterly* 21 (1): 46–60.

Battalio, John. 1993. "The Formal Report Project as Shared-Document Collaboration: A Plan for Coauthorship." *Technical Communication Quarterly* 2 (2): 147–60.

Bennett, Jane. 2010. *Vibrant Matter: A Political Ecology of Things*. Durham, NC: Duke University Press.

Berelson, Bernard. 1960. *Graduate Education in the United States*. New York: McGraw-Hill.

Berlin, James A. 1987. *Rhetoric and Reality: Writing Instruction in American Colleges, 1900–1985*. Carbondale: Southern Illinois University Press.

Berman, Russell A. 2012. "Presidential Address 2012: Teaching as Vocation." *PMLA* 127 (3): 451–59.

Berthoff, Ann E. 1971. "The Problem of Problem-Solving." *College Composition and Communication* 22 (3): 237–42.

Berthoff, Ann E. 1972. "Response to Janice Lauer." *College Composition and Communication* 23 (5): 414–16.

Berthoff, Ann E. 1981. *The Making of Meaning*. Upper Montclair, NJ: Boynton/Cook.

Berthoff, Ann E. 1982. "I. A. Richards and the Audit of Meaning." *New Literary History* 14 (1): 63–79.

Berthoff, Ann E., ed. 1991. *Richards on Rhetoric*. Oxford: Oxford University Press.

Berthoff, Ann E. 1999. *The Mysterious Barricades: Language and Its Limits*. Toronto: University of Toronto Press.

Biagioli, Mario. 2003. "Rights or Rewards? Changing Frameworks of Scientific Authorship." In *Scientific Authorship: Credit and Intellectual Property in Science*, edited by Mario Biagioli and Peter Galison, 253–79. New York: Routledge.

Biagioli, Mario, and Peter Galison. 2003. Introduction to *Scientific Authorship: Credit and Intellectual Property in Science*, edited by Mario Biagioli and Peter Galison, 1–9. New York: Routledge.

Bishop, Andrea. 2018. "(Not) Jacked Up: Actor Network Theory as Lens for Collaboration." *Intraspection* 1: 27–40. www.intraspection.org/index.php/main/article/view/4.

Bizzell, Patricia. 1992. *Academic Discourse and Critical Consciousness*. Pittsburgh: University of Pittsburgh Press.

Blakeslee, Ann M. 2001. "Bridging the Workplace and the Academy: Teaching Professional Genres through Classroom-Workplace Collaborations." *Technical Communication Quarterly* 10 (2): 169–92.

Bleich, David. 1995. "Collaboration and the Pedagogy of Disclosure." *College English* 57 (1): 43–61.

Bogost, Ian. 2012. *Alien Phenomenology, or What It's Like to Be a Thing*. Minneapolis: University of Minnesota Press.

Bourdieu, Pierre. 1990. *The Logic of Practice*. Translated by Richard Nice. Stanford: Stanford University Press.

Boyle, Casey. 2015. "An Attempt at a 'Practitioner's Manifesto.'" In *Thinking with Bruno Latour in Rhetoric and Composition*, edited by Paul Lynch and Nathaniel Rivers, 202–18. Carbondale: Southern Illinois University Press.

Bremner, Stephen, Anne Peirson-Smith, Rodney Jones, and Vijay Bhatia. 2014. "Task Design and Interaction in Collaborative Writing: The Students' Story." *Business and Professional Communication Quarterly* 77 (2): 150–68.

Bruffee, Kenneth. 1982. "Liberal Education and the Social Justification of Belief." *Liberal Education* 68 (2): 95–14.

Bruffee, Kenneth. 1984. "Collaborative Learning and the 'Conversation of Mankind.'" *College English* 47 (6): 635–52.

Bruffee, Kenneth. 1985. "Liberal Education, Scholarly Community, and the Authority of Knowledge." *Liberal Education* 71 (3): 231–39.

Bruffee, Kenneth. 1986. "Social Construction, Language, and the Authority of Knowledge: A Bibliographic Essay." *College English* 48 (8): 773–88.

Bruffee, Kenneth. 1990. "Response to the JAC Interview with Richard Rorty." *Journal of Advanced Composition* 10 (1): 145–46.

Bruffee, Kenneth. 1995. "Sharing Our Toys: Cooperative Learning versus Collaborative Learning." *Change* 27 (1): 12–18.

Bruffee, Kenneth. 2007. *A Short Course in Writing*. 4th ed. New York: Pearson Longman.

Carter, Michael. 2003. *Where Writing Begins: A Postmodern Reconstruction*. Carbondale: Southern Illinois University Press.

Cella, Laurie JC, and Jessica Restaino. 2014. "Lean On: Collaboration and Struggle in Writing and Editing." *Literacy in Composition Studies* 2 (2): 66–76.

Clark, Gregory. 1990. *Dialogue, Dialectic, and Conversation: A Social Perspective on the Function of Writing*. Carbondale: Southern Illinois University Press.

Clark, Gregory. 1994. "Rescuing the Discourse of Community." *College Composition and Communication* 45 (1): 61–74.

Clark, Irene. 1993. "Portfolio Evaluation, Collaboration, and Writing Centers." *College Composition and Communication* 44 (4): 515–24.

Collaborative Futures. 2010. Amsterdam: FLOSS Manuals. http://booki.flossmanuals.net /collaborative-futures/.

Conference on College Composition and Communication. 2018. "Scholarship in Rhetoric, Writing, and Composition: Guidelines for Faculty, Deans, and Chairs." Position Statement. http://cccc.ncte.org/cccc/resources/positions/scholarshipincomp.

Cooper, Marilyn. 1986. "The Ecology of Writing." *College English* 48 (4): 364–75.

Cooper, Marilyn. 2011. "Rhetorical Agency as Emergent and Enacted." *College Composition and Communication* 62 (3): 420–49.

Cooper, Marilyn. 2015. "How Bruno Latour Teaches Writing." In *Thinking with Bruno Latour in Rhetoric and Composition*, edited by Paul Lynch and Nathaniel Rivers, 185–201. Carbondale: Southern Illinois University Press.

Dasenbrock, Reed Way. 1991. "Do We Write the Text We Read?" *College English* 53 (1): 7–18.

Davidson, Cathy. 1999. "What If Scholars in the Humanities Worked Together, in a Lab?" *Chronicle of Higher Education*, May 28.

Davidson, Donald. 2006. "A Nice Derangement of Epitaphs." In *The Essential Davidson*, 89–107. Oxford: Oxford University Press.

Davis, Andrea, Suzanne Webb, Dundee Lackey, and Dànielle Nicole DeVoss. 2010. "Remix, Play, Remediation: Undertheorized Composing Practices." In *Writing and the Digital Generation: Essays on New Media Rhetoric*, edited by Heather Urbanski, 186–97. Jefferson, NC: McFarland.

Day, Kami, and Michele Eodice. 2001. *(First Person)²: A Study of Co-Authoring in the Academy*. Logan: Utah State University Press.

DeLanda, Manuel. 2002. *Intensive Science and Virtual Philosophy*. London: Bloomsbury Academic.

DeLanda, Manuel. 2011. "Emergence, Causality, and Realism." In *The Speculative Turn: Continental Materialism and Realism*, edited by Levi Bryant, Nick Srnicek, and Graham Harman, 381–92. Melbourne: re:press.

Deleuze, Gilles. 1988. *Foucault*. Translated by Seán Hand. Minneapolis: University of Minnesota Press.

Deleuze, Gilles, and Felix Guattari. 1986. *Kafka: Toward a Minor Literature*. Minneapolis: University of Minnesota Press.

Deleuze, Gilles, and Felix Guattari. 1987. *A Thousand Plateaus: Capitalism and Schizophrenia*. Minneapolis: University of Minnesota Press.

Deleuze, Gilles, and Claire Parnet. 2002. *Dialogues II*. Translated by Hugh Tomlinson and Barbara Habberjam. New York: Columbia University Press.

Denbo, Seth. 2017. "Whose Work Is It Really? Collaboration and the Question of Credit." *Perspectives on History* 55 (2): 113–26.

Dewey, John. 1984. "The Development of American Pragmatism." In Vol. 2 of *The Later Works, 1925–1953*, edited by Jo Ann Boydson. Carbondale: Southern Illinois University Press.

Dewey, John. 2000. "The Postulate of Immediate Empiricism." In *Pragmatism and Classical American Philosophy: Essential Readings and Interpretive Essays*, edited by John J. Stuhr, 455–59. New York: Oxford University Press.

Duffy, William. 2015. "Transforming Decorum: The Sophistic Appeal of Walter Rauschenbusch and the Social Gospel." In *Mapping Christian Rhetorics: Connecting Conversations, Charting New Territories*, edited by Michael-John DePalma and Jeffrey M. Ringer, 222–39. New York: Routledge.

Duffy, William, and John Pell. 2013. "Imagining Coauthorship as Phased Collaboration." In *Working with Faculty Writers*, edited by Anne Ellen Geller and Michele Eodice, 246–59. Logan: Utah State University Press.

Dresner, Eli. 2009. "Radical Interpretation, the Primacy of Communication, and the Bounds of Language." *Empedocles* 1 (1): 123–34.

Ede, Lisa, and Andrea Lunsford. 1983. "Why Write . . . Together?" *Rhetoric Review* 1 (2): 150–57.

Ede, Lisa, and Andrea Lunsford. 1990. *Singular Texts/Plural Authors: Perspectives on Collaborative Writing*. Carbondale: Southern Illinois University Press.

Ede, Lisa, and Andrea Lunsford. 2001. "Collaboration and Concepts of Authorship." *PMLA* 116 (2): 354–69.

Ede, Lisa, and Andrea Lunsford. 2002. "Introduction to Janet Emig's 'Writing as a Mode of Learning.'" In *Teaching Writing: Landmarks and Horizons*, edited by Christina Russell McDonald and Robert L. McDonald, 42–54. Carbondale: Southern Illinois Press.

Ede, Lisa, and Andrea Lunsford. 2011. "Collaboration and Collaborative Writing: The View from Here." In *Writing Together: Collaboration in Theory and Practice*, 186–206. Boston: Bedford/St. Martin's.

Elbow, Peter. 2000. "Toward a Phenomenology of Freewriting." In *Everyone Can Write: Essays Toward a Hopeful Theory of Writing and Teaching Writing*, 113–36. New York: Oxford University Press.

Eliot, T. S. 2007. "Tradition and the Individual Talent." In *The Critical Tradition: Classic Texts and Contemporary Trends*, 3rd ed., edited by David H. Richter, 537–41. Boston: Bedford/St. Martin's.

Emerson, Ralph Waldo. 1909. *The Works of Ralph Waldo Emerson*, Vol. 1: *Nature, Addresses, and Lectures*. Boston and New York: Fireside Edition.

Emig, Janet. 1977. "Writing as a Mode of Learning." *College Composition and Communication* 28 (2):122–28.

Endersby, James W. 1996. "Collaborative Research in the Social Sciences: Multiple Authorship and Publication Credit." *Social Science Quarterly* 77 (2): 375–92.

Entes, Judith. 1994. "The Right to Write a Co-Authored Manuscript." In *Writing With: New Directions in Collaborative Teaching, Learning, and Research*, edited by Sally Barr Reagan, Thomas Fox, and David Bleich, 47–59. Albany: State University of New York Press.

Ervin, Elizabeth. 1991. "Review of Dialogue, Dialectic, and Conversation: A Social Perspective on the Function of Writing." *Rhetoric Review* 9 (2): 165–68.

Fessler, Leah. 2018. "NPR's Sexist Blunder Is Proof That Women's Work Isn't Just Over-looked—It's Erased." *Quartz*, July 12. https://work.qz.com/1326146/nprs-all-things -considered-made-a-sexist-mistake-that-proves-womens-work-isnt-just-overlooked-its -erased/.

Fish, Stanley. 1980. *Is There a Text in This Class? The Authority of Interpretative Communities.* Cambridge, MA: Harvard University Press.

Fitzpatrick, Kathleen. 2011. *Planned Obsolescence: Publishing, Technology, and the Future of the Academy.* New York: New York University Press.

Flaherty, Colleen. 2017. "Is Collaboration Worth It?" *Inside Higher Ed*, January 6. www .insidehighered.com/news/2017/01/06/historians-push-more-collaboration-field -traditionally-has-snubbed-group-efforts.

Fontaine, Sheryl I., and Susan M. Hunter. 2006. *Collaborative Writing in Composition Studies.* Boston: Thomson Wadsworth.

Foucault, Michel. 1979. "What Is an Author?" In *Textual Strategies: Perspectives in Post-Structuralist Criticism*, edited by Josué V. Harari, 141–60. Ithaca, NY: Cornell University Press.

Forman, Janice. 1992. Introduction. In *New Visions of Collaborative Writing*, edited by Janice Forman, xi–xxii. Portsmouth, NH: Heinemann.

Foster, David. 1999. "The Challenge of Contingency: Process and the Turn to the Social in Composition." In *Post-Process Theory: Beyond the Writing-Process Paradigm*, edited by Thomas Kent, 149–62. Carbondale: Southern Illinois University Press.

Freire, Paulo. 1970. *Pedagogy of the Oppressed.* Translated by Myra Bergman Ramos. New York: Continuum.

Friend, Chris, Maha Bali, Sarah Honeychurch, and Kevin Hodgson. 2015. Episode 7: "Collaborarion." *HybridPod*, October 30. https://hybridpedagogy.org/hybridpod-episode-7 -collaboration/.

Gale, Ken, and Jonathan Wyatt. 2009. *Between the Two: A Nomadic Inquiry into Collaborative Writing and Subjectivity.* Newcastle upon Tyne: Cambridge Scholars.

Gale, Ken, and Jonathan Wyatt. 2012. "Back to Futures: Diffractions and Becomings of Collaborative Writing." In "Collaborative Writing as a Method of Inquiry," special issue, *International Review of Qualitative Research* 5 (4): 467–77.

Gale, Ken, and Jonathan Wyatt. 2017. "Working at the Wonder: Collaborative Writing as Method of Inquiry." *Qualitative Inquiry* 23 (5): 355–64.

Galison, Peter. 2003. "The Collective Author." In *Scientific Authorship: Credit and Intellectual Property in Science*, edited by Mario Biagioli and Peter Galison, 325–55. New York: Routledge.

Gee, James Paul. 2016. "Ramblings of an Old Academic: Unconfident Advice for End-Times Academics." *Education Review* 23. http://edrev.asu.edu/index.php/ER/article /view/2041.

Geertz, Clifford. 1983. *Local Knowledge: Further Essays in Interpretative Anthropology.* New York: Basic Books.

Glassman, Michael. 2001. "Dewey and Vygotsky: Society, Experience, and Inquiry in Educational Practice." *Educational Researcher* 30 (4): 3–14.

Goggin, Maureen Daly. 1996. "Collaboration." In *Keywords in Composition Studies*, edited by Paul Heilker and Peter Vandenberg, 35–39. Portsmouth: Heinemann.

Goldberg, David Theo, and Cathy N. Davidson. 2004. "Engaging the Humanities." *Profession*. 42–62.

Grabel, Jeff, and Stacey Pigg. 2010. "The Writing Lives of College Students." East Lansing, MI: Writing in Digital Environments Research Center. White paper.

Guttorm, Hanna Ellen, Teija Löytönen, Eeva Anttila, and Anita Valkeemäki. 2016. "Mo(ve)ments, Encounters, Repetitions: Writing with (Embodied and Textual) Encounters." *Qualitative Inquiry* 22 (5): 417–27.

Hamon, Keith, Rebecca J. Hoague, Sarah Honeychurch, Scott Johnson, Apostolos Kout-ropoulos, Simon Ensor, Sandra Sinfield, and Maha Bali. 2015. "Writing the Unread-able Untext: A Collaborative Autoethnography of #rhizo14." *Hybrid Pedagogy*, June 3. http://hybridpedagogy.org/writing-the-unreadable-untext/.

Harris, Jeanette. 1994. "Toward a Working Definition of Collaborative Writing." In *Author-ity and Textuality: Current Views of Collaborative Writing*, edited by James S. Leonard, Christine E. Wharton, Robert Murray Davis, and Jeanette Harris, 77–84. West Cornwall: Locust Hill.

Harris, Joseph. 1989. "The Idea of Community in the Study of Writing." *College Composition and Communication* 40 (1): 11–22.

Harris, Muriel. 1992. "Collaboration Is Not Collaboration Is Not Collaboration: Writing Center Tutorials vs. Peer Response Groups." *College Composition and Communication* 43 (3): 369–83.

Hart-Davidson, Bill. 2018. "Rhetoric and the Art of Bicycle Racing: An Interview with Bill Hart-Davidson." By Jennifer Juszkiewicz. *Rhetoricity*, March 13. https://rhetoricity.libsyn.com/page/2/size/10.

Hartmann, Nicolai, Frédéric Tremblay, and Keith R. Peterson. 2017. "The Megarian and the Aristotelian Concept of Possibility: A Contribution to the History of the Ontologi-cal Problem of Modality." *Axiomathes* 27 (2): 209–23.

Hawk, Byron. 2007. *A Counter-History of Composition: Toward Methodologies of Complexity*. Pitts-burgh: University of Pittsburgh Press.

Hawk, Byron. 2011. "Reassembling Postprocess: Toward a Posthuman Theory of Public Rhetoric." In *Beyond Postprocess*, edited by Sidney I. Dorbin, J. A. Rice, and Michael Vastola, 75–93. Logan: Utah State University Press.

Hawkes, Peter. 2008. "Vietnam Protests, Open Admissions, Peer Tutor Training, and the Brooklyn Institute: Tracing Kenneth Bruffee's Collaborative Learning." *Writing Center Journal* 28 (2): 25–32.

Heard, Matthew. 2008. "What Should We Do with Postprocess Theory?" *Pedagogy* 8 (2): 283–304.

Herndl, Carl G., and Adela C. Licona. 2007. "Shifting Agency: Agency, Kairos, and the Possibilities of Social Action." In *Communicative Practices in Workplaces and the Professions*, edited by Mark Zachry and Charlotte Thralls, 133–53. Amityville, NY: Baywood.

Hesse, Douglas. 2019. "Journals in Composition Studies, Thirty-Five Years After." *College English* 81 (4): 367–96.

Holt, Mara. 2018. *Collaborative Learning as Democratic Practice: A History*. Urbana, IL: NCTE.

Honeychurch, Sarah, Bonnie Stewart, Maha Bali, Rebecca J. Hogue, and Dave Cormier. 2016. "How the Community Became More Than the Curriculum: Participant Experi-ences in #RHIZO14." *Current Issues in Emerging eLearning* 3 (1): 26–40.

Humanities, Arts, Science, and Technology Alliance and Collaboratory. n.d. "History." https://www.hastac.org/about/history.

Hutcheon, Linda. 2001. "Presidential Address 2000: She Do the President in Different Voices." *PMLA* 116 (3): 518–30.

Ingalls, Rebecca. 2011. "Writing 'Eyeball to Eyeball': Building a Successful Collaboration." In *Writing Spaces: Readings on Writing*, vol. 2, edited by Charles Lowe and Pavel Zemlian-sky, 122–40. Anderson, SC: Parlor.

Jackson, Alecia Youngblood. 2017. "Thinking Without Method." *Qualitative Inquiry* 23 (9): 666–74.

Jackson, Alecia Y., and Lisa A. Mazzei. 2013. "Plugging One Text into Another: Thinking with Theory in Qualitative Research." *Qualitative Inquiry* 19 (4): 261–71.

Janssens, Cecile. 2014. "Let's Clarify Authorship on Scientific Papers." *Chronicle of Higher Education*, August 11. https://www.chronicle.com/article/Lets-Clarify-Authorship-on/148287.

Johnson, Robert R. 1998a. *User-Centered Technology: A Rhetorical Theory for Computers and Other Mundane Artifacts.* Albany: SUNY Press.

Johnson, Robert R. 1998b. "Complicating Technology: Interdisciplinary Method, the Burden of Comprehension, and the Ethical Space of the Technical Communicator." *Technical Communication Quarterly* 7 (1): 75–99.

Johnson, Robert R., and Frances J. Ramney. 2002. "Afterward: Recovering Techne." *Technical Communication Quarterly* 11 (2): 237–39.

Johnson, Steven. 2010. *Where Good Ideas Come From: The Natural History of Innovation.* New York: Riverhead Books.

Kent, Thomas. 1991. "On the Very Idea of a Discourse Community." *College Composition and Communication* 42 (4): 425–45.

Kent, Thomas. 1997. "The Consequences of Theory for the Practice of Writing." In *Publishing in Rhetoric and Composition,* edited by Gary Olson and Todd Taylor, 147–61. Albany: SUNY Press.

Kent, Thomas. 2011. "Righting Writing." In *Beyond Postprocess,* edited by Sidney Dobrin, J. A. Rice, and Michael Vastola, xi–xxii. Logan: Utah State University Press.

Kim, Jae-Min, Robert Stewart, Yong-Seong Lee, Hee-Joon Lee, Min Chul Kim, Ju-Wan Kim, Hee-Ja Kang, Kyung-Yeol Bae, Sung-Wan Kim, Seon Shin, Young Joon Hong, Ju Han Kim, Youngkeum Ahn, Myung Ho Jeong, and Jin-Sang Yoon. 2018. "Effect of Escitalopram vs Placebo Treatment for Depression on Long-term Cardiac Outcomes in Patients with Acute Coronary Syndrome: A Randomized Clinical Trial." *JAMA* 320 (4): 350–58.

Kittle, Peter, and Troy Hicks. 2009. "Transforming the Group Paper with Collaborative Online Writing." *Pedagogy* 9 (3): 525–38.

Knappenberger, Brian, dir. 2012. *We Are Legion.* 2012. Luminant Media.

Knievel, Michael. 2008. "Police Reform, Task Force Rhetoric, and Traces of Dissent: Rethinking Consensus-as-Outcome in Collaborative Writing Situations." *Journal of Technical Writing and Communication* 38 (4): 331–62.

Kofman, Ava. 2018. "Bruno Latour, the Post-Truth Philosopher, Mounts a Defense of Science." *New York Times Magazine,* October 25. www.nytimes.com/2018/10/25/mag azine/bruno-latour-post-truth-philosopher-science.html.

Koro-Ljungberg, Mirka, and Jasmine B. Ulmer. 2016. "This Is Not a Collaborative Writing." In *Qualitative Inquiry Through a Critical Lens,* edited by Norman K. Denzin and Michael D. Giardina, 99–115. New York: Routledge.

Koutropoulos, Apostolos. 2017. "Rhizomes of the Classroom: Enabling the Learners to Become the Curriculum." In *Unplugging the Classroom: Teaching with Technologies to Promote Students' Lifelong Learning,* edited by Sharmila Pixy Ferris and Hilary Wilder, 103–18. Cambridge, MA: Chandos.

Kuhn, Thomas S. 1962. *The Structure of Scientific Revolutions.* Chicago: University of Chicago Press.

Landow, George. 1997. *Hypertext 2.0.* Baltimore: Johns Hopkins University Press.

Lanier, Jaron. 2010. *You Are Not a Gadget.* New York: Vintage.

Lather, Patti, and Elizabeth A. St. Pierre. 2013. "Post-Qualitative Research." *International Journal of Qualitative Studies in Education* 26 (6): 629–33.

Latour, Bruno. 1988. *The Pasteurization of France.* Translated by Alan Sharidan and John Law. Cambridge, MA: Harvard University Press.

Latour, Bruno. 2003. "The Promises of Constructivism." In *Chasing Technology: Matrix of Materiality,* edited by Don Ihde and Evan Selinger, 27–46. Bloomington: Indiana University Press.

Latour, Bruno. 2004. "Why Has Critique Run out of Steam? From Matters of Fact to Matters of Concern." *Critical Inquiry* 30 (2): 225–48.

Latour, Bruno. 2005. *Reassembling the Social: An Introduction to Actor-Network-Theory.* Oxford: Oxford University Press.

Latour, Bruno. 2009. "Where Are the Missing Masses? The Sociology of a Few Mundane Artifacts." In *Technology and Society: Building our Sociotechnical Future*, edited by Deborah J. Johnson and Jameson M. Wetmore, 151–80. Cambridge: MIT Press.

Latour, Bruno. 2010. "An Attempt at a 'Compositionist Manifesto.'" *New Literary History* 41 (3): 471–90.

Latour, Bruno. 2011. "Networks, Societies, Spheres: Reflections of an Actor-Network Theorist." *International Journal of Communication* 5: 796–810.

Latour, Bruno. 2014. "How Better to Register the Agency of Things." In Vol. 34 of *The Tanner Lectures on Human Values*, edited by Mark Matheson, 79–117. Salt Lake City: University of Utah Press.

Latour, Bruno. 2016. "Life among Conceptual Characters." *New Literary History* 47 (2–3): 463–76.

Lauer, Janice. 1970. "Heuristics and Composition." *College Composition and Communication* 21 (5): 396–404.

Lauer, Janice. 1972. "Response to Ann E. Berthoff." *College Composition and Communication* 23 (2): 208–10.

Lauer, Janice. 2004. *Invention in Rhetoric and Composition*. West Lafayette, IN: Parlor.

Lauren, Benjamin, and Joanna Schreiber. 2018. "Emerging Forms of Project Management in Technical and Professional Communication." *Technical Communication* 65 (2): 125–28.

LeFevre, Karen Burke. 1987. *Invention as a Social Act*. Carbondale: Southern Illinois University Press.

Leonard, James S., and Christine E. Wharton. "Breaking the Silence: Collaboration and the Isolationist Paradigm." In *Author-ity and Textuality: Current Views of Collaborative Writing*, edited by James S. Leonard, Christine E. Wharton, Robert Murray Davis, and Jeanette Harris, 25–40. West Cornwall: Locust Hill.

Logie, John. 2009. "The (Re)Birth of the Composer." In *Composition & Copyright: Perspectives on Teaching, Text-making, and Fair Use*, edited by Steve Westbrook, 175–89. Albany: SUNY Press.

Lowry, Paul Benjamin, Aaron Curtis, and Michele René Lowry. 2004. "Building a Taxonomy and Nomenclature of Collaborative Writing to Improve Interdisciplinary Research and Practice." *Journal of Business Communication* 41 (1): 66–99.

Lunsford, Andrea. 1999. "Rhetoric, Feminism, and the Politics of Textual Ownership." *College English* 61 (5): 529–44.

Lynch, Paul. 2013. *After Pedagogy: The Experience of Teaching*. Urbana, IL: NCTE.

MacClure, Maggie. 2013. "Researching without Representation: Language and Materiality in Post-Qualitative Methodology." *International Journal of Qualitative Studies in Education* 26 (6): 658–67.

Mara, Andrew, and Byron Hawk. 2010. "Posthuman Rhetorics and Technical Communication." *Technical Communication Quarterly* 19 (1): 1–10.

Markel, Mike. 2014. *Technical Communication*. 11th ed. Boston: Bedford/St. Martin's.

Markel, Mike. 2016. *Practical Strategies for Technical Communication*. 2nd ed. Boston: Bedford/St. Martin's.

Martorana, Christine. 2017. "Through the Lens of Figured Worlds: A Heuristic for Productive Collaboration." *Composition Studies* 45 (1): 59–73.

Mason, Edwin. 1970. *Collaborative Learning*. London: Ward Lock Education.

Mazzei, Lisa A. 2013. "A Voice without Organs: Interviewing in Posthumanist Research." *International Journal of Qualitative Studies in Education* 26 (6): 732–40.

Mazzei, Lisa A. 2017. "Following the Contour of Concepts Toward a Minor Inquiry." *Qualitative Inquiry* 23 (9): 675–85.

Mazzei, Lisa A., and Alecia Y. Jackson. 2012. "In the Threshold: Writing Between-the-Two." *International Review of Qualitative Research* 5 (4): 449–58.

McDonald, Frances, and Whitney Trettien. 2017. "A Threshold Is an Opening." *Los Angeles Review of Books*, November 27. https://lareviewofbooks.org/article/a-threshold-is-an -opening/#.

Mead, George Herbert. 1932. *The Philosophy of the Present*. Chicago: Open Court.

Mead, George Herbert. 1934. *Mind, Self, and Society from the Standpoint of a Social Behaviorist*. Chicago: University of Chicago Press.

Mead, George Herbert. 1964. *Selected Writings*, edited by Andrew J. Reck. Chicago: University of Chicago Press.

Menand, Louis. 2010. *The Marketplace of Ideas: Reform and Resistance in the American University*. New York: Norton.

Micciche, Laura R. 2011. "For Slow Agency." *WPA: Writing Program Administration* 35 (1): 73–90.

Micciche, Laura R. 2017. *Acknowledging Writing Partners*. Fort Collins, CO: WAC Clearinghouse.

Miller, Carolyn. 1996. "This Is Not an Essay." *College Composition and Communication* 47 (2): 284–88.

Miller, Naomi J. 2003. "Which Half Is Yours? The Art of Collaboration." *Chronicle of Higher Education*, January 20. https://www.chronicle.com/article/Which-Half-Is-Yours-The -Art/45332.

Miller, Susan. 1994. "New Discourse City: An Alternative Model for Collaboration." In *Writing With: New Directions in Collaborative Teaching, Learning, and Research*, edited by Sally Barr Reagan, Thomas Fox, and David Bleich, 283–300. Albany: SUNY Press.

Mirel, Barbara. 2004. "Advancing a Vision of Usability." In *Teaching Technical Communication*, edited by James B. Dubinsky, 218–39. Boston: Bedford/St. Martin's.

MLA Task Force for Evaluating Scholarship for Tenure and Promotion. 2007. "Report of the MLA Task Force on Evaluating Scholarship for Tenure and Promotion." *Profession*, 9–71.

Mullen, Carol A., and Frances K. Kochan. 2001. "Issues of Collaborative Authorship in Higher Education." *Educational Forum* 65 (2): 128–35.

Myers, Greg. 1986. "Reality, Consensus, and Reform in the Rhetoric of Composition Teaching." *College English* 48 (2): 154–71.

Nagar, Richa. 2014. *Muddying the Waters: Coauthoring Feminisms across Scholarship and Activism*. Urbana: University of Illinois Press.

Noddings, Nel. 1984. *Caring: A Feminine Approach to Ethics and Moral Education*. Berkeley: University of California Press.

Nordstrom, Susan. 2013. "Object-Interviews: Folding, Unfolding, and Refolding Perceptions of Objects." *International Journal of Qualitative Methods* 12 (1): 237–57.

Nordstrom, Susan. 2018. "Antimethodology: Postqualitative Generative Conventions." *Qualitative Inquiry* 24 (3): 215–26.

Nordstrom, Susan, Amelie Nordstrom, and Coonan Nordstrom. 2018. "Guilting of Loving You: A Multispecies Narrative." *Qualitative Inquiry*. Epub ahead of print. https://doi .org/10.1177/1077800418784321.

Oakeshott, Michael. 1959. *The Voice of Poetry in the Conversation of Mankind: An Essay*. London: Bowes and Bowes.

Oatsvall, Neil, and Vaughn Scribner. 2017. "Growing Your Wolfpack: Why Collaboration Is 'Worth It' in Historical Scholarship." *The Junto: A Group Blog on Early American History* (blog). February 20. https://earlyamericanists.com/2017/02/20/guest-post-growing -your-wolf-pack-why-collaboration-is-worth-it-in-historical-scholarship/.

O'Brien, Timothy L. 2012. "Changes in Academic Coauthorship, 1953–2003." *Science, Technology, & Human Values* 37 (3): 210–34.

O'Meara, Anne, and Nancy R. MacKenzie. 1998. "Reflections on Scholarly Collaboration." In *Common Ground: Feminist Collaboration in the Academy*, edited by Elizabeth G. Peck and JoAnna Stephens Mink, 209–25. Albany: SUNY Press.

Palmeri, Jason. 2012. *Remixing Composition: A History of Multimodal Writing Pedagogy*. Carbondale: Southern Illinois University Press.

Paretti, Marie C., Lisa D. McNair, and Lissa Holloway-Attaway. 2007. "Teaching Technical Communication in an Era of Distributed Work: A Case Study of Collaboration between U.S. and Swedish Students." *Technical Communication Quarterly* 16 (3): 327–52.

Pell, John, and William Duffy. 2015. "Freire in the Agora: Critical Pedagogy and Civil Discourse." *Literacy in Composition Studies* 3 (1): 95–107.

Petraglia, Joseph. 1999. "Is There Life after Process? The Role of Social Scientism in a Changing Discipline." In *Post-Process Theory: Beyond the Writing-Process Paradigm*, edited by Thomas Kent, 49–64. Carbondale: Southern Illinois University Press.

Petraglia, Joseph. 2000. "Shaping Sophisticates: Implications of the Rhetorical Turn for Rhetoric Education." In *Inventing a Discipline: Rhetoric Scholarship in Honor of Richard E. Young*, edited by Maureen Daly Goggin, 80–104. Urbana, IL: NCTE.

Pineau, Elyse. 2012. "Haunted by Ghosts: Collaborating with Absent Others." *International Review of Qualitative Research* 5 (4): 459–65.

Poska, Allyson, and Susan Amussen. 2018. "Two Heads Are Better than One: Collaborative Writing in Early Modern Women's History." American Historical Association Annual Meeting. January 6, 2018. Washington, DC.

Porter, Kevin. 2001. "A Pedagogy of Charity and the Student-Negotiated Composition Classroom." *College Composition and Communication* 52 (4): 574–611.

Poulakos, John. 1983. "Toward a Sophistic Definition of Rhetoric." *Philosophy and Rhetoric* 16 (1): 35–48.

Poulakos, John. 1984. "Rhetoric, the Sophists, and the Possible." *Communication Monographs* 51 (3): 215–26.

Pratt, Mary Louise. 2004. "Presidential Address 2003: Language, Liberties, Waves, and Webs—Engaging the Present." *PMLA* 119 (3): 417–28.

Preston, Jacqueline. 2015. "Project(ing) Literacy: Writing to Assemble in a Postcomposition FWC Classroom." *College Composition and Communication* 67 (1): 35–63.

Qualley, Donna, and Elizabeth Chiseri-Strater. 1994. "Collaboration as Reflexive Dialogue: A Knowing 'Deeper Than Reason.'" *JAC* 14 (1): 111–30.

Ramage, John D., and John C. Bean. 1987. "A Comment on 'Reality, Consensus, and Reform in the Rhetoric of Composition Teaching.'" *College English* 49 (2): 209–11.

Rancière, Jacques. 1991. *The Ignorant Schoolmaster: Five Lessons in Intellectual Emancipation*. Translated by Kristin Ross. Stanford, CA: Stanford University Press.

Reed, Cynthia J., Mary-Claire McCarthy, and Bonnie L. Briley. 2002. "Sharing Assumptions and Negotiating Boundaries: Coauthorship as a Tool for Teaching and Learning." *College Teaching* 50 (1): 22–26.

Reid, Alex. 2017. "Big-Data Assemblies: Composing's Nonhuman Ecology." In *Assembling Composition*, edited by Kathleen Blake Yancey and Stephen J. McElroy, 26–41. Urbana, IL: NCTE.

Reither, James, and Douglas Vipond. 1989. "Writing as Collaboration." *College English* 51 (8): 855–67.

Restaino, Jessica. 2014. "Writing Together: An Arendtian Framework for Collaboration." *Composition Forum* 30.

Rhodes, Jacqueline, and Jonathan Alexander. 2014. "Reimagining the Social Turn: New Work from the Field." In "Reimagining the Social Turn," special issue, *College English* 76 (6): 481–87.

Rhodes, Keith, and Monica McFawn Robinson. 2013–2014. "Sheep in Wolves' Clothing: How Composition's Social Construction Reinstantiates Expressivist Solipsism (and Even Current-Traditional Conservatism)." *JAEPL* 19: 8–22.

Richards, I. A. 1930. *Practical Criticism: A Study of Literary Judgment*. London: Kega Paul, Trench, Trubner.

Richards, I. A. 1936. *The Philosophy of Rhetoric*. New York: Oxford University Press.

Rife, Martine Courant, and Dànielle Nicole DeVoss. 2012. "Teaching Plagiarism: Remix as Composing." In *Critical Conversations about Plagiarism*, edited by Michael Donnelly, Rebecca Ingalls, Tracy Ann Morse, Joanna Castner Post, and Anne Meade Stockdell-Giesler, 78–100. Anderson, SC: Parlor.

Ritchie, Joy, and Kate Ronald, eds. 2001. *Available Means: An Anthology of Women's Rhetoric(s)*. Pittsburgh: University of Pittsburgh Press.

Rivers, Nathaniel, and Lars Söderlund. 2016. "Speculative Usability." *Journal of Technical Writing and Communication* 46 (1): 125–46.

Roberts-Miller, Patricia. 2001. "Post-Contemporary Composition: Social Constructivism and Its Alternatives." *Composition Studies* 30 (1): 97–116.

Robidoux, Charlotte, and Beth Hewett. 2009. "Is There a Write Way to Collaborate?" *Intercom* 56 (2): 4–9.

Rogers, Melvin L. 2007. "Action and Inquiry in Dewey's Philosophy." *Transactions of the Charles S. Peirce Society* 43 (1): 90–115.

Roig, Miguel. 2015. *Avoiding Plagiarism, Self-Plagiarism, and Other Questionable Writing Practices: A Guide to Ethical Writing*. Washington, DC: US Department of Health and Human Services. https://ori.hhs.gov/sites/default/files/plagiarism.pdf.

Ronald, Kate, and Hephzibah Roskelly. 2001. "Untested Feasibility: Imagining the Pragmatic Possibility of Paulo Freire." *College English* 63 (5): 612–31.

Ronald, Kate, and Joy Ritchie. 2006. *Teaching Rhetorica: Theory, Pedagogy, and Practice*. Portsmouth, NH: Boyton/Cook Publishers.

Roochnik, David. 1996. *Of Art and Wisdom: Plato's Understanding of Techne*. University Park: Pennsylvania State University Press.

Rorty, Richard. 1979. *Philosophy and the Mirror of Nature*. Princeton: Princeton University Press.

Roskelly, Hephzibah, and David Jolliffe. 2008. *Everyday Use: Rhetoric at Work in Reading and Writing*. 2nd ed. New York: Pearson.

Roskelly, Hephzibah, and Kate Ronald. 1998. *Reason to Believe: Romanticism, Pragmatism, and the Teaching of Writing*. Albany: SUNY Press.

Rowe, Aimee Carrillo. 2005. "Be Longing: Toward a Feminist Politics of Relation." *NWSA Journal* 17 (2): 15–46.

Russell, David R. 1993. "Vygotsky, Dewey, and Externalism: Beyond the Student/Discipline Dichotomy." *Journal of Advanced Composition* 13 (1): 173–97.

Sawyer, Keith. 2017. *Group Genius: The Creative Power of Collaboration*. Rev. ed. New York: Basic Books.

Schendel, Ellen, Michael Neal, and Cecilia Hartley. 2004. "Toward a Theory of Online Collaboration." In *Multiple Literacies for the 21st Century*, edited by Brian Huot, Beth Stroble, and Charles Bazerman, 195–208. New York: Hampton.

Schilb, John. 1992. "The Sociological Imagination and the Ethics of Collaboration." In *New Visions of Collaborative Writing*, edited by Janice Forman, 105–19. Portsmouth, NH: Heinemann.

Schrange, Michael. 1994. "Writing to Collaborate: Collaborating to Write." In *Author-ity and Textuality: Current Views of Collaborative Writing*, edited by James S. Leonard, Christine E. Wharton, Robert Murray Davis, and Jeanette Harris, 17–22. West Cornwall: Locust Hill.

Scripps, Sarah, Soumitra Ghoshroy, Lana Burgess, and Allison Moss. 2013. "Sharing Credit: Public Historians and Scientists Reflecting on Collaboration." *Public Historian* 35 (2): 46–71.

Sekercioglu, Cagan. 2008. "Quantifying Coauthor Contributions." *Science* 322 (5900): 371.

Selfe, Cynthia S., and Richard J. Selfe. 1994. "The Politics of the Interface." *College Composition and Communication* 45 (4): 480–504.

Semenza, Gregory. 2015. "The Temptations of Collaboration" *Chronicle of Higher Education*, April 17. https://chroniclevitae.com/news/978-the-temptations-of-collaboration.

Simmons, W. Michelle, Kristen Moore, and Patricia Sullivan. 2015. "Tracing Uncertainties: Methodologies of a Door Closer." In *Thinking with Bruno Latour in Rhetoric and Composition*, edited by Paul Lynch and Nathaniel Rivers, 275–93. Carbondale: Southern Illinois University Press.

Sosnoski, James J. 1996. "Notes on Postmodern Double Agency and the Arts of Lurking." *College Composition and Communication* 47 (2): 288–92.

Spear, Karen. 1988. *Peer Response Groups in Action*. Portsmouth: Heinemann.

Spinuzzi, Clay. 2015. "Symmetry as a Methodological Move." In *Thinking with Bruno Latour in Rhetoric and Composition*, edited by Paul Lynch and Nathaniel Rivers, 23–39. Carbondale: Southern Illinois University Press.

Spooner, Michael, and Kathleen Blake Yancey. 1996. "Postings on a Genre of Email." *College Composition and Communication* 47 (2): 252–78.

St. Pierre, Elizabeth Adams. 2014. "A Brief and Personal History of Post Qualitative Research: Toward 'Post Inquiry.'" *Journal of Curriculum Theorizing* 30 (2): 2–19.

St. Pierre, Elizabeth Adams. 2016. "Untraining Educational Researchers." *Research in Education* 96 (1): 6–11.

St. Pierre, Elizabeth Adams. 2018. "Writing Post Qualitative Inquiry." *Qualitative Inquiry* 24 (9): 603–8.

Stallings, Jonathan, Eric Vance, Jiansheng Yang, Michael W. Vannier, Jimin Liang, Liaojun Pang, Liang Dai, Ivan Ye, and Ge Wang. 2013. "Determining Scientific Impact Using a Collaboration Index." *Proceedings of the National Academy of Sciences of the United State of America* 110 (24): 9680–85.

Stay, Byron L. 1994. "When Interests Collide: Collaboration and Demolition." *Composition Studies* 22 (2): 30–46.

Stenberg, Shari. 2015. *Repurposing Composition: Feminist Interventions for a Neoliberal Age*. Logan: Utah State University Press.

Stewart, Donald. 1988. "Collaborative Learning and Composition: Boon or Bane?" *Rhetoric Review* 7 (1): 58–83.

Sullivan, Patricia. 1994. "Revising the Myth of the Independent Scholar." In *Writing With: New Directions in Collaborative Teaching, Learning, and Research*, edited by Sally Barr Reagan, Thomas Fox, and David Bleich, 11–29. Albany: SUNY Press.

Taguchi, Hillevi Lenz. 2010. "Doing Collaborative Deconstruction as an 'Exorbitant' Strategy in Qualitative Research." *Reconceptualizing Educational Research and Methodology* 1 (1): 41–53.

Taguchi, Hillevi Lenz. 2016 "'The Concept as Method': Tracing-and-mapping the Problem of the Neuro(n) in the Field of Education." *Cultural Studies ↔ Critical Methodologies* 16 (2): 213–23.

Tarsa, Rebecca. 2015. "Upvoting the Exordium: Literacy Practices of the Digital Interface." *College English* 78 (1): 12–33.

Tett, Gillian. 2016. *The Silo Effect: The Peril of Expertise and the Promise of Breaking Down Barriers*. New York: Simon and Schuster.

Thralls, Charlotte. 1992. "Bakhtin, Collaborative Partners, and Published Discourse: A Collaborative View of Composing." In *New Visions of Collaborative Writing*, edited by Janice Forman, 63–81. Portsmouth: Heinemann.

Trimbur, John. 1989. "Consensus and Difference in Collaborative Learning." *College English* 51 (6): 602–16.

Trimbur, John, and Lundy Braun. 1992. "Laboratory Life and the Determination of Authorship." In *New Visions of Collaborative Writing*, edited by Janice Forman, 19–36. Portsmouth: Heinemann.

Van Cleave, Jessica, and Sarah Bridges-Rhoads. 2013. "'As Cited In' Writing Partnerships: The (Im)possibility of Authorship in Postmodern Research." *Qualitative Inquiry* 19 (9): 674–85.

Vielstimmig, Myka. 1999. "Petals on a Wet Black Bough: Textuality, Collaboration, and the New Essay." In *Passions, Pedagogies, and 21st Century Technologies,* edited by Gail E. Hawisher and Cynthia L. Selfe, 89–114. Logan: Utah State University Press.

Villanueva, Victor, and Kristin L. Arola, ed. 2011. *Cross-Talk in Comp Theory: A Reader.* 3rd ed. Urbana, IL: NCTE.

Vitanza, Victor J. 1987. "Critical Sub/Versions of the History of Philosophical Rhetoric." *Rhetoric Review* 6 (1): 41–66.

Vitanza, Victor J. 1994. Preface to *Writing Histories of Rhetoric,* edited by Victor J. Vitanza, vii–xii. Carbondale: Southern Illinois University Press.

Voss, Julia. 2018. "Who Learns from Collaborative Digital Projects? Cultivating Critical Consciousness and Metacognition to Democratize Digital Literacy Learning." *Composition Studies* 46 (1): 57–80.

Weingarten, Karen, and Corey Frost. 2011. "Authoring Wikis: Rethinking Authorship through Digital Collaboration." *Radical Teacher* 90 (1): 47–57.

Wolfe, Joanna. 2010. *Team Writing: A Guide to Working in Groups.* Boston: Bedford/St. Martin's.

Woodmansee, Martha. 1994. "On the Author Effect: Recovering Collectivity." In *The Construction of Authorship: Textual Appropriation in Law and Literature,* edited by Martha Woodmansee and Peter Jaszi, 15–28. Durham, NC: Duke University Press.

Wyschogrod, Edith. 1990. *Saints and Postmodernism: Revisioning Moral Philosophy.* Chicago: University of Chicago Press.

Wysocki, Anne, and Johndan Johnson-Eilola. 1999. "Blinded by the Letter: Why Are We Using Literacy as a Metaphor for Everything Else?" In *Passions, Pedagogies, and 21st Century Technologies,* edited by Gail E. Hawisher and Cynthia L. Self, 349–68. Logan: Utah State University Press.

Yancey, Kathleen Blake. 2009. "Re-designing Graduate Education in Composition and Rhetoric: The Use of Remix as Concept, Material, and Method." *Computers and Composition* 26 (1): 4–12.

Yancey, Kathleen Blake, and Stephen J. McElroy. 2017. "Assembling Composition: An Introduction." In *Assembling Composition,* edited by Kathleen Blake Yancey and Stephen J. McElroy, 3–25. Urbana, IL: NCTE.

Yancey, Kathleen Blake, and Michael Spooner. 1998. "A Single Good Mind: Collaboration, Cooperation, and the Writing Self." *College Composition and Communication* 49 (1): 45–62.

Yarbrough, Stephen R. 1999. *After Rhetoric: The Study of Discourse Beyond Language and Culture.* Carbondale: Southern Illinois University Press.

Yarbrough, Stephen R. 2005. "Modes of Persuasion or Phases of Discourse?: On the Very Idea of 'Composition.'" *JAC* 25 (3): 491–512.

Yarbrough, Stephen R. 2006. *Inventive Intercourse: From Rhetorical Conflict to the Ethical Creation of Novel Truth.* Carbondale: Southern Illinois University Press.

Yarbrough, Stephen R. 2010. "On 'Getting It': Resistance, Temporality, and the 'Ethical Shifting' of Discursive Interaction." *Rhetoric Society Quarterly* 40 (1): 1–22.

Yarbrough, Stephen R. 2011. "The Temporality and Function of 'Ethical Shifting' in Discursive Interaction." In *The Responsibilities of Rhetoric,* edited by Michelle Smith and Barbara Warnick, 144–50. Long Grove, IL: Waveland.

Young, Richard. 1980. "Arts, Crafts, Gifts, and Knacks: Some Disharmonies in the New Rhetoric." In *Reinventing the Rhetorical Tradition,* edited by Aviva Freedman and Ian Pringle, 53–60. Conway: Canadian Council of Teachers of English.

ABOUT THE AUTHOR

William Duffy is associate professor of English at the University of Memphis, where he also serves as coordinator of Writing, Rhetoric, and Technical Communication. He has published scholarship on the ethics of rhetoric, the rhetorical techniques of America's social gospelers during the Progressive Era, and the work of critical pedagogy in composition courses. His most recent coauthored work with John Pell has appeared in the journals *Present Tense* and *Literacy in Composition Studies.*

INDEX

voice, 72, 107, 124, 133, 136, 144, 151, 152, 168, 169, 170, 171; collective/individual, 64, 148; third, 167
Voss, Julia, 176n12
Vygotsky, Lev, 163, 175n3

We Are Legion (documentary), 178n4
Weineck, Silke-Maria, 174n8
Weingarten, Karen, 181n16
Wharton, Christine, 30
Where Good Ideas Come From (Johnson), 9
Whitehead, Alfred North, 45
Williams, Raymond, 39
Wolfe, Joanna, 181n16
Women's Ways of Knowing (Clinchy, Goldberger, and Tarule), 76
Woodmansee, Martha, 11, 178n4
writing: creative, 53; generalized, 37; informal, 128; materiality of, 116; mixed-mode, 37, 38; practice of, 3; pragmatism and, 164; reactive, 37, 38; separate, 127; sequential single, 37; single-author, 38, 74; social nature of, 36, 39, 50; talking about, 127; theory, 101; turn-around, 128, 129, 145; writing about, 114. *See also* collaborative writing

writing courses, 108, 133, 161
Writing in Digital Environments Research Center, 109–10
Writing on the Edge, 53
writing process, 21, 130, 131; collaboration and, 49; observing, 48; slowing down, 4, 22, 44–51, 74, 85, 93, 109, 116, 132
writing studies, 5, 25, 43, 174n12; authorship and, 20; collaboration and, 33, 44; critical concept in, 103
Wyatt, Jonathan, 137, 143, 144, 145, 146, 153, 154, 182n10
Wyschogrod, Edith, 39–40
Wysocki, Anne, 183n13

Yancey, Kathleen Blake, 75, 154, 155, 156, 182n11, 183n13; academic discourse and, 157; on collaboration, 158; experimental texts and, 157
Yarbrough, Stephen, 8–9, 87, 173n5, 177n1, 179n13, 181n1, 186n8
You Are Not a Gadget (Lanier), 72
Young, Morris, 64
Young, Richard, 61

Zymanski, Stefan, 174n8